Dostoevsky in 1880.

Dostoerskii

THE UNPUBLISHED DOSTOEVSKY

DIARIES AND NOTEBOOKS (1860-81)

IN THREE VOLUMES

GENERAL EDITOR

CARL R. PROFFER

VOLUME III

translated by

ARLINE BOYER AND DAVID LAPEZA

ARDIS   **ANN ARBOR**

CONTENTS

Notebook X (1876-1877), *translated by David Lapeza*   11

Notebook XI (1880-1881), *translated by Arline Boyer*   144

Notes on the Text   181

Index to Vols. I, II, III   195

ILLUSTRATIONS

Frontispiece - Photograph of Fyodor Dostoevsky, 1880

THE UNPUBLISHED DOSTOEVSKY

DIARIES AND NOTEBOOKS 1876-1881

NOTEBOOK X

(1876-1877)

April 8, 1876. Thursday. [1]

April 8th. It is quite possible that Baron Rodić spoke to the leaders of our political bankruptcy without any malice, but quite naively, sincerely believing in the truth of his words. Indeed (he must have thought)—after all, Berlin will never give us to the Russians; even if Berlin swallows us, she will eat up only our German lands and perhaps the rather too civilized Czech-Slavs, who can turn into Germans afterwards. And they will give us the Turkish Slavs in exchange for this. In short then of course, Berlin is now the master of the East/ern/ question, and no one else; let Russia busy herself with central Asia and Berlin will encourage her in it. Oh, of course, Berlin will never give us Constantinople, but then in the first place it is a remote question, and in the second, perhaps we'll somehow take Constantinople afterwards by ourselves. Well, and it is necessary to limit // Russia and besides, Berlin will never give us away to Russia, and that is the whole point. And if so, then Russia will probably not be able to fight either us or Turkey for the Slavs, and probably I am right in saying so. Let the Russians be offended, that's nothing. They will get excited and then get used to it. The main thing is that it is necessary to use harsh measures to break them of the Eastern question. Thus, the agreement of the great Eastern powers is only useful for their completely destroying the Eastern question and its becoming the Berlin question. What is more, they say that Russia does not even have the means to handle the question any other way, she has few weapons, and there's still a lot of bad organization, so that under no circumstances can she get excited, and if so, why shouldn't I have told the leaders what I told them? //

[To Avseenko.] Well what about you, the cultured people who reproach the common people, are you so nice in all ways?[2]

About Potugin (do not forget).

And about the fact that writers are national (Turgenev, Goncharov), etc.[3]

Milord George,—and who has been the delight of Russian footmen for more than 50 years.[4]

[*The Voice*, No. 103.]   For *The Moscow News.*   Ofrosimov's letter on Ryumin's complaint about atheism in the schools.[5]

[The best people.]   Where are our best people? They will surface in time of danger. Above this pathetic clumsiness.

He says that it was necessary to use culture to inspire humanity in the landowners.[6] They hired teachers from Switzerland, but why, O thoughtless child, did they themselves give up everything with violence, they freed the peasants not with land, but without land. After all, in our country the serfs were freed with land not in imitation of cultured Europeans, but because, with the Tsar at their head, they recognized in themselves Russian people and acted according to *Russian truth*.
There it is malice, and not humanity. //

The Mosc/ow/ New/s/, No. 91, Apr/il/ 13. On *paganism* in Germany from German newspapers, etc.[7]

Well and are these cultured people of ours now firmly united, do you think? Do they have their own strongly recognized base, their own solid ideas? Are they not, on the contrary, in disorder, after the peasant massacre, like ants in a broken-up anthill? —And don't some preach only destruction of everything, and the worse the better, but others that they are superior to the peasants even physically, racially.

Scrofulous, gouty—don't you see, he is better by blood.
(The landowner on the railroad.)
And what do you understand in the severe voice of the Slavophiles?
They steal now from Belinsky, now from the Slavophiles.
Even if you are really *loaded up with booklearning*, you won't signify anything, because there's no idea. //

[To Avseenko.]   And what is there in Europe that's any good?[8] (picture).

The Voice—April 13th—praise of Avseenko.[9]

Make-up of April issue.[10]
—Stuck-out tongue.
—To Avseenko.
—On the war.
—Spiritism.
—The Dreamer.
Answer to the opinion about the atypicality of Russian history (Faust

of the Shchigrovsky Region),[11] on the contrary: the period of appanage principalities, the period of invasion, etc.

Future architecture of buildings, no wood, etc. The extermination of criminals. The transition to the herd instinct. /.../

The Voice, Apr/il/ 15. Thursday. On the Chinese history of the Franco-Prussian War...[12]

What a sure idea! One can write down as many ideas like this as one pleases, and they are written because the essence of the matter is not understood. [To Avseenko.] And so with you: you do not understand the essence, and here's proof for you: you say that the Russian people established the Tsarist Empire...and suddenly on the next page, that all their qualities are passive, which means that you understood none of what you yourself wrote about the Russian people on either page. You don't understand now, and you never will understand. There's the rub. //

The New Time, April 15. Lead article on the Herzegovinians, No. 45. Outline of the article on the Herzegovinians.[13]

War. Austria, Prussia will not give it up, the correctness of Baron Rodić. Otherwise, it would have been possible to form a separate new principality from Bosnia and Herzegovina and guarantee Austria that the small Slavic principalities would not join together into something powerful /.../ But Baron Rodić and Russia's incapacity for war? *"The Russian World"* on *shrewd timidity.* Not liberal. On the war.

The New Time, Apr/il/ 15, No. 45. On the unattractiveness of Russian history for the novelist, in the article "Faust of the Shchigrovsky Region." *The New Time.* Remark to Prince Meshchersky of *The Church and Society Bulletin* on the inadequacy of salaries for the clergy. About Lord Redstock.[14] —Correspondence on the insult to a schismatic in Penza: what sort of charlatan threw down the ikon. //

Why disturb their chapels and churches? Does such a law really still exist?

Belinsky on Tatyana. Krestovsky, Fadeev, the high-school students who killed the muzhiks. Perhaps these are chance pimples and scabs. Isn't it so, aren't they generic phenomena? Socialists. Yes, but there are the Avseenko-critics. No sir, I am disappointed in the Avseenkos. Avseenkos—I'll tell you what they are.

(Conservative party—Katkov.)

To Avseenko. Anany Yakovlev.[15] /.../ But in politics: is the destruction of forests a state matter.

It is a pity that those who write such long letters think so little.

All these ideas, by their ease of accusation and by that obvious ease with which they immediately became your convictions (leapt into your convictions), show that you have not thought them through at all. Nor does your fervor deserve sympathy either, because it caused you no suffering, since too little thought was given to these ideas. The most curious th/in/g is that you do not know Russian reality at all (for the possibility of publishing was a foregone conclusion). Considering the blatant fact that you are ignorant of the simplest reality, I have the right to conclude that you are little acquainted with either the Russian man or Russian Orthodoxy in actuality or in action, and all these are merely old, chronic attacks, accepted on faith because of well-known aims or inclinations.

April 16 letters and reread Avseenko's article. //

Final to Avseenko. "After all, any Austrian gendarme in history displays higher principles of enlightenment than her Slavic peasants." You know these words—that's your doctrine. You say not? But if you placed the Russian common people beneath yourself (a cultured man), would you begin to spare the Slavs? //

To Avseenko. Some military leaders even in the 1830's cursed the soldiers with such words that one was ashamed to listen.

Pestel flogged people to death:[16] (see what they make me do!) A certain official said this; I do not want to sully his name, although he is in the grave.

To Avse/enko/. The Odoevskys did exist.

Victor Hugo—historical necessity (Louis XVII) is not necessity but inevitability; I will understand this with the predatory type[17] of the predatory French people.

To Avseen/ko/. *A*, don't be upset, this is not an exclamation (a!), it's only the initial letter of your name.

To Avseen/ko/. And why didn't they free their peasants. Ours is not a rule of blood and iron.[18] —But then these are the most important questions.

[To Avseenko.] The common people are depraved, but they have religion;[19] there, there are ideals and guidelines. Without knowing dogma, they do // know (for the most part) the lives of their saints (I am not considering the 12 million schismatics apart from the common people). Where religion stops, mere dreams begin. Even you spend time in dreams. In *Anna Karenina*. But then you won't understand. V.S. (his words). Civil marriage.

14

I spoke with him; what a good and intelligent chap, and how innocently depraved.

[To Avseenko.] Why that's the same thing as saying that our whole faith is evil because some monks kill each other.

From *The Voice*, No. 105, April 16... "Did we bother," etc.

No, we did not bother, it is beneath our cultural aristocracy, and their faith is a "yokel's faith," like the faith of the Russian people among the Polish gentlemen. But the gentlemen's faith was still the Catholic faith; in our country, the landowners' faith is atheism, indifference and cold, wear/y/ dissipation elevated to morality. On the other hand, we have a few dozen or so liberal anecdotes or mocking stories about the faith of the common people and Orthodoxy; how the priest confesses the old woman or how the peasant prays, etc., // but we don't know anything else. You don't know anything either, critic. If you knew and really understood what you wrote about the faith which "knit Russia together," etc., you would not have mocked the common people for their Fridays, their fasts, their Flor and Lavr[20] and would not have pointed to your silly culture (which has no like anywhere in Europe in the low level of its accomplishments), and underlying the Fridays, the brimstone and underlying the common people's dirty ignorance, you would have recognized a still pure faith, the flame of religion, the *true* Christ, all-forgiving, all-loving (the common people understood him, despite the Fridays), despite the Virgin, our quick defender and aid—in a word, the deification of love, meekness and humility, service to all as servants, and faith, that from this voluntary status of servant itself shall come freedom, equality and brotherhood for all. In a word, you would have discerned that [your life] [the life of the common people] your life is shallow and negative, full of gasping, petty // literary hatreds and [envies] envies, while the life of the common people is full of heart, strength, spontaneity and thought, and that's the thing that you, rushing into it with your stupid culture, want to destroy. O you little, insignificant men!

The common people know their Christ because for many centuries they have borne many misfortunes and in their final woe heard of this Christ from their saints, the representatives in that time of faith and of the common people, who worked for them and who [put down] laid down their lives for them.

Do not scorn the faith of the common people! Or no, go ahead and scorn it: that suits you.

And so your article and all your ideas issued from continuing scorn for the Russian people, who stubbornly held out among the cultured classes (and

15

the longer, the worse it was) against the reforms of Peter and the enslave-
ment // of the peasants, which finally occurred also under Peter. *You*, in essence, are left-over advocates of serfdom who have no serfs.

Though you don't scorn the faith of the common people aloud, but
then, *morally*, you place it beneath culture.

[To Avseenko.] After all, despite 200 years of imitation of Europe, in
its main functions, our Russian life has remained completely distinctive, but
you, a clique of wretched glovers, want to "drive Russia on," bend her into
a ram's horn and make her cultured. This is all out of scorn for Russia and
for the common people.
 I take exception with you also because I take exception to your collective character, for there are still many like you, and even to Potugin[21] along
with you, although compared to you Potugin is a tsar of talent despite the
fact that he is too naively ignorant. I'll deal with Potugin later, but [you
still] I shall add by the way that you are more ignorant than even Potugin
is. Do not // smile with scorn reading this: if you have indeed read a few
books (only a few, however), you still do not have the ability to assimilate
their sense. What you do is, so to speak, loading yourself down with book-
learning, and not reading. And so, I answer as to a collective character.
 Answer: and not to *The Russian Messenger: /The/ R/ussian/ Messen-*
g/er knows all this itself, although it did print Avseenko's article, but there
are really an innumerable number of such Avseenkos. —I myself am in their
train. Red nose.
 In what does their culture lie, what are they so vain about? Gloves.
I shall prove it.

I never believed the vile (practical and predatory) idea that only the top
is to be educated; I wish and I believe that in our country there will be a social order in which the peasant too will understand the great idea (through Orthodoxy), which so magnificently and harmoniously includes a multitude of
great ideas which Orthodoxy already includes within itself. //

You do not walk, you corrupt.
 He sometimes expresses opinions and, so to speak, thoughts; well, every-
thing is there as with everyone else, but he often goes wrong.
 You say that the attractive/ness/ of the common people vanishes and
immediately appears in the form of a blood-sucker and a petty tyrant. And
the nurse? Unhappy man, you did not see this. (And are there no blood-
suckers and petty tyrants in our society?
 Do you demand that everyone there be holy?
 Why then, you are all mad.
 Do you think that passive or *active work is to yield its four hundred ru-*

16

bles. You will say that this is not Russian, but is it cultured? But then there is no culture among the common people.

Gloves are no sin, they are a weakness.

Gloves—give them up. We pay dearly for them and most of the time we wear them without knowing why ourselves. //

[To Avseenko.] And do you know why they freed the common people with the land? Precisely because they bowed before *the people's law*. You don't understand that? Well someday you will.

You will say, the courts and n/ew/ laws, the ord/er/, the authorities which followed the liberation of the peas/ants/. Didn't we copy them exactly as the Potugins ordered. But then nothing that was taken from Europe caught on, but it hangs on when somehow combined with national custom, and this results in a far from European form. But other things so easily turned out to be nonsense and even now only hurt and wait only until the common people make known their full view of the matter—and then they will be reborn in their own way. Much of the sort has already happened in our country. Do you know that that is why they were freed with land, that is why the reforms of the present reign took place, and although there is much that is unsatisfactory, it is still better than something copied directly from the German.

And do you know why the reforms of the present r/ei/gn took place?

These reforms are not satisfactory, but they are not external, they correspond to our inner desires. And now they've untied the hands of the people's forces and they shall be manifest.

You have, like a fakir, a sprout of 18 inches for 20 miles.

And do you know (above). //

Education: full reconciliation, complete impartiality together with full consciousness even of one's moral right (Orthodoxy).

Stand up to them all, servant.

Of course, we will not turn over our land to them, we must preserve our Russian type and therefore preserve the land under us.

And not of the Slavic family alone.

From Orthodoxy—from which all solutions proceed.

We present the amazing spectacle of the common people without usurpation. We will not make the Pole turn into a Russian, but when the Poles or Czechs really want to be our brothers, we [real] will give them autonomy, for even with autonomy our bond will not be destroyed, and they will reach out towards us, as to a friend, to an older brother, to a great center.

The great matter of love and real enlightenment. That is my Utopia! //

Read Petrov's[22] biography; with a great talent—such conscientiousness, such knowledge of art, unheard, unseen on account of duty, all this is silent and unknown and you do not [pay attention] deign to pay attention—[to Avseenko.]   Russian, uncultured, tight-fisted, peasants, swindlers!

[To Aveseenko.] *Krestovsk/y/*.[23] Honor, whose merit is in blind observance of well-known outward forms, and which is not derived from the internal needs of the human soul. //

Final make-up of the April issue.[24]
1) Avseenko and related.
Apropos of Slavdom.
2) Spiritism.

3) The Dreamer (his biography).[25]
4) Should be of the Herzegovinians.
5) From where will the best [Russian] people come?
6) And about the war.

April 18, simply; Avseenko and The Dreamer, without spiritism.
The Dreamer, arrival and father, but the war and spiritism—all from the Dreamer. //

The Voice, No. 108. Monday. John Tindale on spiritism.[26]

Final—to Avseenko: To love everyone (of course, not Turner), [kingd] to establish a kingdom of peace and God's glory on the basis of the orthodox principles of the common people.

"But that doesn't exist," they'll cry to me, "That's Utopia."

"Let's try, let's close our ranks, let's go together, lend a hand, let's lay down our lives.

At Pobedonostsev's, even in the ninth hour.

Andr/ew/ of Crete.[27] //

Read *The Canon* of Andrew of Crete and enlighten yourself. The common people know many such prayers, and if they don't know them, they do listen to them.

I shall ask Krestovsky, the writer, how it is he cannot see that he is entirely to blame. If it really is true that they insulted him—is he still to blame?

They will say: it is boring to talk about that, everything in the world has been said and re-said. But everything in the world has been resaid, there is very little that is new. And if we can say it fifty times, why not say it a 51st. For if you start talking about something else, it will still turn out to be the 51st time. About some things it is not old-fashioned to talk for even the 501st.

This is not a pen, it is a prayer, one must have compassion for that.

Duel—having accepted the letter, we have broadened our ability for evil acts. //

So science does not at all constitute any sort of essential and irreconcilable difference between the two classes of Russian people, i.e., between the folk and the cultured upper layer, and [to speak of] to represent science as our chief and essential difference from the common people, I repeat, will not at all fit present considerations—and it's incorrect; one must look for the difference in something completely different.
Porters, then they started to hire them simply as porters.
To be ashamed of one's dirty faith, a yokel's faith.
They fr/e/ed the common people according to the people's principles. If it had been like the Europeans, then it would have been on a proletarian basis, like the Baltic Germans. In our country, much from Europe did not take, but was reworked in an original manner.
What is an active or a passive act, Mr. Avseenko?
Broadening of viewpoint. Broadening of viewpoint must lie in the direction of our education.

It would be another matter if the common people opposed (20 years) instruction in science, even by some sort of precept, some folk principle or other of their own, so that we would have had to undertake the exploit of entering into a huge and dangerous struggle with them, [to undertake] into a crusade, so to speak. But then this is not the way it is at all, the common people thirst for science; in European science there have been examples of their own sort of // autodidacts emerging from among the common people, and the common people did not disdain them, on the contrary, they praised them. Perhaps you hold other loathsome folk prejudices just as deeply, the fruit of their deep ignorance, but then it remains to be proved that the common people defend them so staunchly, and on the other hand, there are certainly no fewer prejudices in our intellectual milieu than among the common people, and /are/ some are far more malignant than their prejudices, which are sometimes quite innocent ones.
All this is words, no porters here, but here we have science, which at the very beginning you dismissed from consideration, and science is everything. But then you belittle your own culture and your own exploit exceptionally much. So you are not all that much above the common people. It is a matter of a few very short decades, and you will see that an extraordinarily large number of scientific figures will appear from among the common people, and then the common people will compare with you. Where is your advantage and

what do you pride yourself on. My landowner, just like that, simply and openly declared that he is above the common people in body, that his type under-
went a change in comparison to the common people. //

If I said that the plebs are quiet, then it's so precisely in the sense that
they cannot but be quiet midst such an undoubtedly democratic mood of society, journalistic knavery, deception in the accusations of the antagonists,
even slander.

There is much deception in the accusations, but this trend is undoubtedly a good one.

It is an instinctive appeal to the common people and an expectation of
a great deal from them. I shall not speak now. I will put it off in order to say
it in full. But I spoke evil of society. About instability. But then in the end,
it is from it I await salvation. This salvation is in the broadening of the Russian idea. They will try to catch me: one ought not, as I do, speak such evil
of such a society. But speaking evil, I placed value on it, perhaps more than
many. I expect salvation from the broad/ening/ of the Russian idea. I will
explain this later. Not from civilization but from contact with Europe did
broadening arise independently in the Russian. It wasn't from there that we
took it, for it is contrary to the Europ/ean/ idea, and there is nothing anywhere as disinterested as our plebeian [and we, perhaps, much more frenziedly
stand up for them than the common people do for their own.]

But for now, about instability [really] , *disgust* def.
But the women will demand an article, and not fluent words.[28] They
themselves...

And if there are mistakes now, it is not without purpose, a guarantee,
that they will cure them.

Temporary ailments.

But there is scarcely a trace of this broad/ening/ of society's democr/acy/.

I will never go back on my words, if I do not change my convictions. We
are undoubtedly more gifted than the common people in, for example, self-
conceit, unhealthy and hypochondriac aversion to other people, dark hatred,
cynicism, thirst for impersonality, together with an insatiable thirst for glory,
for the most idle self-conceit, desire for well-known customs and an unhealthy
timidity before one's own opinion to throw off these customs, etc., etc.,
there is no way you could calculate it all. We see valor in the gift of *seeing
one evil*, while this is just baseness, but about this later; but I will add a word
about women. I said above that our hope is in women.

But all our feelings of honor, [of liberalism] , all our shaky concepts of
duty, of humanity—aren't they prejudices and aren't they based on prejudices.
Didn't honor exist in ancient Russia? Returning from Europe, we accepted
new formulas, became unusually unstable, cowardly and characterless, and

about ourselves, cynical and utter nihilists. Of course, I speak // only about those who live and think. The rest live years and years and do not know why they live in this world.

How dirty, how unclean the common people are in their domestic principles. That is why I said that they sigh, but this wasn't understood.

Instability of thought is combined with almost infantile unreasonableness.

The common people are depraved; but the thing is that they do not consider their wickedness a good, while we consider the trash which is in our hearts and minds cultural charm, and we want the common people to come learn from us /.../ //

The beauty of gods and the ideal, they appear quite naked, but neither gods nor the ideal will bear this. With commonplace, ordinary people beauty is conventional. And feeling is cleansed only when it comes in contact with higher beauty, the beauty of the ideal. This contact with the beauty of the ideal is in our *byliny*[29] and to a high degree. There are the wonderful types of Ilya Muromets [and of the wonderf.] and of the fantastic Svyatogor, etc. Potugin knew this perfectly well, but he had to spit on the Russian people for their lack of taste, make them ridiculous and arouse contempt and disgust for them; and here he pulled out a picture of past fashions and of the contemporary brilliant lady, showed what a stupid hat his mother wore in the '20's ([All R] i.e. the question was about Churilo, but anyway the meaning is the same). The only thing Potugin forgot to look at was himself, and how he himself was dressed, and what he found beautiful all his life. //

Important. Concluding words of Avseenko (*The New Time*), No. 52.[30] The answer to this is that you consider the principles of the people and their Orthodoxy mere trifles, but we do not. On the contrary we consider them all that could possibly be important. That is why for you the common people are just unknown pilgrims, and expecting any idea or model from them is ironic, while for us they are everything, and the only hope, because they possess everything, namely Orthodoxy and the morality of Orthodoxy, although just in an elementary form. That is why for us the common people are not only unknown pilgrims, but guides, and whatever might await them, whatever torments and reversals might watch from them on the road, they will even turn aside, perhaps, occasionally, but never will they go astray, because what they carry with them, i.e., Orthodoxy and the principles stemming from it, is too valuable and weighty and can under no circumstance be lost, and will even protect those who carry them, so that if we join them even now, we will save ourselves along with them.
Whoever considers Orthodoxy foolishness, etc., for him my words will

be incomprehensible.

In short, you never [were Ru] understood the common people, and despised them all this time, [posi] you never understood Orthodoxy, and never were Orthodox, [and even]   and that is why you cannot even put any value on it, finally, perhaps you haven't been Russian for a long time, but just the misshapen, degenerate product of reform.

Perhaps it's from a deceived but deeply human feeling, but you are, even in your truth, inhuman, so that the very delusions of Belinsky, if he indeed has any, are superior to your truth, and everything that you have created and written. //

The Dreamer.[31] Once he suffered humiliating abuse from his boss for carelessness. —Do you really think that I could live if I didn't dream. I would have shot myself if it hadn't been for that. So I came, lay down and started to dream.
I will tell you about an impression of my earliest youth, he said with a sad face.

No, I don't despise myself much. I have so many magnanimous ideas, that cleanse me so. Funny ones. One laughs by oneself.
About his father.
He makes things up. But this, apparently, he didn't make up.

He—took to drink, he couldn't stand it. I am a dreamer, I can stand it. I would have stood it. //

Spiritism. Well two accidents, that's enough to destroy faith, because I do not want to believe. It's exactly the converse for those who want to believe, divination at cards.

Spiritism. [Con] Pobedonostsev.[32] But why not speak. Social evil. The Commission and the springs. It didn't understand the social evil. The important thing would be to pursue the utilitarian goal, but who would believe you now (from the point of view of mere petty knavery. Not even delusions, desires to delude oneself.) Maikov has no springs. I was myself at Wagner's[33] 7 times, no, I didn't beat them off myself, didn't lay a finger on them.
The Commission did not think through to the simplest fact (of cerebration— — —)

When I approached Aksakov[34] —a strange sensation of unwillingness to believe. Courtesy disturbed me (two names, a year of exile). Little organs under the table. Foma. Mathematic/al/ proofs. Detailed impression of disbelief or rather—unwillingness to believe.

Insignificance of culture. Sechenov. Thirst for miracles. Immutability of understanding. Christianity // and Eastern miracles.

Hypothesis of devils; Keronsky, Maikov. I almost wanted to get angry. No, this matter awaits further investigation, to join battle armed with the establishm/ent/ not of education, but with the excitement of higher interests—than idleness. Spirit low. Is it really so difficult to raise the human spirit. The middle, the bourgeoisie came, capital, merchants.
But then I only believe that spiritism is a phenomenon not explained only by springs installed under the table and the inordinate stupidity of those occupied with them.

Foma. Mathematical conviction. It is nothing. Moral conviction is important. But if you are convinced, what baseness of moral feeling, what baseness of moral needs. // But at the same time it would seem to be contrary to baseness. A rise in spiritual needs, in women especially. A desire to participate disinterestedly, for the deed itself, for prayer. They write letters, study, read, investigate, demand explanations. The rise of woman in our country is not subject to any doubt. Men were unstable, and now have become more corrupted with graspingness, cynicism.

It is a pity that woman is weak, *becomes tired*, cannot stand disappointment. They value an ever fresher feeling, a lively word, but mainly and above all, sincerity.

The Diary of a Writer brought me closer to women. I receive letters and questions about what to do. They breathe such sincerity, a deeply serious phenomenon. She lies—she is not sincere. /.../

Because you use pressure, by this very thing you deceive yourself. Why if only they clarified this, and not so haughtily and imprecisely.
You see I know that I use pressure. Believe me, there is much more distrust of oneself than you think. You consider us very simple fools.

The indifferent deny it. Ah, I didn't think of that.
Sechenov. Keronsky.

Let her, like Shchapov's wife,[35] soothe her melancholy and disappointment in self-sacrifice and love. Not like Mme. Pisarev, but both of them are equally agonizing phenomena. Agonizing in that fate of which both could be worthy and in those good deeds which they could pour out to the world.

In the thirst for higher education there is seriousness. //

Let an employee turn up whom he ruined, or one who would drag him to court for appropriation of someone else's property.[36]
Brother had no incidents in court with male or female employees for misappropriated funds, as I read in the newsp/aper/ 1500.
It is very unpleasant for me to remind Mr. Blagosvetlov[37] about this.

But in the absence of actual proofs to refute the insinuation about Shchapov, I should have explained the source from which it came.

In the editorial office of *Time* these relations were held high, there was no dirt.

No one could call my brother out.

Then I read how a proprietor-socialist wrote laudatory things about the rise in apartment rents.

That is not M.M. Dostoevsky's style in the treatment of people. He never used the word *rot*. It was not a servile seminarist, beginning his career, and impudent, shameless, when he makes it.

Time included Shchapov's articles cautiously, and I certainly know that it didn't especially pursue them. On the contrary, I remember very well that Shchapov himself brought and offered his articles to the editorial staff. //

Shchapov was without a firm line of work. Shchapov was a man who had not only not developed but who did not have the strength to develop.

The Cause is not authority in the cause of honor.

So what if he was tender with those for whom he did good, and especially with those for whom he did something better, as compassionate and delicate people are in such cases.

Deal with the materi/al/.
He could never broaden his viewpoint, did not have European education and wandered about in it blindly.

Would many men have done this, even of those who got into the important homes [with qu] through their liberalism? perhaps even those among them who became famous then for their liberal tendency, wouldn't have done

24

it before getting into (because of it) the important homes in Petersburg.

Well isn't that nonsense? I appeal to the public.

Money in advance—that would be more in accord with all recollections and all testimony of how *Time* was run and published and what tone the editorial staff had, sufficient testimony to which, I repeat, one can collect even now, if it is quite necessary, despite the 14-year gap.[38]

The essence of the communication of these two first-rate poets. //

That is cringing servility—not wishing to hand him the money.

I do not recognize my brother in this conversation, and that is why I conclude that things didn't happen that way.

It wasn't I who published *Time*, I never went into my brother's financial accounts, but I am sure and I know, that it could never happen that he would evade payment under various pretexts.

Spiritism.—One is not struck by the fact that they are satisfied with this, one is struck by the low level of our development.

Spiritism. With spirits they speak courteously, and even in French, as if they were some sort of high society. Really, in the sum of impressions, perhaps there was that too.

Not in regard to the real, but the idea, one side of a triangle is less than the sum of the two others; there's nothing not to believe here (about Lord Redstock).

Christ—1) beauty, 2) nothing better, 3) if so, then miracle is all of faith, after this the sermon of Ioann Zlatoust, even in the ninth hour—remember.

Conversely, now mathematical proofs, scarcely a hairbreadth and lack of faith (without raising the spirit or emotion).

That is ecstasy, a frenzy of faith, all-forgiveness and all-embracement. Let us embrace strongly, let us kiss and begin as brothers.

Where, death, is your sting, where, hell, your victory?

(The 9th hour had begun, if you were Nero the mocker.) Though the hierarch takes absolutions upon himself in an almost impossible manner, this is from the penetration of the spirit of Christ, who pronounced curses on the fornicators and at the same time forgave the fornicatress, both are right.

Without a moment's hesitation.

And will you shake this faith with positivistic proofs?

25

You see I know that there is nothing higher than this thought of *embracing*; what will you, with your positivism, give me in exchange. I will follow you when you give me something better. But at present this isn't in sight from you. You've only chopped heads and you want to chop some more...

And suddenly the baseness of spiritism, knock. No, here is the baseness of society. Where is all that realism, positivism, those student movements, where did it all get to.

They will say: what do you mean, after all it's only one angle. Yes, but in this angle all is collected, *everything*. //

Page 31.

April. *Chapter One*. 1) The ideals of a vegetable, stagnant life. Kulaks and bloodsuckers. Higher gentlemen, driving Russia on. 2) Cultured types. Injured people. 3) Inconsistency and inaccuracy of the disputed points. 4) The altruistic porter, who frees the Russian muzhik. *Chapter Two*. 1) Something about political questions. 2) The Paradoxalist. 3) [For the dead]. Again a word about spiritism. 4) For the dead. //

The New Time, No. 56. On spiritism.

[To Avseenko.] Why did all the Russians, becoming cultured in Europe, even ministers, /beginning/ even with the Empress, always attach themselves to the stratum of Europeans which was liberal (toward the left) and which denied *its own culture*?[39] Didn't this reveal the Russian soul, to which European culture was always hateful, from Peter the Great on, and hasn't it proclaimed itself unconsciously foreign even to the Russian soul. Moreover, those who were the most Russian in feeling. That is why we attached ourselves to the revolutionaries, who wished to destroy their own. About Russia, though, we drew inferences mistakenly, because in Russia it would have been natural for us to become, on the contrary, conservatives, for the Russian order was different and conversely opposed, but we considered it equally barbarous. Belinsky, for example, in his passionately enthusiastic nature, attached himself quite directly to the Socialists, who had rejected the whole order of Europe, and if he applied the same thing to Russia, then it was only because he didn't know her. And really, he understood Russia poorly or rather, prejudicially, and knew her extemely poorly. He knew Russia through fact, although he grasped an awful lot by instinct, by presentiment.

One must note that he applied the whole Europ/ean/ order directly to Russia, without thinking about the distinction, and there lies the distinction between him and the Slavophiles. Besides that, the difference from the Slavoph/ile/s is that renewal is not in the common people.

He saw only the order. But he loved the common people, and the whole

26

difference between him and the Slavophiles lay in the fact that he placed no restorative hopes on the common people [themselves] , while the Slavo/philes/ not only saw independent restorative principles in the common people, but even investigated those very paths by which the renaissance of Russia in a national spirit could proceed. Belinsky did not believe in these paths, but most important, he studied them very little. And read the Slavophiles, it seems, very little. As if in despair, he began to expect world-wide restoration out of the social movement begun in Europe, and was madly carried away with it. Nevertheless, by the seriousness of his denial of civilization, he concurred; denying Europe, he coincided with the Slavophiles, although from the other extreme. To clarify this curious phenomenon of Russian life, I will add that Belinsky was an incomparably more conservative Russian than the Gagarins.[40] Nevertheless, having joined the *extreme left*, he unconsciously showed himself extremely Russian, and in this became much closer to the Slavophiles than our Westernizers of the period, who so idolized the West before Russia that they converted to Catholicism (toward the right).

There really were such Westernizers: precisely from among the higher landowners. They exist even now. These have now completely* become, not Russians, but Europeans, but their characteristic** trait, by which one could always know them, was that, joining Europe and becoming Europeans,*** they immediately joined the ext/reme/ right, i.e., lost their last Russian trait, lost their feeling for Russia. Those, I repeat, who joined the left, the extreme left of Europe, all without exception turned out to be and declared themselves by that very act, Russians, who had denied European culture and had a natural aversion to it. Belinsky, for example. But to proclaim themselves Russian was still not enough: denying the West, they did not know that they were Russian and slighted themselves even worse than the West. This stratum continues even now, and they are Westernizers as opposed to Slavophiles, who have driven out necessity in themselves, and consciously learned not to deny Russia.

Let us consider them.
Their instability, etc.
—Socialism.
—Orthodoxy.

*Above the line: "all the Westernizers toward the right became Germans. All those to the left remained Russian—many to the Slavoph/iles/."

**Above the line: "it is curious, that they went sooner to Catholicism than to Lutheranism."

***Above the line: "on the contrary, all those on whom civilization acted destructively, destroying the Russian in them."

I will dwell on this, although a long theme, we'll manage. But what did they bring from Europe. Politic.

The Slavophiles, who denied Western civilization, taken as the ideal for Russia.

If they drew conclusions thus even about Russia, it was because even then there was no time for them to think about Russia, they were deciding other questions. The Slavophiles thought about Russia.

Miller proclaimed Slavophile doctrine national.[41] But I thought to reconcile the Slavophiles with the West/erniz/ers. For the first time I give my thesis.

If they had been more familiar with Russia, they would have become Slavoph/iles/. But even now this unfamiliarity continues. Slav/ophile/ doctrine even now is uncertain, although they'll side with it.

In Europe, Europeans say of the Russians that they are all without exception revolutionaries, however they are revolutionaries only in Europe, and if they were able to treat themselves intelligently, in Russia these revolutionaries would have to become conservatives (the reason—too little familiarity with Russia). They even take Russia for this same Europe.

For Orthodoxy is even less ritualistic than Stundism. They'll finish with the dishes. Redstock too. //

What treasure do we bear the common people.
The New Time, April 24. Saturday, No. 54. About Shchapov's drunkenness.[42]
We bear a higher idea than to simply survive (v. *laissez-faire*).
What treasure do we [really] bear? And the peoples will say: no, their ideal is better. The Orthodox [people] Christ is better than the one who agreed to the Inquisition in Spain. And how are you to know if Peter understood this. [In a great soul]. If he did not understand it entirely, then he [fel] had a presentiment, in a great soul there must have been great presentiments as well. It is a pity that fate should have given him a too severe soul. Antokolsky and Peter the white-handed.[43]

End with Zlatoust's sermon: Even in the ninth hour, etc.

Strong NB. That is why Slavophilism seems a somehow egotistical doctrine, i.e., that the Russians will save the world. Yes, but on the other side, not absorbing personality in oneself, on the contrary, acknowledging all personalities, but merely *indicating the ideal* (of a world-wide, *feminine* soul).

 Letter of a landowner—this youth is a bewilderment. They should have been Slavophiles, i.e., have gone for universal reconciliation, and not preaching that the worse the better, and be my brother or off with your head. Similarly, *Terner* and *Yanyshev* are only a bewilderment.

 Orthodoxy, statism, but Orthodoxy is the faith of which it is said: you do not know of what spirit you are.

 In my idea: in me is the treasure and salvation of mankind, thinks the German, isn't that so? Not in me, but in my idea, thinks the Russian, be a servant to all, acknowledge everything good, unity. And so my *personality* (sobriety necessary) is a citizen of the world.

 Mr. Terner spoke like a foreigner.

 F/ather/ Yanyshev is an official.

 The duty of a Russian is that. //

	Mother Superior Mitrofaniya	
May issue		
Answers to letters	?+ Spiritism 1).	Byzantine history.
Kairova /.../	2) Women.	Extreme left.
	?+ Foundling home,	Treasure to the common
	temporary insanity.	people.
Left.	?+ Women.	Spiritism.
Pleased plebs	?+ Letter on those go-	Women
	ing to the com-	
	mon people (...)	
Temporary insanity.		Foundling home,
Foundling home.		temporary insanity.
Women.	?+ The Dreamer.	1) The Dreamer.
Spiritism.	?+Language and father.	2)Kairova.
Treasure.	Extreme left of the Europeans.	
Broadening.	Instability of men. Treasure to the common people.	
	Political, if there will be anything.	

The Voice, Apri/l/ 28. Death of non-com/missioned/ officer Danilov.[44]

 Petrov's anniversary (even earlier around the 25th).

 Kairova affair.[45] Conclusion in *The New Time*, No. 60, Friday, April 30.

 Temporary insanity![46] For heaven's sake, then one can say everything, every impression is temporary insanity. And who knows the borderline (what experts?), where can you set the norm that beyond this line temporary insanity is irresponsible. Why any sort of incident is temporary insanity! Sunrise is temporary insanity, a glance at the moon is temporary insanity, and what else! It means an inclination // to lunacy.

 She scalded the child's hand, means temporary insanity, she was sick and tired of him, he jangled her nerves. (In the family, she said, there were drunkards: why whose family hasn't had drunkards.)

The main thing is learning about the environment. After all there is the line of environment.

Who pities the destroyer does not pity the victim. We will get to the point that we not only justify, but praise him. "She protested," she said.

She bought a razor beforehand. What do you mean, unpremeditated? Without temporary insanity, premeditated. "No, she did not strike any blows" (the jury). Who struck them, then? Went home. "She cut herself up."

The journals in our country praise such a verdict.

They will always protest in the name of common sense.

What sort of experts in the human soul are these?

What science can be learned in the university? Don't they attribute a lot to it? Our prejudiced ignorance to a science unenlightened and unaccustomed to the reasoning of the crowd and the mean.

In the system of criminal punishments:

Expulsion from society all together (the only punishment, without even tortures) and certain return to society if he is worthy of it, so as not to leave the soul in despair—these are the principles which certainly ought to be adopted. Their organization is another matter—that is a great task for the future. But I think that I settled these two principles like a Russian.

Removal from society is essential for *social justice.*

The New Time, No. 64, Tuesday, May 4.
Ieroglifov's broil at Bazunov's.[47] //

Mr. Grigorovich[48] who to the Russian peasant was a le/arned/ foreigner. (This foreigner in Russian national life was for some time considered a Russian.) Now he is precisely this for art.

The New Time, No. 66, May 6th, on the women's question.[49]

Stundism (proselytism). *The New Time* from May 12, waits for some Khlystism and then will weaken.[50]

NB. Contingent of priests and monks. Convictions. Terner and Yanyshev.

When the fathers lose their status, both sects and atheism will be destroyed, for the atheist contingent still yields clergy.

Status is abstraction, socialism.

Peter the Great. Great souls cannot but have great presentiments. Peter could not but be a Westernizer, but he could scarcely have been one in such a narrow sense as the Petersburg Westernizer or the Jesuit Gagarin. And if he had seen the Slavophiles, he would probably have understood them, he would have taken Khomyakov and Yury Samarin and said, here are fledglings from my nest, although seemingly they have spoken against me. //

This aristocrat was in the highest degree a Russian aristocrat, i.e., he had no aversion to the axe. True, he took the axe in two cases, both for ships and for the *streltsy*.

The Empire, after the Turks, should be not pan-Slavic, not Greek, not Russian—each of these solutions is incompetent. It should be Orthodox—then everything is understandable.

On instability. Terner.
With Orthodoxy we set forth the most liberal idea there can possibly be, collectivization of men in the name of collectivization with those who will not be in agreement with us.
Kairova. —But the jury could endure this, knowing firmly that they could not make any other decision. Russians are the most patient people in the world, and Russian jurymen especially. Our juries endure everything, even Utin. Public prosecutor Sluchevsky alone would have been enough.[51] Apropos: Mr. Utin began his speech with thanks to the prosecutor for defending Kairova. Mr. Utin did not just want to be rather original, or else after hearing the brilliant defense of the prosecutor, he should have directly begun to accuse Kairova. I do not think that the jury would have been very surprised.

But either she was temporarily insane, or she acted just "as we all would have acted." What, must everyone be mad? Madness, is that praiseworthy?

Distrac/tion/ and madn/ess/, are probably in nature. There was none, but through the newspapers partly one gets precisely this impress/ion/. Utin.
As much mercy as you please, but do not praise the act: call it evil.
"In the end, one must be merciful" (not by obligation alone). To display mercy does not mean to pity Kairova and laugh at Velikanova.[52]
Hands-'n'-footsies—a monstrous word! A most ordinary word. // [Why al] //

Our attorneys and jurymen (and, it seems, the bench too) suppose, it seems, that when you go knife someone you are cold-blooded.

Who pities the offender does not pity the offended.

[Utin.] Let Velikanova catch Kairova and cut her with a razor, and it seems to me that besides dirt and hard labor, she would get nothing in court, in her horrible capacity of legal wife.

She loved much. I am sure that Mr. Utin is an exceptional Christian, but still, Christ certainly did not speak his eternal words about such love, and this sort of insinuation is rather vile. Despite the fact that in the temple (before suffering) he forgave even such love, [but] but such love, about such love he said clearly: go and sin no more.

After all, you yourself said that Velikanov is an impossible man and that the fact of Kairova's love attests to her madness more than anything. How can you be surprised, then, at Velikanova's words: hands-'n'-footsies. It's impossible to live with an impossible man. Well, once they say /two words indecipherable/ howl later

Velikanova settled in another apartment. I understood only that Velikanova settled at her repentant // husband's, who summoned her. But then in no way does it follow that Velikanova figured that Kairova would go on paying after her arrival too. So I understood that as soon as Velikanova arrived, she reserved the apartment for herself. Then it was difficult for her to recognize who was paying: her husband or Kairova? Her husband called her to him, which means her husband reserved the apartment for himself, especially since Kairova had gone away, and her husband believed that Kairova had gone away.

But Velikanova played around for two weeks. Why this comment? Or is Mr. Utin sorry that they didn't murder her? You can't say that Velikanova hadn't endured a lot: she bore the feeling of mortal fear, of suffering. On the whole, the moment was not entirely attractive. Why, I'm sorry that Kairova was in prison for 10 months, but of what shall I reprove Velikanova? And to say that she alone had suffered is too strong. And you can't place the blame on Velikanova. She threw out her step-daughter.[53] The girl was saved by a miracle from the fourth floor, does that really excuse the step-mother? *The New Time*, No. 73, May 13.

I only timidly dare to say that one must call it evil, evil, and not an exploit.

Kairova, all these razors can be very nice. I don't love all these loves without responsibility. Lies and deception. Disgusting. i.e., not love, but everything they draw out of it, even the facts, God help them, all are sinful, and I am no judge.

⑥ Foundling home (step-daughter out the window.) Scalded hand from the samovar. The foundling home is a responsibility. Temporary insanity is a terrible word. The environment was oppressive—does that really save her from responsibility. But there is more bliss in responsibility than in living merrily with little intrigues, having a foundling home nearby for the consequences. But still, the blissful with little intrigues are blissful. These passionate natures are suicides.

Of course, it is fun to give reign to all one's powers and, so to speak, delight in life. I remember a nice plan by the French writers of the '40's, who proposed establishing, so to speak, Saturnalia in order to return everything taken away from the body through long centuries of monasticism. It is terribly strange that these same writers portrayed the monastic life and the monk not otherwise than in the form of plump rosy fellows with a bottle in hand, winking lecherously at some little beauty, so it's difficult to imagine what was taken away from mankind. True, there were a few ascetics in all countries and in all ages, but then so very few.

⑤ The caricatures are undoubtedly deserved.

Beginning of the novel. The Dreamer. Two critics. But I have no right to write a novel: I have two articles behind me. But I will not write about what I promised. I will speak only about Russian Europeans of the *left* and the *right*. On those going to the common people (letter). And what do we bear the common people? Broadening of thought. Orthodoxy. Apropos, Te/r/ner. (Samarin. Miller's speech). —Kaulbach,[54] etc. Constantinople and Orthodoxy. (On instability and why the common people are superior— till another time.)

More on spiritism.

On women.

Read a letter about a lady who committ/ed/ suicide.[55] There is no higher sense of duty and justice that alone constitutes happiness. And how tired she was, oh, how tired she was, what a material understanding of happiness, allocation of funds. They'll come *to howl. How disgusting*.

Through Christianit/y/, on the contrary, many have realized that they are righteous in their souls, really realized in Christianity that the idea is in mor/al/ responsibility.

[Foundl/ing/ home] Foundling home.[56] Recompense for the children through education, professions, laws, raising the spirit (otherwise they despise them, they are ashamed, that is why they're bad). Love for the fatherland.

Yes, but a temptation for the legitimate. True, you are legitimate, from the fourth floor, hand under the samovar. —But elevate the idea of the legitimate too. The government must understand that children belong not to the fathers alone. Advocate the idea of mutual burden.

Break them of science, of nationalities.

through a long period of decorous generals and banned books not prepared intelligently, without knowledge. //

Come into my house. All this is wonderful. —Perhaps a dream? What sort of dream, if our juries do not recognize crime.

But then the Kairovas are hateful.

Utin. Blasphemy.[57] If he had said it naively, it would only have been ignorance and a crude understanding of Christ—and nothing more. But then Mr. Utin added: if it were not blasphemous. This means he knows that it is unsuitable himself. Why did he say it? Of course, he felt like joking about his client Kairova—a feeble joke, in bad taste, but the jury endures everything.

Really, let's dream. Why shouldn't the government give them an education. At a loss? Nothing more profitable, more workers.

Is the idea of broadening the idea of children, as of citizens, really impossible. The necessity of education. Let's talk about that. But now *laissez-faire*. Industry itself will manage the business, give bread /.../ —It would be to direct the general activities in a new direction, state, social, Orthodox /.../ We shall speak about instability after, // later. I promised to say how the common people are superior to us, there is no instability in the common people. But this another time. And now only about the right and left.

The place is cleansed, the Yid arrives, sets up a plant, makes a fortune, tariff is the savior of the fatherland. But after all, he's got it in his pocket. No: he gave bread to the workers. And that's it. But the government supports the Yid (Orthodox or Jewish—it's all the same) with all the duties, tariffs, statutes, armies. And that's it. The Russian idea is not like that, the *Orthodox* idea. Be free, but bear everyone's burden. Love everyone and they will love you (not beneath the lash). Stand up even if alone. They won't take children from their fathers, but let the fathers be imbued with the idea of collectivization. The children together. It's impossible to destroy the family. Benefit. Wonderful. *General responsibility* (and not lechery). /.../ Time of instability. *Etc. Right, left.*

The New Time, No. 74, May 14. Friday. // /.../

In the same issue of *The New Time*, No. 74, from a German pamphlet on Bismarck's mediocrity.

One can answer some "great Russian" who made the excerpt about Bismarck, that "otherwise you don't even compare with Bismarck."

The Moscow News, No. 119, May 13. Article on *the Czech immigrants in Volhynia, on our instability* (as an example). Granting them their faith and language out of liberalism, supposedly so as to avoid unliberal chauvinism.

The Mosc/ow/ News, No. 119, May 13. In the same article about the Czechs, evidence that our clergy wasn't itching to convert the Czechs who *wanted* to join our church.

The New Time, No. 76. Murder of two girls in Kiev in the University Botan/ical/ Garden.[58]

Temporary insanity, the girls. Temporary insanity, the child pushed out the window. //

What, are you firmly convinced that there does not exist a line beyond which one cannot go in temporary insanity. All is from the environment.

Mercy is another matter, but do not corrupt the common people, do not call evil a normal condition.

Why not rape girls, etc.

Now they are still ashamed and plead temporary insanity, but soon they will stop being ashamed. Barristers like Utin hint at the future. Innocent, laws, just as it should be.

The Mosc/ow/ New/s/, No. 120, Saturday. Correspondence on the slap in Ratkov-Rozhnov's face. /.../

On Kairova. On non-com/missioned/ officer Danilov, on Petrov.
On the fact that she pushed her step-daughter.

[Kairova Utin] Where does freedom lie? In abandoning oneself to all these possible trends or controlling oneself and one's aspirations? //

The teacher who shot himself in Ostankino. *The Mosc/ow/ New/s/*, No. 122, May 17.

Kairova. //

Was at the foundling home,[59] all children of mothers sitting on the steps of dachas and sharpening razors for their rivals. Distortion of vulgar

35

feelings, not knowing themselves if they should kill or not. —In my opinion, if she had known for sure that she would kill, it would have been better because of the firmness of the concept and the decision, while not knowing for certain, only mischief resulted, from ambition, from voluptuousness, from hatred. What do you think, that I despise this? No, I know how far it can lead, anarchy outside of you, in the external law (for society is law, not to speak of official law) and anarchy within you, but still *it is a sin*, do not say it *has* to be, do not proclaim *irresponsibility*. —But of the foundling home later. /.../

But I like our Schillerism.

Children in common. //

Kairova and the foundling home.
Temporary insanity.
A letter on youth going to the common people. Right, left. Vacillation. Left is closer to the Slavophiles, Belinsky and Boborykin.[60] Boborykin on my lyricism. After all, denying himself. And you are not only denying, but still believing that you served even European humanity. About this in the next issue.
On women.
Spirits.

/.../ On the Czechs, on Orthodoxy.

Terner. —Let the Cath/olic/ churches on Nevsky Prospekt remain, but the Czechs. It's necessary to convert them.

Treasure to the common people.

On women.

Salvation from education and from women.

Spirits.
Take the questions of / ... / deforestation, instability, among the common people there is none for the present, about this after (and later, what we bear the common people), but for the present only the consideration: right-left, but Belinsky did not know Russia, about this later, but now to the correspondent on youth, optimism, the time of instability will pass, education, women.
Spiritism.
They themselves will shake off the common people.

Cosmopolite. Since I see that there is no cosmopolite besides the Russian, it is consequently an essential characteristic of the Russian, that's his peculiarity.

Spiritual Unity. Orthodoxy. Instead of material unity, through the strength of Catholicism, Roman unity.

But to be sure the Slavophiles and cosmopolites begin with this, with the destruction of an exclusively Russian idea, by comparison with Slavdom. But then, Slavdom is only the first assembly. It will extend to all Europe and the world as Christendom. You laugh at Orthodoxy, but the Redstockists, you will see, will end after all by dancing around the punch bowl and eating every one of their cups, the Stundists too. It is a characteristic of mankind. —I am very glad that I wrote that. Perhaps our very descendants will live until then and remember.

But not the destruct/ion/ of Russia, the humility of Russia's idea. //

Foundl/ing/ home.

When will that first moment be, when these children learn that they are *not ordinary children*. Probably there is no moment, from the first instant away from the nurse. They will learn that they are *worse than everyone*. Why? This (though much later), but not very: because, they say, your father and mother were dishonorable. Why dishonorable?

Feelings. The middle and talentlessness are base. The top.

Villainy or nobility, or both together. That's where to get the hero of a novel. In *Victor Hugo*—the *enfant trouvé*, the detective. —*Of course*, all these razors on the stairs are nice, but...

Purity does not bother us, especially in our country, especially in children. Or fade into nothingness. But not extol. *They carry the coffin.* How do you know, a look, a word didn't do harm? etc.

Evil is evil

...It was necessary to destroy the causes of crimes (the environment). But crime is not in the causes alone, not in the environment.

Do not destroy the personality of a man, do not take away the high image of struggle and responsibility. We will have a great deal more to say about this.

Peter the Great worried about the most immediate benefit, but we do not know his presentiments.

In his life was dreamin/ess/, rigorism, he could not have been acquainted with philosophical questions.

Means define the circumstances of the affair. The Knave of Hearts or a father who stole for his hungry child.

Says incessantly: did she love him like her own creation? But what did she make of him. Childish words.

Judging by this kind of defense, that's how it will appear to the public, that if Velikanova were in Kairova's place, hard labor, while perhaps it would not have been that way.

Perhaps profound Christianity suggested this idea to Mr. Utin, but it came out all wrong. It is a cadet's idea. Cadets really imagine that Christ, speaking of the fact that she loved much, implied precisely this kind of lechery.

This night, this sharpening of razors is hard.
What's more, one can almost certainly say that she did not know what she was doing. I.e., I do not believe in temporary insanity, not for a plugged nickel, and no one else does, I don't think, but she did not know, does that end it? Raskolnikov, the lowered axe. True, it's repulsive. But it still arouses deep compassion. But Utin destroyed everything, over-stepped the bounds. He said, it had to be so. The very fall of man arouses compassion. Why after all, she was not his wife. The correspondent is right, there are no limits. (excerpt) It does not matter that it had to be so.
Hard burdens. True, they acquitted her and certainly would acquit her, but she still suffered. —Perhaps the feeling of justice is satisfied.
But then this same Velikhanov, who lied so much, could have not lied about having paid or now paying, the bed is his.

He is born, writhes, cries, declares his right to existence, as if he has one. But into the latrine with him.
And now the lawyer appears, saying that he loved much, I am not speaking now about Mr. Utin. But apropos, if she had killed Velikanova—hard labor. //

One pillar of politics. The Sultan.
Orthodoxy and Slavdom. Constantinople as capital of Russia is inconceivable, but Constantinople as capital of Orthodoxy is necessary.[61] Orthodoxy and Russia as its senior element.

The Voice, No. 138, Wednesday, May 19. On *The Idiot*[62]—in answer to *L*, to his review of "The Paradoxalist," You have, sir, instead of a heart, a little piece of banality.

38

That there is no crime is one of the crudest prejudices and one of the most corrupt principles.

Alchevskaya's story about a little boy murdered for 10,000.[63]

Found/ling/ home. It is well known that infants acquire terribly complicated ideas and this process is imperceptible. So there is no reason for us to be so proud of our intellect. *Caspar Hauser.*[64] //

Velika/nova's/ words hands 'n' footsies.
And you, gentlemen, in your family, despite all your good breeding, never had such words.
I pursue deception.
But Mr. Utin flew off the handle and praised crime.
And if one is to be conspicuously humane, one can be humane towards Velikanova as well (though it is funny, this method is crude).

Politics. Murat. Sell dear to France. Early. Austria hinders a great deal.
Right, Constantinople is the capital of the Greeks, must split it up, for they will fight with the Slavs, —without Russia it won't come off.
Capital of Orthodoxy. —Great Russian.
Disturbances in Turkey, in which England, not knowing what to do, will probably follow its traditional policy of support of Turkey with all its might. But this policy is impossible without alliance with France. It will be necessary to tempt France. France's decision means everything. Will a head turn up in France that will manage to sell itself dearer.
Will Bismarck want to give up the Eastern question's coming to be in Berlin. //

Applause. —The court cannot but be for definition of what is evil, what is good, for unity of thought and defin/ition/. Punishment can be altered.
Obliged to send others away, reform them, make them over through labor, they want to suffer.
Who knows, afterwards, you aren't right, brother, leave us. Let them take him in another community, or even in another people. But all this is still amusingly fantastic.

Schedule[65] 21, 22 /May/	—Utin
23-24	—Environment
25	—Foundling home
26-27	—Alchevskaya's story, etc.
28	—2nd correspondent.
	Young generation.
	Beginning and Turkey.
29	—End of Turkey.

Plebs. Even in England, even in America you will find a section of society more isolated, more aristocratic than in our country. Only about instability and what we bear with us, etc.

But Mr. Utin exaggerated almost everything, I do not want to speak evil; she is too unfortunate. She loved much. If he had treated the matter more humanely, he would have been more circumspect, would not have said such nonsense. But apropos the junker.

Out of an excess of junker (barrack-room) strength at the sight of a woman.

Junkers, high-school students, cadets.

So it's as though he acquitted her. It seems they have (support) this from unnecessary excess/es/ of youthful strength.

And old lady-supervisors, even speaking in French.

Foundli/ng/ home. Heavy-handedness. *L*—about the war.

I / :/ simply that it wasn't worth preserving.

Punishment. How is one to know, perhaps, the court will decide you're guilty, brother, and he will embrace us. //

NB. *Right-left*, whether in the highest society or among nihilists—a single *phenomenon*.

Foundling home. Dunya, leg, at least she got a mother out of it. And with what reverence you look at that breast, the nurse, love—for their maternal feeling, and—what loathing Kairova. No, in our society there is still a lot of sentimentality and false conceptions (false views).

I liked these old women's clear views, for they hold *their own*. Mothers.

May

Chap/ter/ one. 1) [Excerpt from letter] From a personal letter. 2) New regional word. 3) The court and Mme. Kairova. 4) The counsel for the defense and Velikanova. *Chapter two*. 1) Something about a certain building. Corresponding idea. 3) Undoubted democratism. Women.

Women.

Foundling home. Second correspondent. Plebs. Plebs (Alchevsk/aya/) On our instability. I promised to speak of it, what we bear, but now I'll give merely an idea: right, left. In the right-left, according to Boborykin.

Instability, which does not exist among the common people, despite even Kilikinsky *volost*. What we bear despite instability, and now merely right-left.

Where are my spirits? They promised too much. //

On our instability. *The New Time*, No. 82. Saturday, May 22, 1876.
Excerpt from *The Church and Soc/iety/ Bulletin* on Stundism and Redstock.[66]

NB. An unscholarly, crude lack of faith is better than a subtle, scholarly one.

NB. Kilikinsky *volost.* Orenb/urg/ Prov/ince/.

On our instability. About the fact that we are afraid to punish the criminal. Crime is an illness (apparently), Surovin. The aggrieved lady at Palkin's. The police officers are afraid to lose their dignity. They hit and shoved the policeman. Nearly hit and shoved the area superintendent of police (assistant).

Murder of two girls in Kiev.

On instability. Terner. And about *The Ch/urch/ and Soc/iety/ Bullet/in/,* praise of Redstock by a non-believer in God. //

June issue.

Answer to critics *L.* Crime and punishment. Alchevskaya's story, etc. Women.

Answer to the correspondent about the plebs (to the common people).[67] Kilikinsky *volost.*

[Right-left]
[Turkey, Russia's role] Instability.
Russia's role.
Memento. Call on Prince Golitsyn.

Why did Pisareva die? An old lady's specialty fatigued her. She was going to receive an education, broaden thought and fell in love with the old woman. Weariness, apathy. Lively nature. She could not stand it and was disappointed. She cursed.

May 27 (June 8) George Sand died, a great, beautiful name.[68]

The New Time, No. 88. Saturday, May 29, biography of George Sand.
In the same issue our newspapers on the East, on the war and on the taking of Constantinople.
Karamzin. Shidlovsky.[69]
George Sand. My youth. Guber's *Faust.*[70] *L'Uscoque* School.[71] Phil-

anthropy! Venice. Socialism. George Sand most of all in our exile. Humanity. //

Mother.
She was a proprietor.

As usual all to a man socialist, denying property in general, but themselves owning at least some property—Victor Hugo, Herzen, G. Sand, etc., then it wasn't the same, afterwards this set off a series of writers studying the Russian peasant.

Instill the beautiful in the soul. She doesn't know. Pictures, Madonna. Egor Sand,[72] she did not believe. —Something honest, firm, I will not give up the idea.

An idealist, chiefly.
Those who studied the Russian peasant were foreigners.
Land of holy miracles.[73]

Since then a litter of trashy people has appeared, we are trash, so let everyone be trash. But why are we trash? There is nothing great and consequently, if you want, you can become great. Bourgeois
Only poetry remained then, next all science was destroyed, and the railwaymen set off.

That was the time of whole-hearted faith in the great.

She loved the aristocracy, but based it on perfection of the human soul, with which she appeared proudly, not in the form of humor, nor in the form of Belkin, Goriot, or /one word indecipherable/ but simply made them tsaritsas.

Jeanne,[74] Shakespeare.

Women should cry and wear mourning.

She took a lot of our more Russian strength (of general humanity).
End with broadening of thought.
There are no allies, all are aginst us, but there would be well-known consequences. They liberated their people, they would liberate another. Liberators. And they would firmly apply the idea in their own country. Not all /.../ banks. I speak because, if not now, then very soon, we will come to an understanding. //

42

She was a poet of the bourgeois social (educated) branch. The common people did not have a poet. Not ennobling, without beauty.

It seems George Sand expressed all her ideas before the '50's, —her wonderful later works no longer contain any sort of new word.

They considered themselves above Christ.

There is no humility in the heroines, but there is a thirst for voluntary sacrifice, for exploit.[75]

What did she mean for Belinsky? A soc/?/ poet in France is not the same as in our country. It bears on all mankind. Such was 19th century poetry in France.

Chapter 1. [1) Death of George Sand. 2) A few words about George Sand. Chaper Two. 1) My paradox. 2) Solution of the paradox. 3) The Eastern question. 4) Utopian understanding of history. 5) Again something in
Again about women]

Chur/ch/ Bulletin. Redstock.

Better coarse atheism than scholarly. They'll end with atheism, and if not, they'll become quakers and peculiar cups.

Religion is not form alone, it is everything. From father to son the atheists acted like the Orthodox. You regard Orthodoxy condescendingly. Gilbert, Archbishop of Paris.[76]

But what a comic [insc] statement: But you see we weren't able to retain faith in God, so don't hinder even Redstock. They confess themselves.

Vasiliev at Redstock's.
Liberal Orthodoxy.
(For the August issue, combine everything together and an article on *priest's bigamy*. And constant account of receipts.)

[*The N/ew/ T/ime/*] *The New Time*, No. 90.[77] Monday, May 31.

Heretical article from *The Chur/ch/ and Soc/iety/ Bulletin*. On Bigamy. //

Future ideas
July—August

Russian autocracy. On the security of autocracy. All liberties at once and all Assemblies of the Land, because the power is too secure. Only in our country. Our distinctiveness. —It could be even now, but our society is still holding out. It does not understand the Russian essence, for they lost touch with the soil. Decembrists (Westernizers). The Slavophiles *lead to true freedom* reconciling.

Russian pan-humanity. Our idea. Pan-human. It would seem to have spread. But no. In this it is to the highest degree a unity. Merge this article with the treasure *which we bear* the common people.

The Mosc/ow/ New/s/, No. 134. Sunday.

Ticket-man, drives out an old veteran. Reported by *The Mosc/ow/ New/s/* from "Week" (Masha's story concerning this).

NB. I spoke in the May issue about democratism[78] Does democratism consist of supporting unrestrained debauchery and scaring capital, hands and minds off the land. At the same time destroy the forests, for the peasants destroy them like maniacal /.../ —Mitrofanushka, they're all his nurses, feed him till he gets a stomach ache, cause his death.

They distract from reconciliation with the common people. They say he exploits them. But don't they understand that just let a capitalist have money and with any lack of civil rights, he will turn it to exploitation. Consequently, if there's anyone our liberals should pursue, it is only the honest landowners, farmers who among the common people could devote themselves to their strength and enlightenment. // Oh, do not [trouble] debauch the common people with lack of civil rights. Our time is a sort of Time of Troubles during an interregnum. They will say to me: But why did you shout about the common people and sing them eulogies? Now you admit that they're dogs and rascals? Nonsense, I love them, as I want to save them from debauchery, while you are their undoing, *it would be liberal of you. Accordingly, you exploit the common people, debauch them for the liberal appearance of your newspapers.* What will happen to Russia without forests? The situation is worse than Turkey. /.../

About the fact that literature (in [our age] our time) must carry the banner of honor high. Imagine what would have happened if Lev Tolstoi, Goncharov had turned out to be dishonorable? What temptation, what cynicism and how many would have been tempted. They will say, "If even these, then, ... etc."

Same with science.

NB. It would be concerning Strousberg and the case of the bank in Moscow.[79] //

The Eastern question. Orthodoxy, treasure to the common people. Servant to all. This from Orthodoxy. Orthodoxy not Catholicism (difference) not Lutheranism (victory hymn), not sects (cups, and today they'll take me to heaven), but in Orthodoxy a servant to all, comforts all, helps all, preserves all personalities, does not swallow them, there will be no factories. Universal service to all—broadening of view, treasure to the common people /.../. //

But the idea has not matured. The Slavs do not understand. It is only in Russia. And that is why we must merely serve the Slavs and ease their lot, but there as they wish: join the federation or not, it does not matter.

Federation of all Slavic lands, but a Russian Constantinople (banner). Capital of Orthodoxy.

The New Time, Thursday, June 10, No. 100.
Included in the Political review is my phrase about "the key in Prince Bismarck's coffer," but as if not I, but someone else said it. Keep this in mind.

The New Time, No. 103. Rober's speech to the teachers (national) at Maximovich's school, at the final examination.[80] //

One of the comparisons. The tarantula, which strayed into my bedroom at night. They did not catch it. *Piccola bestia.*[81] Florence. It was a most unpleasant sensation to sleep in that room. Half asleep, asleep, I dreamed.

Death of Apollon Grigoriev, relate fact.

George Sand is not an idea, George Sand is a conviction. A noble nature, an artist, not without mistakes.
Literature is the banner of honor.

Right-left. Apollon Grig/oriev/ on Belinsky (to the Slavoph/iles/).[82]

Apropos of Apollon Grigoriev.

Constantinople, broadening of view, Orthodoxy (we do not protect our personality, but give it up).
(v. bl/ue/ notebooks)

Political article.

Answer to letter.
Suicides (Herzen's daughter).[83] Are they afraid—the suicides? Depression, the Russian needs life, Russian thought, Herzen's daughter. Spider in Florence. *Ekkov.* Answer to a letter (about Kairova).

Herzen's daughter.

Spiritism. *—The Church and Soc/iety/ Bulletin.*

Insult to a lady at Palkin's. /.../

Letter of a suicide. //

Ekkov. Let me do myself in, just so they don't. Protect someone. He does not even think of that.

George Sand. Types.[84] Need of sacrifice and personality in types. She saved herself through that, otherwise she would have gotten muddled. She based her socialism on moral feeling, and not on ant-like necessity. She herself not knowing she was Christian (types, personality).
NB. There is no moral satisfaction, but there is moral necessity, discovered by science. In order to destroy personality, they fabricated an environment, laws, and imagine that personality will submit to these laws.
Her spiritual needs and requirements, personality, and she was the only one who was.
/She based/ h/er/ soc/ialism/ on the necessity for the moral renewal of mankind in conformity with the growth and development of the human, the civic and the political. G/eorge/ S/and/ is not an idea, but a conviction. Her convict/ions/ were through the greatest faith. In types—the necess/ity/ for sacrifices and the develop/ment/ of personality. After Christ. Latest conclusions of *science.*
And then②
On broadening of view.

(NB. and conclude: all this has to be repeated 1000 times more and explained.)
She was one of those dissatisfied with the fortunes of the Revolution of '93 (did not want to [be] see in the bourgeoisie as the ideal).

Man does not live by bread alone. On the necessity of sacrifice.

She is ours, though the Senkovskys and Bulgarins spurned her.[85]

She went drinking with Leroux—debauchery at Ledru-Rollin—a most decorous woman, mother of a family, hen-house and even a proprietress.

Girls especially beautiful. [I]
She died by the '50's. I speak only of her ideas. Artistry continued.

Ours. She was important for us. So far as she entered our exile.

She did not know Christianity. Curse remains. //

It is not humanity we are to learn from the Western poets, but *broadening of ideas and what of theirs is beautiful and sound.*
 Lately there has been a lot with which one can disagree.
 But Mr. Turgenev still lost his reverence early.
 He was ashamed of praising very much.

 —George Sand.
 —Broadening of thought, Rober in Tver. —Literature is the banner of honor. Tarantula.
 —Political (Get ready soon, and there would be war—*apropos*.) NB (when are they ready for war?
 —Right-left.
 —Apollon Grigoriev.
 —Suicides—answer to letter. Herzen's daughter.
 —Answer to letter: *why Utin.* On evil and good, *on the devil, on environment.* Is there crime or not.

[Politics] War declared. I am not my paradoxalist, but sometimes I'm better. Of course, it would be good if the peace is not broken, but *quand même,* even taking a beating, like the Bulgarians, is no good. Russia is terribly much stronger at home. If they roll out Turkey, which is beyond question, will they give them something to gain. (Austria) —Russia. Capital of Orthodoxy. Constantinople is Russia's ruin, but as capital of Orthodoxy, not.

 Semyannikov—June 15 and March 3   in all 2R. 70k.
 Kekhribardzhi—June 25   3R. 75k.
 Rober in Tver.

[Suicides] *Ekkov* here. —Herzen's daughter,
letter of a suicide.
 Piccola bestia.
 Selin—Prachkov.
 Ragozin—heart.[86] //

 Rober in Tver.
 Constantinople is the capital of Orthodoxy.[87]
 Broadening of thought lies in the fact that we do not live within ourselves like England, and do not consider achievement of goals within ourselves,

but in general familiarity and concepts.

[Suicides] Preserve Slavic units, uniting them in one Orthodoxy,

   The Russian view was formed by the fact that we are Orthodox, but this is narrowness—the glasses and spoons of schismatics, through reform is active Orthodoxy. Pardon and reconciliation with all the ideas of Europe. Of Europe we can now, after two centuries, conclude that they did not succeed by means of Christianity, they want to succeed by means of science, socialism. Denial of Christianity, not to offend Nikolai Mikhailovsky.[88] We have Orthodoxy, but the important thing is unity. Unity, first, in the destruction of the spoons and glasses. Second—in familiarity with European ideas, third—disinclination towards political usurpation, ability to reconcile.

   The capital of Orthodoxy—that is our idea, which Europe fears.
   —Russia will stay in Russia, but will become sovereign of Constantinople as the custodian of Orthodoxy.

   Here. June 29. //
   One should note that if Europe looks at the Slavs so unfeelingly at the present time, it is precisely because of Russia, because the Russians are also Slavs.

   Pisareva,[89] nat/ural/ sciences, great thought, one whole of the land, and not specialties, study dyeing for manufacture of chintz (it doesn't matter if different than the other), Pisareva, midwifery, what it gave the soul, the heart, the burn/ing/ questions, cynicism of *uneducated* people who pecked their specialties out of the bread.
   Great idea, will sustain her, and will remain, be miserable (pedagogical exam).

   Appeal. Aid to the Slavs. Europe helps—even came later; a *complete* university education is essential to calm the agitation. The enthusiasm is too serious, and only in the highest science is there enough seriousness to quiet the agitation.

   Pisareva. —(Besides what was published in *The N/ew/ T/ime/*, I know nothing about Pisareva.)

   Herzen.

   Letter of the woman who shot herself.

   Announcement, what until August.

How she excused herself. Pedagogical courses, nothing will be found on the back of the medal, be miserable.

But the laws which give education will progress of themselves.

In serving mankind, she did not find satisfaction from the bookish world, from bookish, abstract convictions. //

Chapter one. 1)	Departure abroad, something about Russians on trains, 2) [Something about Petersburg [Baden-Baden] Baden-Badenism] [3] On the bellicoseness of the Germans. 4) Last word of civilization.
Chapter two. 1)	Idealist cynics. 2) Is it shameful to be an idealist? 3) Germans and work. Incomprehensible tricks. [Wittiness] On wittiness.
[Chapter three.]	1) What helps at the waters: waters or good form? 2) One of the beneficiaries of modern woman. 3) Children's secrets. 4) Land and children. 5) An unusual summer for Russia. //

Themes for August.
About the fact that the Russian peasants, the people are not at all so foul-mouthed (foul-minded) as they were portrayed by Gogol (patched /.../) and the generals commanders of soldiers in the '40's.

Story of Father Ivan Rumyantsev about *Sesitsky*, swearer and slugger (police superintendent).

[Gogol didn't know the Great Russian people at all.] [90] //

Make-up of the Aug/ust issue.

NB. *Apropos.* Ragozin's letter. Pierce the heart.[91] —That is a profound argument, for what does it mean to pierce the heart? To foster morality, [need] thirst for morality. You won't get anywhere through intellect.

NB. Apropos of Selin (Kiev professor) and his dissertation about the fact that we have entered complete uncertainty.[92]

NB. Anonymous letter on spiritism. (Vibration of particles in the organism.)

NB. Read Potulov on spiritism.

NB. Portetsky's letter (got angry).
NB. Russians abroad are not of respectable form. Respectable form consists of sincerity and honesty. There is none because the Russian intellectuals are immoral.
Abroad even the criminals are more moral (*Zola—la belle Lise*).
Selin on the loss of ideals since Napoleon's invasion.
"Complete uncertainty." In our country, perhaps, they would be glad to believe but do not know in what.
Why Pisareva became tired and poisoned herself: she did not find the needs of the spirit. A great many women go that way, the back of the medal.

Colonization of the Crimea.[93] *The Mosc/ow/ News.* The government must. Besides, it will fortify the borders. /.../

In Germany, they say that we are not ready for battle (about the Ministry of War), about the officers. (Bah! where did I read that about officers who steal). It's nonsense they're talking—I thought to myself. //

Orang-outang.[94] —If he's going to be, then how is it that in 2000 years, he didn't invent anything, not even arithmetic. But he didn't invent anything, not only not arithmetic, but not even a word to express his thought. But is that natural: for if there is thought, then nature would certainly give a word.

There is not a common cause, and for this reason everything has broken down to personalities.

Parallel of the social family. Marriage, *association libre (esclave)* Zola and marriage according to Christ, where *esclave* is inconceivable.

Why has the real world been governed until now by a mere ideal? The ideal of the sacrifice of all of Rothschild's 1000 millions, by comparison with the realist's feeling of self-preservation.

Piccola bestia.

Democratism alone remains for us (with immorality). But this national principle was consoling.

But instead of aristocracy, the best people. Who in our country are the best people? They will establish themselves. //

Make-up of the August issue.[95]
1) On Zola, etc. (I just knew they'd start screaming about paradoxes.)
2) Pobedon/ostsev/ on Herzen.
3) On spiritism (my card-reading).
4) Ems, Journey to Ems, road, /.../ spat, lakes—the Germans' good nature: *was suchen Sie?* Character of the German, lady *pour hommes*, most curious trait. Russian and his daughter (hostile views)—didn't laugh.
(NB. Description of my spring-time adventure at the police station.)[96] In '71 the mood of the Germans in Dresden. Countess Kusheleva-Bezborodko who cursed the Germans.
—Description of the mass in Ems, etc.

5) On the Slavs Europe—the crown of mankind—permitted the Turks everything. (The idea is so far from the deed in mankind!)

Death of Apollon Grigoriev.[97] Women, according to Strakhov.[98]

Stuck-out tongue.

—Crimea (*Mosc/ow News*).
—German beggar (gave 1 mark). Old woman with mignonettes.
—Death of the province or not?
1) Lizaveta Smerdyashchaya (try).[99]
—(Antony the Roman).
—Not fully expressing the idea!
—Kurilenkov's letters about missing mail on the railroads.
Levitsky's letter on the lawyer Chigirentsev, who sold out his client's case to the opponent. (Right of dishonor, Mosc/ow/ captain.)

Too little morality. Comparison with foreigners: here there is no deliberate crime, here even among criminals there is belief in honor and honesty. In our country not only is there no honesty, but not even a thought about it. Simply immoral. Naked depravity of egoism, unashamed of its foul nakedness and only afraid of the lash, and not even afraid of that. It is all pictures of an intellectual uneducated society. But the higher intelligentsia is preserved, but it's terrible to think: they are all gray, all in their 40's. And the new ones—in the new ones there is only cynicism, they stripped naked and stripped not even for depraved pleasure (Rousseau)—not at all, without any thought at all, simply like savages, like beasts. A dog gnaws a bone, another growling. Here's the emblem: for one to drag off the bone and chew it up. Savages! savages! Orang-outang.

Safonov's letter on the officers who came to blows. The right of the strong, hallowed by society, the right of revenge. The personality is not well-provided for (Karlov irritated). A society has no rules of morality. From Europe, consequently, it brought nothing, and although there are individuals of high honor, since they have no influence, one must consider them *for now* as special cases, unable to rally from among themselves a civil society.

All this because there is no common cause and it has broken up into personalities. —And there is a common cause, but it is not visible to all. Points of view have broken up according to personalities. The Germans do have a common cause. Unification of Germany.
—As regards the repute and honor of the Germans: they say, that's the way we Germans are. But their bourgeoisie is more so. It was produced by lively business and is dear.
NB. Read Lebedev's sketch in *The New Time*. //
Make-up of the August issue.
For Karlov's main illiberality lies in the fact that he is a soldier.
Take from Herzen, from "The Stankevich Circle" for objection to Selin.[100]
Two objections to *The Stock-Exchange News* (Baden-Baden, Constantinople).
"You imitate those who have started to look at Russia like Baden-Baden" (Herzen's phrase). This does not at all guarantee the future, but makes it extremely *possible*.
In order to know what the best people are.
The best people.[101] The question of the best people should not even be asked: any sort of force, if only a bad one. But what are the best people, really? Simply an honest man, a Christian. Consequently, there is nothing to envy. But it is necessary, so that even the aristocrats will respect such a man, it is necessary to attune social opinion that way.

The best man always was so, but not where there were aristocrats. Strong men. It is not the strong who are better, but the honest. Honor and self-respect only are stronger than everything. (Insert about the Russians in Ems, no self-respect.)[102]

And in Berlin I saw an orang-outang.

Parallel of the Christian and social family. Beauty of the Christian family.

Paradox. Yes, but when will it in fact be different. [No] But the ideal. *Parado/x/.* No, although it is better the ideals be bad, and reality good. —But principle, principle is higher, etc.

War now would not be altogether bad for us, at least not entirely bad. /.../ It would set moving and bring together many separate forces and would give much new stimulus.

Talent, and talent is necessary in everything, even in a movement.

In our country there has already been an experiment in which ideas turned, formed during the time when in the universities, instead of science, parade-drill appeared, and how distortedly these ideas were later belched out.

Because woman is a great power. //

Make-up of the Aug/ust/ issue.

What does it matter that I have enemies? An honest man lives with the fact that he has enemies.

Honest men always have more enemies than dishonest men.

To take cover, chuckle and avenge oneself on another for one's own insignificance.

Paradoxalist. In our country one must tell every doctor: doctor, heal thyself.
For heaven's sake, he's advertising here that he treats confidential illnesses, and that will be impolite.

Certainly about the Russians who speak French (v. 5) and teach their children. What an old theme (tool for the expression of thought). Foreign languages are terribly useful, but only when one has had one's fill of Russian. Also in classical languages, there is no benefit without Russian. But it is the Russian lauguage that is kept down, and it will learn to think in French and will be an *international mediocrity* of which we already have enough.[103]

Emmigration of the gentry, Crimea—agriculture (v. 7).

He lies on the bed like a bundle.

He is proud and unshakable⎯⎯⎯⎯⎯
Sneaking around ⎯⎯⎯⎯⎯⎯⎯⎯⎯ meetings with a Russian

They quickly become irritated. *Everyone* wants to avenge himself on someone for his own insignificance.

Everyone must have the right to land. In our country it is a national principle. The Decembrist Yakushkin.[104] We're yours, but the land is ours. Propert/y/ is a most sacred thing: personality. But up to a certain point. The German barons, independent sovereigns united into one state. Unlimited property may be compared with a barony. They have proletarians. But that unlimitedness is not right. Prop/erty/ should be limited. But in our country and in the West! Complete abolition of propert/y/ is terrible.

One need not fear social unnaturalness. The Paris Commune is harmful because it is riot and violence. It is better to allow the enthusiasts their province. What is unnatural in these dreams will be destroyed of itself, and the sooner the better. The best acrobat (head over heels) will end by walking off like everyone else on his feet. //

Thus:
—Ems, road, all the anecdotes. English woman, Strakhov's opinion.
—Death of Apollon Grigoriev.
—Description of my spring-time adventure at the police station.
—Ems, children all. —Newspaper room. Turkey and Europe, etc.
—Crimea, opin/ion/ of *The Mosc/ow/ New/s/.*
—Paradoxalist.
—Zola. *Notes of the Fath/erland/* and *The Stock-exch/ange/ New/s/.*
—Review of correspondence. NB. Here about Herzen. (On the death of Mme. Pisareva.) Here. Death of the provinces or not?

Church in Ems. *The Church and Soc/iety/ News*'s praise of Redstock's Stundism.
—Spiritism. //

—*Ems. Pictures.*
—Sleeping roll-vendress.
Children. Three girls and a boy consulting. Girl with orphan. Children swimming.
Boy going to school. Children's loud laughter. Infants in arms with nurses. Children of Russians dancing to music. Dressed-up children.[105]
—Old beggar woman with mignonettes. Sick woman leaning against a wall. Beggar, pressed, with tooth and bundle. They put him to dry in a book so that now it's a profile that walks about, not a man.
—Service in the church.
—Russians shoving.

—German honesty, she stole a penny for wild strawberries.
—Food, the farther along, the worse it is.
—Neighbor. Greek ladies.
—Picture of Ems at sunset.
—The foulest goods, Emperor Wilhelm inspecting them.
—Girl at the springs.[106]
—Crowd at the springs.
—Russians cannot have good form. No morals.

The lawyer Gagarintsev. Free institutions are good when they are those of people who respect themselves, and accordingly, one's duty is the duty of a citizen. But the Russian man has no faith, according to the professor—lost all ideals and faith in them at the beginning of the century—went wrong, like, f/or/ examp/le/, the Decembrists, the Russian man lost all respect for himself. But he worries about decorum. Jealously fears for himself. Lies incessantly. Has no conscience at all.

Our lawyers will end by becoming so unscrupulous that they will be absolutely impossible; people will not go the unscrupulous ones, and the conscientious, or those who consider themselves such, will be so few, and they will be so sought-after, that they will become expensive in spite of themselves.

In our country, it is precisely because everyone has lost all faith, and consequently all opinions, that denunciatory literature is so dear. All who do not know what to hold on to, how to act and whom to believe, see guidance in it. And though this guidance is only negative, it is precisely what our people need, the more convenient it is—and because if someone appears with a positive ideal, they are the first to turn away, embittered, he lists all their vices, protecting himself, and they ridicule him cynically, but the negative does not commit them to anything, but on the contrary gives guidance to sneer at everyone and even at the very best people. And that is easy and fun. Man sneers and thinks that he has fulfilled his duty toward virtue.

Lahn. Not faraway, they took Arminius's wife. Tacitus.
On music.

Sent the letter myself from the post office.

The highest gentlemanliness is to be able to understand a joke, ours [somet] will understand (ours is very grand), but will be offended: Isn't he referring, he'd say, to me. Drives himself to insult. //

Ems.
Palkinskys; God bless them, let them play around.
Ems. She found 20 marks.

Germans in the Russian church.

An English woman suddenly ran, not into the ladies' room, but the men's. They didn't manage to hide from her. She clasped her hands. //

On dirty tricks. Avseenko. —Dirt in souls.

Two maidens, who landed in the police station to investigate maidenhood.

At the spring of Hebe. She was not at all bad looking two years ago, but now is definitely turning into a German.

A Russian woman has no one to imitate, and there is no need to. And if she starts imitating someone, she sets off on the very worst path.

Something warm, children, what sort of happiness is this for children.

Dried up, civilization. Here they're content, they do not notice the gathering clouds.

In our country, people are discontent, they do not believe themselves. The best people.

(Anecdote in the police station. Their 10,000.)

The best people.

What *awaits* us? Opinions have become muddled.

Chapter three. Paradoxalist, muddle of opinions.

The best people will be known by their higher moral development and higher moral influence.

The word *I* is such a great thing that it is senseless if it is eliminated. Here no proofs are needed, any proof is incommensurate. The idea that *I* cannot die is not proven, but sensed, sensed as living life. My finger lives, and I cannot deny that it exists. Exactly so with me: once one has said: I am, I cannot admit to myself that *I will not be*, there is no way I can.

Everyone must have a right to land, even if others work it (to die in the garden) (stifling factories are unnecessary).[107] Our atheism is only a separation from the common people, an isolation from the land. If you would settle on the land and work it, you would believe in God. //

A very detailed plan of the Aug/ust/ issue (shorter).

Chapter one—Having finished this issue, got on the train. To rest. Alas! to Ems and not there—(Ryleev's poetry).[108] Corner. I see more than you. In the train-car, so as not to be with Russians, the newspapers.

On Russians, especially abroad. Knew one like that. Changes views, etc.

Unfolded the newspapers, *The Stock-exchange /News/*. The problem isn't in *The Stock-exchange /News/*, but Baden-Baden.

Bore retribution, why spoke out.[109] To speak in negati/ve/ innuendoes is better.

On the East/ern/ question *The Stock-exch/ange News/*. I do not hold Granovsky's opinions. Short but powerful critique of Granovsky. (Take into consider/ation/ the anger of a patriot.)[110]

The Stock-exch/ange News/. Baden-Baden. But the ideal will always triumph. [Literatu]

This is all in regard to *The Stock-exchange News/*, I have no business with *The Stock-exchange /News/*, but as a matter of fact *The Stock-exchange /News/* amused me. Literary dishonesty. Well so what.

Kireev.[111] The East/ern/ quest/ion/ is always national. But it will be really national when it is truly the Slavs and Orthodoxy.

[Germans on trains better] War and confidence in it. Conversation of uneducated people. On the war. Denied. Countess Kusheleva. Timid shrewdness. Weapons. Bankers. Germans on trains better. More fellowship, care for one another. Conductors. *Was suchen sie?*

Story about the English woman. They didn't laugh. Dirt. [This af] Av/seen/ko found dirt in *A Raw Youth*.[112] [This afte] This in the mother's story. Improbability, but this was taken from a true event. This after the detective and the two maidens. This after the story, repeated in Moscow, about a lady, on the Seine two ladies. Announced that *The Russian Messenger* was correcting my dirt.[113] [This] I didn't answer. There was none of that. From what sources. Stavrogin (non-believer, and triumph of living, reproach of a certain dirty act). Is the English woman dirt. The English woman is better than all of them, etc. Apropos: took a pamphlet on the subjugation of women.[114] Well written. Mill's blunders. Not at all hostile to women. But suddenly it slipped in that the English woman is better. Untrue, Polish women, French women. Law of nature, that our own Russian woman should please more. Types [Most]. The Russian woman is best of all.

Apropos: Apollon Grigoriev published. Do they know how he died? His death. Woman.

However, there was something to look at from the train window, and there was something to think about. Agriculture, agriculture. The Decembrist Yakushkin.

Chapter two. *Ems. Polyglot crowd. Solitude.*

Russians again. French language. Germans, Englishmen—go about their business, —the Russian becomes acclimatized, *comme il faut*. [self] There is and can be no self-respect. (There was among the deniers. Special cases, etc.). Post office. Sent letters. How the Russian bureaucrat would be [Description of Ems] In /1 word indecipherable/ and leave 5 pf. Lermontov monument. Russians in church. Germans out. Redstock, Protestantism.

—Description of Ems.[115] Foul goods. Old women and a withered old man and all. Spring. Girls. Muses. Local female workers. Our maid would be horrified.[116]

—Reading room. Turkish question. *The Mosc/ow/ News*. Crimea. *The Mosc/ow/ New/s/* best of all, though risky. Crimea. It is gratifying that Russia stood up so and sacrifices. What do they say about England's contribution? Is it true? They reproach them. It would be interesting to know the figure. And about Austria, they scream of many millions of guldens. That's interesting.

—5-er a shirt.

—[On the best people] Russians again. There's no self-respect. There's no cause. About the best people.
—Description of the adventure at the police station.
—Children, all about children. //

Chapter three. Conversation with the paradoxalist. I said that he was a dreamer. I will explain of what sort his dreams were.
"—But you know, I was in love twice."[117]
Chapter four. Answer to correspondence (NB. Already in Petersburg.) Conclude with Herzen's daughter, and begin with Selin. Duel.

To Selin *most important*. (Ideal) Union with the common people was lost, it's true, but (Herzen's article) the need to unite with them again began only by two paths: through Europe (Belins/ky/) and the Slavophiles—(see the article: "My Paradox" in June)[118] —otherwise the Decembrists and Belinsky on the one hand and the Slavophiles on the other, would not have appeared. On both sides there was the most naive understanding of the common people, they discovered its secrets and laws, its principles (and by that bore witness to the rupture which occurred after Peter). Undertanding [was] of the common people was more sincere and conscientious. They argued about the Russian people (Belinsky and the Slavophiles), decided the matter, how to act and on what bases to unite with them. The Decembrist Yakushkin was sincerely surprised that he could not satisfy them. —One can say simply that all the ensuing arguments and disagreements of the Westernizers and Slavophiles had as their essence and main theme the problem: *on what principles and bases to achieve once again a union with the common people*. But that this union was lost—no one argued about that.

But you will agree that until 1812, union with the common people was proceeding unconsciously: no one valued them and no one bothered about them. On the contrary, they placed everything European higher, although there was no way they could give up many Russian customs and tastes, and they weren't even ashamed of them (v. Catherine's memoirs, bath house).[119] But they really began *to be ashamed* of these tastes in 1812. But at that time the concern and anguish over union with the common people begins (Slavophiles and Westernizers) (NB. One and the same union but different paths). Pushkin began it, and so it continued [nearly] until the emancipation of the serfs. The elite agonized and reinforced their idea of anguish in society. But the terrible mass of the non-elite middle ran parallel. These, considering themselves the cream of learning, continued more and more to be ashamed of the common people. Our time is that point when the anguish of the elite concerning union with the common people is already beginning to penetrate the middle. When they understand the idea, union will ensue.

Landowner/ship/. Worker at the factory—children not in stifling basements. What about private property? I don't know. Proprietors must make concessions. Communal landownership in our country.

Would that that withered beggar and that old woman not hold out their hands in their old age. Brotherhood. //

Stellovsky. That remarkable literary industrialist ended by losing his mind and dying.[120]

Afterward (or in Ems. But another *postscript* in August *then*, whatever kind turns up) /.../

Strakhov. [I'm not sa] The Englishwoman an absolute woman. I'm not saying where the excerpt is from, or whose, because I don't have the time to analyze the pamphlet.

In the police station. I consider this adventure petty, but the petty too sometimes has its abstruse side.

Piccola bestia.

Landowner/ship/. Landownership now, after the peasant reform, is chaos. (Laws on workers.) It's only just being settled. When and on what bases it will arise is a riddle. Future landowners will be *the best people* (however, I will have more to say about the best people), but now the former gentry threatens to turn into a proletariat, a dangerous proletariat. —Only when landownership is settled will there be order in our country. (A tie with the community of future landowners is desirable.) //

Third /chapter/.

[After] Begin the third chapter with the French language,[121] isolation and then situation, the Romans. And then historic/al/ position. War declared, Wilhelm etc., children. Englishwoman, withered. Landownership. *A few words.* (Perhaps, adventure in the police station.)

Chapter four, answer to Mr. Selin, etc.

It's a bad sign when they stop understanding irony, allegory, jokes. Decline of education, intellect, sign of stupidity. *Correspondent*, a sage with notices. Ball—indeed I praise the ball. If not a ball, then drinking-bouts. But here something holds the captain back. Vice is a tribute to virtue. Paraphrase of a sage, a fool. Who does not know that virtue is degraded, but virtue never pays tribute, and if it agrees to, it is not virtue. It is constrained. But the thing is that this is a fact: however vice may exult, why does it not become higher than its opposite. Vicious people are always constrained by someone to say that nevertheless virtue is higher and nevertheless they pray to virtue. This is a fact of the first magnitude and of terrible profundity, one of the most insoluble facts, —have you thought it over?
They don't know how to use the letter "yat."

Children. —Children. *La population reste stationnaire*—Malthus's mistake.[122] Dumas-*fils*. //

European diplomacy interceding for the Slavs.
Russia gave pledges of peaceableness.
Piccola bestia.
Robes, my idea of Constantinople.[123]
Dimensions of Baden-Baden.
Fürsten Lippe-Dominald /?/
Fallen officers. —Mutilated.[124]
Disappointment. Mark/ov/. *The Mess/enger/ of Europe.*

Young people ask for work.
[Answer to Selin] NB. Is it true that there was a national movement.
Answer to Selin. Prachkov—on the duel, to Ragozin, to Herzen.
September issue.

On *bureaucrats*, what is done for whom, they for Russia, or Russia for them. *Peter the Great* a landowner. Idealist.

France destroyed, she does not exist in Europe.
Union (10 million Frenchmen at the present time refuse to be Frenchmen and defend their homeland).

Answers to letters.

NB. List of amusing incidents for the month (NB, I am starting a separate heading). *The Voice* and *pronunciamento*.
The Messenger of Europe. Ironically about our proclaimed *maturity*

(asses!), but any good unity is already maturity, while you preach disunity.[125]
Moreover: unity is the highest maturity, its *last* word. The French would
give the devil knows what for unity.

Russia's only possible word on Constantinople: Yes, it is neutral, but it
is neutrality under *my* protection. Constantinople is an international city,
which means an eternal fight over it and that the Eastern question is not finished. Constantinople is Russian.[126]

Russia gave pledges of peaceableness, unprecedented in almost her entire
history.

Letters: Find work, tasks. If you are a good man. It is more difficult
than ascending the throne. Project of society. Personal. Fiscal million.
The state will give. The pride of their philanthropy should not be offended: the educated members of society will come out—perhaps, obligation of
reimbursement from salary.
Hot-bed of bureaucrats' demands for the government. //

On the fallen and *mutilated* Russians in Serbia (officers and soldiers). I
propose to call attention to this. Money already collected.

European diplomacy, interceding for the Slavs, more and more takes
away our fascination with the Slavs. Baden-Baden.

It is impossible to drive the Turkish horde out of Europe. Not necessary.
Ivan the Terrible and Kazan. They'll be selling robes. (They say there will
be a terrible shock.) Here there will be absolutely nothing and no shock.

Young people, work.
Factory worker who killed his wife, well, wherever it happened.
Peasant on a skewbald horse.
Letters of Herzen's family.
O/n/ hard-drinking officers in Belgrade, dying in two days (Viskovakov's
pamphlets).
About Suvorin and the coarseness of the attack upon him.

Articles of Markov, *The Messenger of Europe, The Voice*, No. 252, Sep-
t/ember/ 12.

Piccola bestia.
Question of the duel.

—"Prince, I do not believe your appearance," etc.

The backward moment, the moment of doubt. Drunk officers (Suvorin, Viskovatov). Has Russia improved or not? (*The Voice*, September 12, on Nemirovich-Danchenko).[127]   Above articles: Markov's and *The Messenger of Europe*'s.

The Messenger of Europe: It was so with the Candians and with the Slavic minorities, and what resulted? —And what was so bad? Why is it bad to gather in a union. Sit in a corner and pant: how smart we are, oh, how smart we are![128] //

—"Miss something-or-other in the role of a young widow, expressed the energetic type of young girl..."
That is what it means to write in set phrases (made up in advance).

Duel, wild disposition, incident in May in the district of the insulted captain's wife.

Landowners and their children, descending upon the type-setters.
There were no ideas of honor, etc. There was nothing with which to replace serf ownership. (Where are the best people?)
On the other hand, the brotherhood of men (A. M-ch).
Without the best people, the land isn't worth it. Where are the best people?)

There is no family (says Shchedrin).[129]

In France society is the Commune and the bourgeois. Two clear parties. In our country no parties have appeared, chaos. The best people are necessary.

Answers to letters.

Our stupidity always shows itself. (Kraevsky/y/ on *pronunciamento*.)
Enthusiastic recognition of Milan's kingdom. Here is a protest against the Porte, against the *status quo* and against all of Austria's claims to the Balkan peninsula. This is really in the Russian spirit. Hurrah![130]

Quotes Marlinsky's (meaningless) words on the historical purport and is in rapture over them.[131]

The Voice, No. 249, September 9. "Idea and Figures"[132]

Answer to Selin (Prachkov).

Visiting young people—officers, in comparison with the common people—
also sincerity. //

The New Time, No. 196. Extremely weak lead article on the fact that if
only Russia would declare her disinterestedness and that she will not acquire
any territory, all of Europe would be behind her. Nonsense. *Independent* Slavic principalities are even more dangerous for Europe: she understands that
they will always listen to Russia.

Idea. The problem lies not in an equilibrium in Europe now: Russia has
nothing with which to appeal to it or to appease it, but must boldly break it
and create a new combination of two or three powers. Germany and Russia.
That is why the question: who will permit us to take Constantinople, is
stupidity.

True, two huge neighbors always end by eating each other up, but when
will this be. (England will cause us to quarrel.)

The New Time, No. 196. [Protest]   Agreement with the Skupshchina
commission of the princely title.

But in No. 195 they cite how *The M/oscow/ New/s/*, in answer to Kraevsky's *Agence Russe*, declares that it had never presented such a stupid opinion
as Kraevsky thought up in his telegram.[133]

NB. Kraevsky simply out of stupidity (*not without secret monies, of
course*, where should he receive them from).

But I was speaking of *The Citizen*, which I presuppose to be on someone's secret pay roll. But on whose? Well, for example from F.P. Baymakov.[134]

Legion. What sort of legion? Something civilian. Squadron. /.../

Equilibrium in Europe is a contradiction in terms. Under Napoleon I
there was none. It was established later, but whoever wanted to or could, upset it, and for others, it was an excuse for captious objection. I have already
written: swept an empire from the face of the earth. Russia must be independent. We believed in equilibrium because we did not believe in our independence, or rather, in the seriousness of our independence. We bowed
down before Europe. Now our emancipation from Europe has begun.

To *The Messenger of Europe.* Wit is a gift—a gawky situation. You con-
tradict, but do not know what to say. Zaitsev. You are not like the earlier

ones—Belinsky, Herzen. You who trade in liberalism and come out number 1. The old—the sand will run out, [libera] degenerated from the past into something grovelingly liberal. Be witty in that direction. Oh, you barbers!

I don't say you lack intellect: you do have an ordinary intellect, but a little higher up, you really are lacking something. You are the mediocrity.

The liberal-Westernizing party, wishing as little independence as possible for Russia.

Wittiness is a gift, and if you don't have it, why do you start in?

The Messenger of Europe. On feeling and not conviction—child, give a penny, sir, for Christ's sake (p. 351), and the child dies, and the beggar commits a burglary. —(Vagner as incoherent.) "We don't know whom to wage war against." "One shouldn't want war. Who wants war, but we have to free them'" With whom are we to wage war? [Lea] A profound question, but they'll bite off their own noses.

What concern for the Mohammedans: what will happen if the Kazan Tatars contribute? They'll thank them, take the donation and be reassured on their account, that they are not given to fanaticism and that Moslem preaching did not concern them. Why are you so concerned about the Tatars and the Caucasian tribes. Clearly: you want // to demonstrate that having a single religion is reaction, fanaticism, and that we, in vengeance for the Slavs, will start burning our Tatars alive? Why do you distort the facts? And then they started talking about the criminal investigation department. Malicious insinuations: Groveling liberals.

But the Slavs really are slaughtered for their faith, like a *rayah*, a foul *rayah*. If they convert to Mohammedanism, they would immediately become equal—just you advise them!

"Even more elevated than a single faith." Why even more elevated? A single faith, i.e., [faith in] common faith in the fact that in the Gospels Christ has said the final word on the development of mankind. Faith comprises within itself all things humane and all the most elevated points of view, and the men of the Gospels are fairer than you. Why am I to be sorry for 12,000 who were slaughtered for their best cause and quality, for their Christianity and faith in Christ.
And most of all, that the common people regard it that way, but you cannot understand that.

It's a fact, no matter how much you dislike it.

Garibaldi: la république avant la France.

Two powers of equal strength waged war and Garibaldi would not come to their aid. But Napoleon died and the Republic began and Garibaldi came to the aid of the young republic and the republicans.

We'll ask ourselves, what came of all this maturity and have we become more mature? Of course we have. If we hadn't met Palaetsky and Condiore, we'd have been playing cards. Allow us to be happy that we're not playing cards. You want everything to congeal in grandeur, you don't allow people to sneeze, living life. Why not more mature. After all, we've read *The Messenger of Europe.* And how is it so bad that // we are perhaps a bit prematurely happy at our maturity? But this is with all peoples, in all peoples, this is living life.

France didn't do that for Italy. Note that in this area France and Napoleon didn't do anything. That France after all looked very unsympathetically upon Garibaldi's feats afterwards and said *"Jamais."* France was very quiet at that time.

Has it really come to consider itself more mature than before? That's funny. Society was dissatisfied with Napoleon. A mixed period, based in France, but during the first revolution, France was proud and really considered itself more mature. And then under Napoleon I how proud everyone was, 2/3 or even 3/4 of his reign, until the bourgeois rapture gave way finally to disappointment, and at the same time the suppressed revolutionary forces awoke.

Simply a pedant, a pathetic teacher, a certificate of maturity. But this is something completely different. [Who cannot] To you it seems easier to die (but to publish *The Messenger of Europe,* of course, is more your line). So it's easier, but then someone who can't manage the easier thing won't do the harder one. If we consider sacrifice for the Slavs our duty, we cultivate in ourselves, as a result, at least the sense of duty. But you propose turning directly to the trifling task of internal perfection, but where will you find the feeling of duty towards that if you do not cultivate the duty beforehand. One won't come without the other. The perfect/ion/ of man, as of the nation, is a whole integral task. You say that you do not condemn donations, but you want us, in sacrificing, not to feel any satisfaction. With you, no life will come. A stupid, dull teacher. A hollow man. Perhaps you will say that you are afraid that we, satisfied with exploits, will give up the struggle for the future. But what // fool would do that, and what a stupid idea. But it's precisely here that the feeling of duty to the future will spring up, intensify and increase. The only way it will come is as gradual life. You would like us not to be happy for ourselves, not to feel ecstasy: but then there would be no sacrifices at all. And we would sit here and play cards, as we have [two hundred years running]

65

all these centuries before this. This is the only way life happens. And your worries about a certificate of maturity are so naive that it is frightening to imagine how so much paper and ink could be wasted on such nonsense. Maxim.

Cultural and mystic/al/ creeds.
I still haven't given you a single mystical creed.
You consider philanthropy higher.
This is because you don't know the first thing about the question. I define Orthodoxy not as a mystical faith, but as philanthrop/y/ and I rejoice in this.
They have the harlot and the mystery, but we don't have them.

This load of grovelingly liberal moralizing.

Witticism.

How stupid we are *to drive the Turks out of Europe. Constantinople is ours.*
Young people work

No, better I should not give. At this point the worse it is, the better it is. It will multiply them more, [and onl] and then the State will see that it must make them all rich, and destroy the poor, etc.
But meanwhile I will think about how my stomach aches, or how painful it is to sleep in the cold, I'll give one last time, and consider principles later. —You'll say that there won't be such a fool, but then it's you talking. I acknowledge an ordinary intellect.

Meanwhile, with all the eminence of their roles, so much baseness!
And they knew whom to set as an example. It is difficult to imagine to what extent the European peoples are capable of giving themselves certificates of maturity and being in raptures over themselves. To the point that they do not notice how much there is in them that is vile. //

Sept/ember/ 13.
The New Time, No. 195. Raevsky's funeral, from Tambov a sect of the purified. *Address* of the Nikolaians.
The Mosc/ow/ New/s/'s protest against *The Voice*'s senseless telegram.
The Voice, September 12, —doubts, etc. *The Messenger of Europe.*

Mole.[135] But have we developed. What do you mean, no? (don't ask us for exact proofs beyond the word). Everything that could happen did happen. Birds of paradise are not yet flying. It's true, but then no one even expected them, however society has become more serious, become complaisant and come to be acquainted with a certain series of ideas and political views, and not to playing cards or listening to cringingly liberal, comfortable, self-satisfied didactic chatter. But you talk about the mirror, no, if they're going to look in the mirror then let them look. Otherwise where did such a load of idle and completely unnecessary moral admonitions come from? To whom would it occur that a certificate of maturity would make us indifferent? Apathy, on the contrary, will make us indifferent.

You say that there is no maturity in donations, in service or in dying. No, allow me to take their part, there is considerable maturity. It would be wonderful if such a feeling were to seize everyone: is indifferent apathy and egoism better, or cards, or raw vodka, French women, etc. And even if those have not ceased, they have at least diminished. The idea and the feeling has gotten to everyone, which means they have attained to ideas and feelings. This is some and even a significant degree of maturity, and why not be happy at that. Can't we boast about them? But why not? Don't you boast (in the mirror). The misfortune will be if we stay that way and don't go farther.

Allow me to tell you that France did absolutely nothing for Italy. Here Napoleon and polic/y/ (partly after Orsini). Such personal psychological things have a terrific influence sometimes. There would have been another policy, it would have come out different. And France would have moved. [This does not me] [Then] This does not mean that there are no supporters, workers, bourgeois there. The majority loves the idea of the subjection [to France] of Italy, even the republic/ans/ looked at Garibaldi, and then *Jamais*. And anyway, I do not think that it would have been so sober. Some other killingly funny example about Garibaldi. //

NB. First about maturity, and then about single faith, about the Tatar [Tatars o] church and Orthodoxy writes Dost/oevsky/.
Witticism.

Are there any national minorities in our country which have been destroyed for the advantage of the Great Russians. There is after all the desire to make do on such conventionalism.

Separate the mystical fate from the civil. Here we're not talking at all about [faith] what you're thinking.
Although the element of faith is very important among the common people. Here, in the present case, the element of faith in living life, there is honor, conscience, philanthropy, the source of everything is Christ. What, are you better than Christ?
I did not present you with a single mystical idea.

Yes, of course, on the one hand...

67

But if we start from the other.
What is better: on the one hand and on the other hand, or naive Vagner?
You are *fruits secs*. You are not Granovsk/ys/.

That, well, they say, they've all gotten carried away, but one will stop them.
Certificate of maturity, only writers gave it, but sympathy for the Candians was still sincere.

What is it you want? For us to sacrifice our heads. Not be carried away, without poetry. No, you refuse. So now what? But we should not forget that in any case we are not mature, and in pride abandon causes, by which in our own country, etc.
Who will forget that, what a fool!

The theater. The opera. Everyone is in raptures. —Opera is opera, but we should not forget that we have a question about the police,—or a ball—not forget literac/y/. —And we won't forget, everything in its own time! But you say that it won't work, if not, //
incommensurate.
So they sit in school, but don't forget that there is more.
So on Borodino field,—and it's good that you fought so, but don't forget, that there are many civic matters.

Conventional liberalism.

Stereotyped philanthropy, grovelingly liberal tendency.

Liberalism's "gloomy blockheads."

The main thing. The theoretical attitude toward the matter, i.e., if you like, not even a theoretical one, but simply—a lazily domestic one, there's no thought here, this is a stereotype.

Concerning political maturity, I am not to blame if I see it only in the national sense (the presence and the possiblity of this sense is a very important fact and the result of maturity) and even more, perhaps, in the fact that even many members of the educated class have agreed in both feeling and deed with the common people. As for an intelligent attitude toward the matter— the periodical press has not really distinguished itself. Only *The Moscow News* is at the height of maturity in its attitude toward the matter,—and of the others, I would call few, very few newspapers serious, and if one were supposed to always believe them, almost not a single one.

Orsini, or more correctly, the future guardianship. France and the Romanic tribes. Thiers. Remember that France is very true to its historical traditions.

And later when Cavour went on with his affair, and Garibaldi seized Naples—do you think that it was pleasant for France, and if not, what of Napoleon, and France?
And that famous *Jamais*! (Don't you remember?) //
But France does not like to play the benefactor gratis. Seizure. Napoleon I. But in our country—unselfishness. They pointed it out to you, poked their fingers at it, but you don't pay any attention to the Orthod/ox/ cause. But that's why this formula is beautiful, because there is unselfishness in it. It will have an influence on our diplomats.
And again: "France did more." But then it's not over with Serbia. But the national movement is still more reliable than the political calculation of Napoleon III.

Imagine that they will even forget their certificate of maturity. Most important: all this is fantastic, all this is not the way it happens in life. Old incorrigible idealists.

A frightened crow is scared of a bush.

Nor do I think that one can accuse the Germans of very great modesty and temperance. Certainly not the English? They are so modest, so humbled, one might even say.
Here's an axiom: there will never be a time (a state of things), when Constantinople will not (would not) be someone's (not belong to someone). This is an axiom. One ought to note it. —Even now there could be (in fantasy, of course) a combination by which the East would fall to one power and the West to another, and who would stand up to these two powers? I do not say that this will be or ought to be, I am against such a solution, I say only that this in fact could be.

Run-of-the-mill folk go on blissfully and suddenly there appears a Napo-//leon, a Bismarck, a miracle, but they again become used to it, again continue blissfully and suddenly again a combination, again a miracle. The characteristic of simple people lies in the fact that with every combination they consider the whole matter finished, then the word "equilibrium" (which never existed) appears etc.

While Kazan existed, [woul] it was impossible to foretell to whom European Russia would belong: the Russians or the Tatars?

We thank the Tatars, and what then?

What did you want to say? Did you want to say something?

You concerning maturity. This phrase has recently begun to create an unpleasant impression, you have seized upon it... But who thinks that we have completely matured and that we *must* stop. To what idiot would that idea occur? But that's why it occurred...to such a pedant to pose.

About the fact that the Turks broke truces in every possible way and moved their forces from one place to another.

The N/ew/T/ime/, No. 197, Sept/ember/ 15. Up-to-d/ate/ news.[136]

Eastern affairs. Times correspondence from Vienna.

Our poor soldiers, our poor Sevastopol men, with George Crosses, old majors, medical divisions and field chapels,—it's all socialists and communists! Depraved men and women![137] However they can attain *some* goal. Mikhail Grigorievich, poor socialist.

Here are *The Mosc/ow/ New/s/*'s words on socialism and the slaughter of the Bulgarians by the socialists, No. 234 (Septemb/er/ 14).

Lead article.

Equilibrium in Europe did not exist. True, diplomatic pressure from Europe [was so] in favor of the rights and responsibilities of equilibrium was sometimes very strong for other powers... But these were sheep. For the wolves never once was there a law written. I will only note that in the present century never once was Russia a wolf, but always a sheep, true, a voluntary and chivalrous sheep, but a sheep nonetheless.

The Mosc/ow/ New/s/ is the best of the newspapers. The rest are green. Even the hoary newspapers are green. It pleases me that here I still pass judgement on politics, and about such affairs too. [Especially] There are fine traits of greenness: to call the English first minister, premier (probably they call him that in English). When /.../ Disraeli was made Earl of Beaconsfield—in our country, it was practically a holiday for the newspapers. To think that some purposely wrote about England, in order to use the phrase Lord Beaconsfield. And in general foreign personal names arouse fascination in us. How can one compare, for example, in euphonious grandeur such personal names, as for example, Lord Derby, Lord Somerset, Harrison Devonshire—[or] with Naryshkin, Repnin. In comparison with such names as, for example, Saltykov, Pleshcheev, Prince Kozlovsky, Rostovsky, Kutuzov, they are definitely inferior. Somerset is so prominent because he is a Somerset. That's something important. But what is our Russian name. Montano, for example, is just as graceful, both severe and graceful. And here's Ivanov, Kupriyanov, —ugh, how uneuphonious.

What is this? Admiration that he is premier, and not simply first minister (well, this could very well be) or simply the most innocent boast that, see, they say, I know that in England the first minister is not called the first minister, but the premier.

And really: when he writes "premier", this increases his self-respect, as if he were premier or at least equal to events and of course now he understands all of politics.

[And if not the premier, then he runs in the same circles as the premier]

Beaconsfield.

Beaconsfield, /D/israeli a novelist, he has probably written himself, how charming. And if there were such a land, etc.

Of course these are all insignificant [notes] proofs (of the political greenness of the newspapers). But then all the rest is in line with this. //

Perhaps we shall give a certificate of maturity: why not let the little one pass, we'll get worked up.

Somerset—and then in comparison with him Stasyulevich.[138] What disharmony!

Borodin/o/ Field, you die, but that's easiest of all, it's much harder to pay attention to one's civic imperfections, to understanding the land.

"Leave us alone, sir, you've paid attention, just let us finish the business here, don't get in the way."

I'm not saying anything and I don't even want to get in the way. I'll step aside a little farther, to a withdrawn spot, that's where I'll make my observations on this business, a very simple one by the way, but I'm only afraid that you will become proud, give yourself a certificate of maturity, while...

"But you will be good enough not to look at us, you see, we would strike right now."

No, I'd better move off elsewhere, and I will empathize from there.

"Let us live, sir. Well, we'll celebrate a bit, can't do without that, and then we'll go farther. And there isn't anywhere, not anywhere where people don't celebrate a bit." —Do we boast. The French, over there, how they boast to the whole world! And the English! And the Germans.

But it's precisely about the French that he writes and even gives them as an example. Liberation of Italy. What a strange conception of fact.

Constantinople. It's most likely that England will win it by lawsuit, i.e., she will still support Turkey, her liberalism, grandeur, necessity and independence , but when it comes down to the last minute and she sees that she can't any longer, she'll go and occupy it. She has already started: with Egypt and the Bezik bukhta.[139] So that Russia will have to deal with England, and I don't suppose she will ever decide to take Constantinople from Turkey.

Chernyaev, Egypt, *The Mosc/ow/ News*.

I left it unanswered, for what can you answer, [it's nec] to answer, it's necessary to start from the very beginning, and in some societies and with some questions that's not only awkward, but even indecent.

In our country the most able men do not understand the Eastern question. //

2) Who is afraid of a tarantula: I don't think the stock-broker Yids and the heartless diplomats are. Honest men, they are firm, but they couldn't not be afraid. War is a good thing, even. We have doub/ts/ about the officer, about the movement of society. Greenness of the newspapers.

NB. 1) Perhaps nonsense, but perhaps a terrible and radical political upheaval.

Piccola bestia. People don't die from tarantulas very frequently.

Effaced himself.
1) *Piccola bestia.*[140]
2) Words, words, words!
3) Combinations and combinations.
4) Robes and soap.

1) Inveterates.
2) Kifo-Mokievism.[141]
3) [The same] Continuation of the preceding.
4) Kifo-Mokievism article.
Terrors and fear.
—To Maslennikov.[142] //

[it was enough to turn up]   [Sergei Nikitich Kolontarov]
[well they'd hide somewhere there]
Robes and soap
Weighty words.

They made do on hundreds of anecdotes about the common people, which amused them [terribly] terribly, to which I am witness—frequently behind the dullest incomprehension of what is transparent and quiet/ly/ shines in his humble simplicity. //

Current:
Reread what is written in the book (on the duel, for example).

Then letters, etc.

The best people. *The main thing.* Where are the best people? We didn't stick to the estates and prejudice, but only to the ideal. The literary ideal is the plebian. The national one—the ideal of the good man, is better. Moreover principles like learning is light. [you hi] All together is to a higher degree democratic—just note that. Bureaucrats, created by Peter (they didn't hold on to the ideal of the good man), it wouldn't occur to anyone that the rank of state or real councillor is given for moral perfection, while in the strict sense it ought to be that way, and when the system was set up that is how they calculated, it is undoubtedly so (with them they wanted to replace birth, hereditary positions; the hereditary system is somewhere portrayed as a crushed monster and in its place pure angels appeared—the registrar, the court and the state counsillors). But at least the rank was set up to inspire due respect, and the person bearing it was appointed to hold it with dignity, so that both society and the common people would recognize it as all the very best. But not so. Democratism triumphed. But that's just an ideal, and in reality... But the basis of honor... [etc] 200 years of engrafting, besides *man is man*: the highest ideal is to forgive and in the grandeur of one's imperturbability, of one's tranquillity in injury—subdue people against their will. But when will men be like that? Meanwhile the law // clearly demands the ideal: forgive. And does not understand the answer: but you see I wear a sword, where is honor, otherwise it's cynicism for you, and harm for society. But then forgiving because of an ideal only is pious, while forgiving because of cynicism, shame, the cynicism of egoism, i.e., because of cowardice—is base. But there are laws, says the law. That's just it, there aren't.

Elusiveness is the most powerful thing.

Karlov, dogs. Well, what justice of the peace—

On the children, on the wife (which /?/ society always supports. Letter of a correspondent).

Yes, the correspondent is right, and one cannot bear it. Society will begin to despise and not respect you. You can rehabilitate yourself only by having murdered yourself.

Final abstract of the Sept/ember/ issue.[143]

—They heard the schemes of some Germans—and not mine. *Piccola bestia.* Robes. East/ern/ question. Egypt. Chernyaev. Constantinople is ours, there is no equilibrium. New phase of politics (twins).

The Messenger of Europe (whole answer).

—[To Selin] To Ragozin.

—[To Selin] On Herzen's daughter.

—To Selin. On the duel and Pechorin.

Last page on events. //

The Contemporary News steals from me, but writes stupidly. *The New Time* delighted, No. 198, September 16.

Oh, *The Messenger of Europe* says that it does not want to hold back the common people, and yet the common people's movement is terribly offensive to it. This Granovsk/y/, after his article, saw the movement of the common people in the very sense in which he denied it.

Candians. This affair appears in stages: first the Candians, then the Slavic minorities, then battleships' encounters, —why all this should not be.

We have matured—this will never happen. If such eccentrics were to appear, then immediately others would appear beside them, and nowhere as in Russia: the spirit of contradiction, the spirit of doubt. Nowhere more than in Russia, and you hold up France.

The foundation in Europe—two powers.

The Englishman seems modest? Or the German: ,ndeed, here's a really humble person, and what modesty! and what dissatisfaction with himself, from Bismarck and Richard Wagner to the Revel... [Ger. English(man)]

Wittiness. And if God didn't give it to you, it's no use deciding to use jokes. A respected creature loaded with moral admonitions.

The Eastern articles from *The Messenger of Europe* are useful for the intellect, but...don't you see, I much prefer—I'd better stop. //

Only Russia is bound to European equilibrium.

You were the idealists of the '40's, but you have grown old and turned into something which, though very much respected, is loaded with a whole pile of antiquated, inappropriate, ready-made moral admonitions, superfluous, primeval, so [antiquated] that one's almost ashamed to read them. However, perhaps this is simply a lazy attitude toward the matter, something mechanically, grovelingly liberal.

Granovsk/y/ is inferior to Belinsk/y/. Well who is frightened that we won't go any farther, because we will put on airs and rest content? And who can take that for something serious and profound? But then, perhaps you really are frightened it can happen from you.

Study Orthodoxy, it is not only ecclesiasticism and ceremonials, it is a living feeling, fully those very living forces without which nations cannot live.

There isn't even any mysticism in it—there is in it only philanthropy, only the image of Christ.

This

I do not deny you have intelligence, but of course it's not intelligence proportionate to the Russian movement and the Eastern question.

Oh, of course; the Eastern articles from *The Messenger of Europe* are useful for the intellect, but...but I'd better stop here.

And why not boast? After all everyone abuses us so, and we have been abusing ourselves 30 years running.

Admit that you wanted to be witty—eh? But don't you see: witticism is, first of all, a gift of nature and...however, I'll break in here: why touch upon the most ticklish points. Irritated. I would like...for them to behave better, otherwise we'll manage to answer.

You shall perish beneath your pile (load) of liberal moral admonitions, etc.

...Many men who, though ordinary intellects and backward ones, because of their limitations, consider themselves in the fore of the movement.

You turned out not to be in the fore of the movement, you do not understand it. That is not at least, it is at very most. Here we have our meeting with the common people: we turned out to be incapable of thinking, feeling correctly, incapable of deciding on anything. //

The main thing.
The New Time, No. 201, Sunday, September 19. Article: "What is to be done?" From the English *Daily News*. Program of the English liberals.[144]
Most important. September 22, *The Voice*. Opinion of *Journal des Débats* on publ/ic/ opinion in Russia, arises just as easily as it is quelled. Insert in answer to *The Messeng/er/ of Europe* in the section on the *Cretans*, etc.

For a single faith or not for a single faith.
Why, simply help.
You see, you're standing up for the Tatars.
One's for faith, one's for what they're for.
freedom, but still weak, oppressed and slaughtered. //
Most important.
If they were developed enough to fight for freedom. —But they would turn out to be cowed to the point that they no longer dreamed of freedom, but simply wailed over their kids, whose tormentors would cut off a finger every five minutes to prolong their torment before their fathers' eyes (that's how it was), and suddenly a coldness comes over us; no, they have not risen to the concept of freedom, to that single blessing of men, and therefore I will

keep my five rubles in my purse. Your understanding [th] , Christian shoulders, eh? what do you think? And that's why there's no use your standing about *with your arms folded* before the national formula, but Orthodoxy is the cause.

Go off to lie on the stove.
They will never deign to investigate the real truth of things, but go off into their theoretical definitions, made sometime at a great assembly /by/ Her/?/, Odoevsk/?/, which meanwhile turned out in *some cases* to be terrible short-sightedness and injustice.
Inexperience in the conduct of any business—that's what we've got.

You want it not to be too much, to be a bit less.

Right now, right at this moment the English and the German press are advising our government to get to calming the arisen Russian spirit. But this is, of course, something different, you advise society itself to calm down. //

The New Time, Thursday, Sept/ember/ 23, No. 205, proclamation of the Sufis in Constantinople from the newspaper *Temps.*

You get mad at the rubric, let's assume it is your business—but why analyze the reason you say, for which the don/or/ is or is not noble. The common people simply give.
Finding denominational intolerance in the Russian man is sinful, simply sinful.
What accusations haven't been piled on the head of the Russian man. It's shameful.

Final
If it were only from the irritability of your self-esteem: I think I'll speak, you'd say, more wisely than all of them, then it would be perfectly excusable.
An unresourceful man likes awfully to distinguish himself.
But since you really believe in these qualities (don't deny it, you do), it only shows your pathetic ignorance, etc.
Harmf/ul/ abstractio/n/, harmful dissemination of false ideas. Gray-haired sinners against the Russian people. //

One Faith
NB. The Gospels do not allow searching for reasons to help. Simply accept, the Samaritan.
And if you once allow a reason for helping—you'll immediately get into intellect and reasoning, there is no sufficient reason, no, help him, he does not love freedom—that first blessing of men.

Why do you want to cancel out a historical necessity, which is preserved in real life, and put in its place another, academic and incomparably more inconsistent, erroneous and base idea.

Not to speak of how absurd it is to try to move the wall. You won't move it, you know. Westernizing Kifo-Mokievites.
And what if an elephant hatched from an egg.[145]
And what if there were no history and consequently neither Orthodoxy nor any single faith, then we would have furthered a higher ideal, freedom—that first blessing of men.//

Single faith.
The Samaritan: the Gospels teach one not to pay any attention to faith.
Instead of faith, yourself, but it's worse for you.
But once you put down the rubric, freedom—that first blessing, I will not *help* the Bulgarians (but the Montenegr/ins/).
They lead to ecclesiastical questions, etc. But is this applicable in this case at all?
Certifica/te/. *Certificate of maturity*. What senile pedantry!

Final. You've had it, a different time is coming.

Self-flagellation in our society. //

October

Notes.

Notes. Committee for the relief of widows and orphans of those fallen in the war and donations to the following address: Sergievskaya, House No. 17 (from 11 am. to 1 pm.). In all, through Octob/e/r 1 (6258) rub. received (*vide The New Time*, No. 214, Saturday, October 2).

Shariat—the spiritual and moral-juridical code of the Moslems. The interpreters of the Shariat are the clergy, and they preach war against the Christians (*The Russian World*, October 2).

October issue (initial program).[146]
4 elements.
1) On assistance for youth.
2) Answer to letters.
3) Story.
4) Easter/n/ question (at the very end).

Beginning:
About what the best people are. Rank and wealth (landowners), then merchants. [The landowners have died (the gentry)]

The common people have their own ideals. Insinuated themselves (into even the best). Many testimonials. (Different ideals, inconsistency, muddle, Pechorin.)

The landowners have died off, the best people have died off. Reforms, /.../ merchants.[147] Talent, education passes fleetingly, but the main thing is *money*); *wants to give up* rank, courtiers. The common people are silent (debauchery has touched even them). National ideals. The preaching of socialism (it has success because there are no better ideals). [ai]

Aid to the Slavs came just in time (the landed class and the family are collapsing). In Russia, a riddle.

(Strousberg, Polyansky weep ignominiously.)

—Herzen's daughter.
—Tramps. Pauperism.
—With an icon out the window.[148]
—The best people. //

Current—October.
Current for the Oct/ober/ issue.

Youth. —Check of horses. [Police-officer] District officer, who deals with them: aren't there any who did military service, —shock in society and on the exchange.

Correspondence. The editorial staff of the publication (Gaydeburov) not finding it suitable (NB, to all appearances, the word *suitable* means possible according to the censor, etc.).

Society. Ideas from which I start (axiomatic):
1) The positive advantage of the fact that educated people will turn up. The increase of intellectual forces.
2) The decrease in the intellectual proletariat, *flight to the common people.* Strengthening of the domestic principle.
3) They *will yield.*
4) Faith in the strength of the young in their nobility.
5) Hope from future unity. They have their own *alma mater.* Feeling of general gratitude, inculcation of principles and rules which they themselves have already deduced from life, and not those taught in school in the form of compulsory formulas, etc.

Throughout the university towns, but with the preservation of general unity.

To the common people. Knaves. Tramps, closeness to swindling, disunity, bad elements. —*Incalculably more bad than good for the State*. For 500,000 one could eliminate it. Is 500,000 a lot for such a blessing? //
Unifying the young people and their acceptance of their *moral unity* and rules from the educators, straight from free society.
And conversely, both society's and the State's (in its best representatives') knowledge of youth, of society. Recognition of what to accuse and what to [pardon] excuse. Justice. More profitable than a battleship or Popovka, [149] which cost not 500,000, but four million (although Popovki too are essential).

There cannot be clashes between society and the government. Indeed in society itself there may be and certainly will be elements [from the gov] of wishing the government well, even higher and stronger than the officials of the government themselves.

Society. I could talk a lot of nonsense, though I still am not presenting a plan, the basic ideas (axioms), from which I proceed are *faultless*, I believe in that. —And I can always be corrected of nonsense by those who understand it better than I.

Ironclad battleship, here I see such *iron-handedness*.
Soc. Nekrasov, who left his father. //

A lot of scandal—and no result. Everywhere playing the stock-market, everyone's a stock-broker (Russia's highest governors). Budget and finances, fine, but what is worth a ten-kopeck piece, they give a ruble for. /.../ Merchants /.../ No education, no development, mammon, peasants grown rich.
The best people. Where and what are the best people now. The ranks have declined, the landed class has declined. The commonfolk's ideals have remained (crazy, unpretentious, but direct, simple. The bogatyr Ilya Muromets is also one of the offended, but honest, just, true). In society even a professor, even a learned man, talent, but let them be honest and true. It's clear that that kind of outlook would have to take hold among the common people—our only salvation. But if they are going to respect the merchants, mammon. These struggle, these want to overpower the commonfolk's worldview. As long as there's money, as long as there's white fish on the table. Vast national upheavals, like war, would be salutory.

There is a war every 25 years. Nor does progress stop it, nothing does. Which means, it's a normal condition.

The simplest consideration: if there is a truce for the possibility of talks for 6, 5, 3 months or 6 w/eeks/ (it doesn't matter)—then, let's assume military actions and all those lines of demarcation will be strictly fixed. Well, and the slaughter of the Bulgarians, which is continuing. Isn't it // all the same for Russia? (NB. Death in Petersburg, Octob/er/ 4 of a Christianized Tatar soldier, killed by two of his former co-religionist Tatars, of course, because he was baptized.) *Here's an example of the Shariat for you, right under your nose.* If this was in Petersburg, how are we to protect the Bulgarians, —who are *there*, at home, i.e., by the Turks? (On the Tatar soldier see *The New Time*, No. 218, Wednesday, October 6.)

Axiom

We must always know and remember and be convinced that in the decisive world-wide questions, Russia, if she wishes to say her word or carry on her outlook independently, will always find *all* Europe against her, without exception, and that *in the strict sense of the word*, we have *and never will have any allies in Europe.*

It would be better for Europe to divide into two powers, the German and the Pan-Slavic (England aside). Then it would be finished, and both powers could get on together, absolutely not disturbing one another (a final and radical change in the map of Europe).

Elimination of the Romanic tribes. Perhaps only the Pope could unify them. The other // little European peoples could flourish individually. But politically there would be only two powers.

Of course, this opinion about *The Messenger of Europe* is made for the ancient old *Messenger of Eur/ope/*, and not for today's, edited by Mr. Stasyulevich, of course, moreover, it's in a completely different format and not at all on the *same* paper, *but*...and the paper is not at all the same.

in a completely different format, and the paper is not at all the same, but...

The Mosc/ow/ News. The sufis' preaching according to the Shariat (*The Mosc/ow/ New/s/*, October 5, No. 253).[150]

For our society, this summer is a whole course in a universit/y/ faculty.

The Voice. Octob/e/r 7, No. 277. Larosh's article, praise of *The Messenger of Europe*, "we would do better to make donations to the schools."[151]

Without this, as you say, *inert* (?!) indefinite feeling, there will not be contributions to the schools either. What a silly idea, what a petty idea, an artless idea. Old sh/.../t.

The Voice was about to chime in, in unison with the noble impulse, because its issues are not selling, but in the satirical articles it has both *L* and em. Where will you get raptures over the schools given our stockmarket, without sacrifices of blood (militarism! The ass!). //

See.

Is it possible now *to suppress* the *common people's* movement on behalf of the Slavs, and would it not be a much greater danger not to satisfy the common people, to whom reports of the suffering of the Slavs have already come through. See *The Mosc/ow/ New/s/*, Oct/ober/ 6, No. 254, Wednesday. Letter to the editor.[152]

More about *Constantinople.*

The New Time for October 3rd, No. 215.[153] Article from the provinces, on the eve of the solution of the Eastern question. The newspaper prints it as an example of purely Russian views on the Slavic cause. —Again Constantinople is a common place, neutral (both Ignatiev and Danilevsky and examples of views, that is all). But is there any sense in these heads! Could Constantinople, is Constantinople ready to be neutral, no one's. *Free cities* worked out their form themselves through long life, but what can you make *out of nothing* in this case. For what is Constantinople—a huge mass of Mohammedans. The center is Mohammedans, and the Jews, the Armenians and even the Slavs will side with them against the Greeks. A war will start for predominance, just exactly the same as in Turkey now. //

The Greeks cannot but demand greater freedom. The Turks, as the stronger, cannot but slaughter them as now. The Patriarch will quarrel over Sofia, over Christianity. They will quarrel over capabilities. The Greeks are more capable, cunning and educated than the Turks, while the Turks are stronger in the mass. But the Greeks can no longer look upon them as masters, for the Turks have lost the authority of the caliphate.

And all the Greeks (Athens) will be at one with the Constantinople Greeks.

War and butchery (the Slavs, perhaps, for the Turks), an international garrison will have to be installed. A free city with an international garrison is fine. It will not even be a common place, but a rotten place.

It will end of itself with the English turning up for the sake of order and appropriating everything.

An international garrison in the Dardanelles is also surprising. (The intrigue: each chief of the garrison pulls for himself. So a general governor is indispensable, isn't it, but who will install him, by choice the Turks.)

As soon as there is war with Russia, Europe bars Russia from the Dardanelles! And are we really supposed to sit locked up forever, never to see the sea!

Constantinople is ours, must be ours and no one else's again (Pozzo di Borgo).[154] See Soloviev's article "The Eastern Question."

In order to control the sea, it is necessary to seize a passage to the sea once and for all.

Immediately after this a second article: *Europe and Two Powers*. France is a desolated nation and has said all it has to say. And there are no Frenchmen there. For—to the socialist and to the common people—to the worker—it is all the same. The bourgeois—all the same. The Bonapartists will go over to the Germans. The legitimatists are a corpse, that leaves the republicans, the ideal *république*, a name without a body. //

An important page.
On Molchalin.

The Russian World's stupid article against *The Voice*'s article on aid to a Turkish captain (gone over to Christianity).

Orthodoxy is not a disunifying, but on the contrary, an all-unifying motive. This "rubric", by which the whole Balkan peninsula, with not only the Slavs, but the Greeks and Constantinople, will side with us.

In the Crimean War, Russia proved not its impotence, *but its power*. Then it was possible to speak so for future *reforms*, but now the situation is *different* and it is necessary to tell the truth. Despite the *rotten* state of things, all of Europe could not do anything to us, despite its expenditures and debts in the billions.
And our internal state is stronger than anywhere else. Autocracy. The European view of it among the kings (they defend themselves with the Guards) and its future turn toward the Russian soil, i.e., all freedoms, for they *are not afraid* (as in the West) of the common people and their subjects. //

Apollon Grigoriev.
They will request transfers. /.../
I am ready, that is the direct responsibility of a Christian. But one should not strengthen, consciously strengthen a *status in statu*, but I am not speaking of that at all, but of a great idea.
The New Time, No. 224, Tuesday, October 12.
On Strousberg and his *great idea*. Even the flies heard the news, honeyed souls, —means of communication.
—I suffered from the denunciation, but not you.
—Not only will they not fine you for that, but even at the present moment of disorderly risings and cries of: "To Serbia!" or "For the Slavs!" — they will give even you a cross for moderation and thoroughness.
They will give distinctions for that, for moderation and thoroughness.

—But if you do not love Russia, I will not insist that you do love her. Do excuse me for that! I want to remain free not only on the one, but on the other side too. My motto is for a just cause, who is not just has only himself to blame.

You wanted to speak more wisely than all the rest, but that's not the way it came out.

The New Time, No. 226—Thursday. —"Does not the command that Loftus leave for Livadiya mean England's complete impotence?"[155]

Just you wait. She'll show you impotence.

Journal de Pétersbourg. A newspaper for lackeys.

The Moscow News, Thursday, No. 262. Strousberg on bankers (great idea).

Is it a great idea? Because of your great idea someone must suffer.

(The best people.)

Here *The Voice*'s article, October 7, Larosh, praise of *The Mess/enger/ of Europe*.

We will start collecting for the schools. There will not be schools either without this *inert feeling*. With Strousberg's great ideas. //

Strousberg. From the tearfully repentent scoundrels to the [seriously] truly non-comprehending, why they are scoundrels.

The Moscow News, No. 263, October 14.[156] Leader on the workers' congress in Paris, renaissance of socialism, parallel with the Eastern question. *Splendid comparison*.

The Mosc/ow/ News. Same issue on the Red Cross[157] (Tokarev). Non-comformity of the doctors. Isolation. He should begin to distinguish himself.

The Mosc/ow/ N/ews/, same issue. On the sale of women and children *in Constantinople*.[158] The Loftuses[159] permit it, the students in Pest in honor of Turkey.[160] An unstable peace.

Instability, glad that they fell on Strousberg.

Members of the council did not look: but then everyone in our country always looks at things that way.

The New Time. Saturday, October 16, No. 228.

Ketcher's toasts.

Stupid NB society. Artlessness. Since I borrow, I must say: from Suvorin. Many expressions have been lost. One from the other. *To efface one-self*.[161] (Molchalin. Triangular wound. Died on the sword, like a dragonfly, but was austere.)[162]

Shakespeare perishes from stupidity.

The Stock-exchange /News/ for Saturday 16 (*The N/ew/ Tim/e/*, Oct/ober/ 17).

On the harm in the taking of Constantinople, etc.

On the pettifogger Noreyk.

The N/ew/ T/ime/—a newspaper which I read not always with great pleasure, but whose success shows how sick we are of *The Voice*, endeavoring to say something to *The Stock-exch/ange News/. //*

[Reality] Fantasy can never withstand comparison with reality. *Shchedrin.*
I knew that.
1) Two deaths. Herzen's daughter. Cold gloom and tedium. Step-mother.
2) Then out the window with the icon.
Humble suicide. God's world is not for me. Somehow, afterwards, it seems a long time.
On madmen.

—Tramps. Pauperism. —Rumors about the university. Believe it.
—Transfers? Leaves pangs of conscience.
—Who will be our best people? Those who understand of what happiness consists. —In wealth? In moral freedom? /.../
—It is dangerous to suppress Christianity. About Russia, they think that it is all too easy to do anything with her (Westernizers). Meanwhile everything goes by its own laws. Larosh's article. For the schools. Nonconformity of the doctors.
—Isolation. Tokarev, doctors. The lady who answered me. There is no unity in the upper crust. However unity is in the common people.
—On Constantinople. On England. Everyone drags that in, so why not me.
—On Loftus. Yes, just you wait.

Stellovsky, Apollon Grigoriev (best people, only money).
But there are still the poets, or else Stellovsky.
I before nationalities.

and: latest news.

With the icon—and how dare one think so much of oneself?
The lady served.

NB. Words and wordlets.

This time England will not fight. Mark. But she will occupy all the places which she ought to, and which Russia should have occupied before her, and you sure won't drive her out of those places. But this time she will not fight, attack, interfere as in '54.

The New Time, No. 229. Satirical article (Polyansky).
October 17, Sunday.
The Petersb/urg/ News. Sun/day/. Octob/e/r 17. *On the step-mother.*

That the Commendatore is great is a difficult idea, not out of envy for the Commendatore—but by his own judgment of himself, that he is himself a lecher.[163]
But he is not a lecher.
Reflect bravery.

I tried an example of a critique.
Such critiques are long unheard of. I wanted to play around. //

Strousberg is still better than Ovsyannikov. The Ovsyannikovs are a corrupt crew.
Pushkin—that chief Slavophile of Russia.

Not 25 years have passed in sum—and not a generation has passed among any people of Europe without war, and this as long as history recalls, so that progress and humanity is one thing, and any sort of laws, something else. Nevertheless the ideal is just. And it is said by the Ideal Himself that the sword shall not pass and that the world shall be reborn *suddenly* by a miracle. But then it is said that the second appearance of the ideal shall be greeted by the select best people, whose number all earlier best people shall augment.

If he really is one of the best men, then now when he has lost all the privileges of the best men, even now will he remain one of the best men, even now will he preserve honor and conscience.

The soul rises against the artlessness[164] of events.
How to be the executor of Europe's commands (*The N/ew/ Time*, October 20).

Even with the Order of Vladimir round his neck, he is a peasant, he is simply depraved. Ovsyannikov throwing out...

We would have done everything, everything exactly the same, but it ran into trouble, that everything that boasted of itself and posed as the best, considered itself and intended to be so. That summer they often said to Russia too—whatever she requires. //

The common people have declared this war. *Le peuple c'est moi.*

Either because of the artlessness of the views reported to her, or because she could not bear artlessness, the soul demanded something more complex.

The Voice, 20, Wednesday. Zhemchuzhnikov's article.[165] Object more briefly and energetically. (You are in the way.)

Is not Zhemchuzhnikov ashamed to speak of consciousness, the common people know much more and better than yourself what they are doing, because, in addition to a lucid mind, they have a heart and [here] you have only old, inconsistent, abstract liberalism, which moreover turns out to be a heartless liberalism. Look: the common people help the Slavs in order to help the unfortunate, their heart aching (and they were always so compassionate and were always ready to give both blood and life to the unfortunate, it did not just fall from the sky last year, as you write). What does heartache for the Slavs, real compassion (for us, the intelligentsia) matter to you, because you consider that the least important matter (you almost despise it—i.e., living life, the very first and most important thing), but for you, on the contrary, a dead principle is the very first thing in the forefront; you say, as they do in Europe, using the principle of humanity, so must we do as well. It is this acknowledgment that you demand, that they acknowledge that this, as you say, is more humane and we, so to speak, have been ennobled and have moved closer to Europe, but still the common people have much more knowledge because they not only know, but feel! Here's an example for you: those, like you, Zhemchuzhnikovs, Europeans, men of principles, freed the peasants not because it was hard on them, I think (oh, I am not speaking of the exceptions) but because the principle of serfdom had been condemned in Europe. Isn't that so? For the huge mass of those who desired emancipation it was just that way.

You are pedants, asses, loaded down with book-learning.

On the Russians, who fell in the battle of Krevet.

The Moscow New/s/, Wednesday, No. 268, Wednesday, final of lead article.

A relief society will be organized, I believe.

I believe it because, for me the question of who our best people are has been decided.

A soldier goes to die. What if there is something better. That is not what is important. What is important is the resoluteness of their souls. He sees that it is the best and will certainly want the best, to the point of laying down his life. To the point of heroism.

Pedants! You have even forgotten how one lives living life and you live through books.

Do you really think that he does not realize it?
And which is better: to realize, or to act.

You bought yourselves your convictions and artlessness cheap.
What sort of bargain is that!

Lead article. —On autocracy as the reason for all liberties in Russia. (NB. Here is the difference in the views of the alien Russians and the Russian Russians. According to the aliens it is tyranny, according to the Russians it is the source of all liberties. //

NB. Chernyaev's desperate position—intrigues.

Picture. This is not the common people. Rubbish.

The New Time, No. 234, October 22.
The Stock-exchange News, October 21.

Young and old. Not [by the enemy] through the enemy did the Slavs fall, but by their own discord.[166] Homunculus like Poletika Neuletika.

Abstract.	Zhemchuzhnikov
	Schools.
	Poletika. Chernyaev.
	Serbs.
	Best people.

In *The Russian World* the Serbs and the artiller/y/ /are/ defended, while everyone knows that they ran. Chernyaev's delicacy (they did not write about the duel,[167] they did not write about the pressure of the ministers). But *The Stock-exchange /News/* charges that Chernyaev slandered the Serb/s/.
See *The New Time*, No. 234.

1) No genius (*The N/ew/ T/ime/*). But to stand at the head of the movement of all Europe is an insight of genius. And [it comes easily] only a genius

succeeds at such a task.

A new word—well say it—so, Poletika, dying of jealousy, *will not do it* brilliantly if he is ambitious, brilliantly if he is a Pan-Slavist. In military terms our staff officers will be at a loss, but even Suvorov would have turned back with artillery which refused to fire. —Chernyaev's name now belongs to history and will never die, but Mr. Poletika will disappear without a trace. //

Who is immortal? —Mr. Kraevsk/y/ is immortal.

Instead of reinforcing the army with a Russian contingent, they did not send Russians to him, but to Novoselov. But not only Russians, but bullets too. The ministers started an argument at the last minute. Duel. We heard beforehand that *all* of Chernyaev's actions were paralyzed. And *Prince* Milon does not accept the resignation of a minister who caused *the betrayal of the nation* in the artillery the next day. These are the Serbian political heads, the arguments of Slavs unworthy of independence. We are helping the common people, but not that trash. They need a head and a strong hand. The Slavs need an emperor.

They hated the Russians. Tokarev fell in step with that hatred (Tokarev and Chernyaev).

Tokarev should have shown Chernyaev and the Serbs in general the thoughtlessness of their behavior. Suzerain.

Chernyaev, rousing the Russians, could have taken Constantinople—(Russia was ready).

But the Tokarevs and the Serbs resisted, while that played into the hands of our government. The affair would have ended without a declaration of war, but Russia had the right to fight *herself*, since England was fighting openly.

If the bureaucrats (Kartsov and Tokarev) had supported Chernyaev, Russia would have entered disposing patronizingly near the end and prescribing the terms. //

Chernyaev did not act alone. He had an enormous council of Russian officers (they left from hunger, out of disappointment).

But the Serbs trembled for their glorious future, and, most important, from personal irritation at Chernyaev.

Meanwhile the bureaucrat proclaimed to Europe that the Russian people were in discord with their Tsar, which could not be. The bureaucrat newspapers *The Voice, Journal de St. Pétersbourg* and near the end, in an exraordinarily low article, unprecedented even in our country, *The Stock-exchange News* sided with the bureaucrat.

[Long] In vain do *The Stock-exchange /News/*, *The Pet/ersburg/ News* prophesy punishment for Chernyaev. No, now it is a different phase. On the contrary, *The Stock-exchange /News/* will find support on the editorial staff. Everything that was against the movement—/.../ everything base, all the Knaves of Hearts—all are now happy at Chernyaev's misfortune.

The Turks compromised, —now they will be angry that they compromised and will take revenge. We must keep the sabre out of its scabbard. All or nothing from Turkey. If we compromise, *against our will* we shall have to fight the next year. Besides, the Shariat, and not only the Caucasus and Central Asia, but even our Tatars will start acting up. It will be a spur to the Mohammedan world. With the destruction of the Great Russian the borders crumbled. /.../ //

Minister Nikolić.[168] The ability to kill the leader of one's people on the eve of the decisive battle.
    Chernyaev regenerated the whole Slavic cause—that is what Chernyaev did, Chernyaev is, perhaps, unreasonable, of bad character, but he is a genius. If he were more intelligent (not a genius) he would lick Nikolić's boots, but he got round them. An ordinary intellect would certainly have done that. Chernyaev did not find it necessary to restrain his perhaps arrogant, petty irritability, but he did not find it necessary, believing too much in his own powers.

/.../[169]

Even to shooting at the leader of his people, and that in the most decisive moment of the struggle, [when death]

The New Time, No. 235. Saturday, October 23. Excerpts from all the newspapers *in favor of Chernyaev.* //

                              Here.

—Order.
—Herzen.
—With the icon.
—Chernyaev and reaction (all).
  and suddenly
—Both Zhemchuzhnikov and the *schools* concur with officialdom.
Final—Best people. Strousberg. /.../.

NB. Best people, noblemen, seminarist. A merchant is merely a depraved peasant. /.../ The very best thing about him was love of bells and deacons. But there is his Order of Vladimir with distinction round his neck and dinner, kinsfolk with the barons. Finally ideals in the common people.

Now I have seen what the best people are, at least they shall be, the common people want them to be, etc. This summer the best people were formed.
NB. Mark NB
In my article on Chernyaev perhaps much is incorrect and based on rumors, but as a whole and *in essence* it is correct. //

The Slavic cause had at all costs to begin, 3) i.e., enter the *active phase*, but *no one wanted* to begin in this sense. Chernyaev began.
4) They will say he began not at all for the sake of the Slavic cause, but from ambition. From brilliant insight. He believes in the strength and necessity of the Slavic cause, otherwise he would not have taken it up, especially if he were ambitious, because ambitious men in such cases like to strike more sure.
But let us leave this ticklish subject of ambition.
[Nik] Minister. —Shooting at the leader of his own people. However in subsequent battles the artillery had already rebelled and the militia fought lousily (confidence in the general was destroyed). The Russians fell. But *The Russian World* speaks of shortages and shells—we heard about these shells long ago.

5) One can scarcely compare Chernyaev with Garibaldi, a man simple-hearted to the point of eccentricity, and also perhaps very ambitious. But certainly brilliant. But Garibaldi did not begin by himself, but started on Cavour's initiative, while Chernyaev began by himself. (Unification of Italy. Unification of the Slavs.) True, the very fact that Garibaldi joined Cavour[170] shows his genius. Zhemchuzhnikov would not have joined. When Gambetta went to Thiers, —*that* set him higher than the initiative in the balloon.[171]
True, Garibaldi only followed Cavour, while Chernyaev started everything himself, but... //
The defender/s/, like diplomats, demanded *all*. This is false tactics. The best tactics would be that they be *ordinary* people.
The Russian spirit was above the Serbs. Now they have learned what valor is and what men are. From the Russian blood, spilled for them, shall grow their valor—not right away, of course. Now the arguments will start. Envy. Their intelligentsia will curse the Russians, say that through us the whole misfortune came about, but there will be, as always, a reaction of opinion. The Serbs will remember the Russians, killed *for them*. They will start to bless us and marvel at us.

The Petersb/ur/g News, No. 208. Friday, Octob/e/r 22 answered *The Stock-exchange /News/* splendidly.[172]

Again diplomacy. Again *skim off the cream*. And the Bulgarians, the Bulgarians—what will happen to them now. Ignatiev.

Conference.[173] They speak of a conference of the great powers in Constantinople no less. That would be completely superfluous. Russia must not compromise. Most likely, they will not invite her. They will invite her when Russia's actions appear too dangerous. But now some Frenchman will talk about his agreement or disagreement and object to Russia; as if we need his agreement. Rubbish. Constantinople will turn into a nest of intrigue. Austria-Hungary dared to say that Russia is afraid of her. Why, Russia is not afraid of their whole union, i.e., France, England, Austria and Turkey together. Now she is settling accounts with them alone, if only we had stayed friends with Germany. //

Under// these conditions any war is incomparably more advantageous, because peace costs too dear. Therefore if there is war, we must wage one so that everything is finished at once.

After such propagation of the Shariat, they need food, and suddenly submission to Russia. Need food, and here are the Bulgarians, Timur. For proof that the Russian Tsar cannot forbid it, we have so many taking care of the unfortunate, the appropriate role after the ultimatum.

Newspaper—so that moderately, not boastfully//

The reaction in our country immediately seized at the misfortune. The Serbs, "Chernyaev," they say, "is not worthy of [his] the cause, which he took upon himself." No genius.

—No, a genius (*The Peters/burg/ News* Garibaldi) etc.

Splendid article on the Serbs and intrigues. *The Mosc/ow/ New/s/*, No. 270, October 22.

Shaven chins—with severe and malicious views of disorder.

Really funny, if another official, a privy councillor or acting privy councillor had turned up there, with severity towards Chernyaev. And it is around them that those dissatisfied with the ministry were grouped. Reaction in this country too.

The Russian World, Saturday, 23, No. 260, rejects all disturbing news.

The Stock-exchange /News/, No. 293.—Saturday, Oct/ober/ 23. Nonsense and baseness.

Program

This, right now, on the war.

On Chernyaev, on rumors, in more detail, while *The Russian World* now refutes them, now does not believe them itself.

But from all this it is clear what the intrigues of the ministers and the higher intelligentsia are. (Two Serbias.) Irritation with the Russians. In more detail. We have already spoken of that. But a horrifying degree of pettiness. My artist is right, saying that reality transcends all fancy.[174] On the eve of battle, at the leader of the people, etc., the shells, Novoselov. Tokarev. Officialdom. /.../

    The best people, Knave/s/ of Hearts, and then at the end Zhemchuzhnikov and the schools.

    We predicted the Knave/s/ of Hearts. //

    There were, even among Russians of significant rank in Belgrade, those who looked at Chernyaev condescendingly and encouraged the ministers (intrigues of the English). Chernyaev's position is a terrible one,—he argued with the prince. The shells.

    The best people have appeared. For this alone one can pay much money and much blood.

    The people's Russia has said whom she wishes to consider her best people. Not the stockbrokers, measuring short-sighted profit by the yard. A shame about the blood, but let him die, the Russian will say. But must look what *The Stock-exchange /News/* says: why so little advantage? But there is great advantage in the fact that we learned that Russia does not want you. /.../ And Russia is sorry even for those who robbed the common people and shot them when there was unrest, it's not for me, one who has been in Siberia, that these are fairy tales.

    Shorter to find *a way*.

    What is Russia's advantage? Russia's advantage is in her perhaps having re-lieved the sufferings of the Slavic tribes, even though this might not have brought her immediate material help. But Russia's great idea has been raised up and the halo shines. If you do not comprehend the advantage in this, be silent or publish your journal for those like you or for Strousberg's followers.

    Russia's advantage is in the fact, finally, that she moved forward for a cause at one with the common people. //

    Knaves of Hearts.
    The New Time, No. 236, Sun/day/, October 24.
    Answer to *The Stock-exchange /News/*.

    Best people.
    Briefly. Formerly, the boyars were around the princes and the tsars.
    —Then classes were fixed, officials.
    —The boyars managed to transfer new power to themselves, but the demo-cratization of events, the seminarist, the isolated man.
    —After that, in the present reign, the *formal rank of the best people* was abolished.
    —But then with much greater force began attempts, lawyers—merchants— /.../ Strousbergs. Heart stopped at success.
    —The common people remained, and hope in the common people, but they

had holy fools, certain Ivanushkas, Ilyusha himself a hero.

—And then this summer the whole of the common people suddenly speaks and points out who their best people are—not the Strousbergs /.../, still the same naivete full of faith /.../

—One's heart rested easy.

/.../ *And after that Bulgaria and Chernyaev is a genius* (so shortly as to be incredible), the officials' influence.

—Alexei, man of God.

—Suffer. I myself was witness.

—Thirst for glory, what is money, spiritual glory is better. They ask where Christianity is, it is right here.

From the Caucasus//

Our local "civilian soldiers."

"Rouse the cause of Slavdom and place it right on the present point at issue... i.e., that it *absolutely* has to be decided."

What great man is great in the eyes of his servant.

Hope in the common people remained, but it lay in an inert mass. They had Alexei, man of God.

But this summer, they showed what the best cause for them was. Coming out of serfdom, not yielding to debauchery or raw vodka—they said what it is they consider the best cause, and consequently also pointed out their best people, those who march toward glory.

7) And if our Petersburg attackers of Chernyaev knew, how *impossible* it is now to have it so that the common people renounce him! They would not have attacked him.

But they still do not believe, and for that reason do not understand the national movement.

Councillors of State with shaven chins and with those who—*forbid*.

Petersb/urg/ army leaders.

All these soldiers are for the present still civilians and they are imagining gunpowder they have not even smelled yet, and want to imagine powder without having smelled it. //

Men of science, but men of science do not exhaust everything. Not through any science will you construct a society, if there is no noble material, living life and the free will to live honestly and lovingly. Science will show the advantage and prove only that it is more advantageous to be honest.

About us, they write that the Wellington /?/ was plundered. The Polish counts (who? the government), while we [are ashamed] i.e., all the press are ashamed of *The Voice's* blunder about Beaconsfield's profit, but *The Voice* has not blundered that way again at all.

That the common people pointed out the best people to us—that is so indisputable. But is the best man of science defined?

What is advantage in Europe is sacrifice in our country.

Lately one has started to become *terrified* for the common people: whom do they consider their best people. /.../ Lawyer, banker. Intelligentsia.

—And suddenly—

Undoubtedly everyone, the whole intelligentsia, all the powerful of the earth who stand beside the Tsar, must side with the national view.

Democratism does not frighten us.

We have nothing to be frightened of.

The power of the Tsar.

To such a people all the freedoms may be given, — they will not violate them. //

Answer to the anonymous author.

Your power is spent for nought.

You write that: that you do not repent.

No, I would have acted better in your position, I would have—not simply have begun offending, much less anonymously.

Only forgot that they are almost all such scoundrels.

The merchant. True, he sacrifices, but a European (Vladim/ir/ round his neck) does not even sacrifice. //

October

Chapter one. 1) A simple but strange matter. 2) Several notes on simplicity and simplification. 3) Two suicides and 4) Sentence.

Chapter two. 1) New phase of the Eastern question. 2) Chernyaev. 3) Best people. 4) The same.

Current. October-November /1876./

Review old material of story topics (from the novel *Children*.[175] The girl with the ikon).

On S. Soloviev's article about the East/ern/ question (in the arch/ives/).

Anna Petrovna Boreisha supervisory assist/ant/ warder in the jail for pre-trial detention of criminals.

Commerce Commissioner Colonel Fedorov.

Kornilova's lawyer Mostich, Kirochnaya, No. 8, Apt. 15.

Kornilova. —As if my will were not my own, but someone else's (when she threw her out the window). I really didn't want to go to the police-station, but somehow went by myself.

Stepan Kornilovich Kornilov in the department for preparation of governm/ent papers (abstracter, 30 years) //

November
Current: November 1—Kolya. Kornilova—*Fuks*. At the notary's with Sokovnin. November 2—Bykov. Answer to the anonymous writer. Answer to Rossek.

November
1) An article a bit more caustic about our Russian kindness. "Weak, does not hold up." England will suddenly say what, the Tsar, Gorchakov, the courtiers, the press—all are terribly kind. Let England praise us, and we will hand everything over to her, maybe even the Slavs.

2) On Constantinople w-i-t-h-o-u-t f-a-i-l.
Anyone who doesn't recognize the necessity of capturing Constantinople (Tsargrad) is not a Russian. Are we equal to the resolution of the Eastern question if we understand it so abstractly. The Slavs and Russians in the future. /.../
France in the future (nothing).

3) The major mistake in Russia's policy is that her aims are so *moderate.*

4) On the fact that Russia should take on herself the maintenance of the Slavic family in general, those tucked away in Serbia and Montenegro, now, even before declaration of war (and whether there is war or not). This absolutely must be after those most lofty words from the Kremlin on *the heroic struggle of the Slavs for a just cause.*[176] To *do honor* to these words [we must] Russia must send the Slavs at least a million for sustenance. A firm demonstration to Europe (in view of winter). Charge the Slavic committees which have their own managers and representatives. //

5) *Femme cosaque*—we surprise Europe. But in our country life is still not settled, we are just beginning to live.

6) A colossal slap in the air: and what can be done, since it is impossible not to strike this cheek (excluding the common people).

7) But treaties (Paris, 1856) are contravened only through *actual* contravention, i.e., military, without war they do not change, and have, on the contrary, a terrible vitality.

8) Thursday, November 4, No. 247, *The New Time*. Infantile article on the Eastern question.[177] Control of Constantinople decided only from the *naval* point of view and decided nonsensically. But control of Constantinople is important from other points of view as well, for example, if only that the Slavic people who first gain control of Constantinople will also *repress* all the other tribes of the Balkan peninsula, and secondly, that hostilities will begin between the Greeks

and the Slavs. And for this reason, so that there be hostilities neither between the Greeks and the Slavs nor among the Slavs themselves, and that there be therefore neither *treachery* toward the common Slavic cause, nor its *betrayal* to England, —for this reason is it necessary that Constantinople fall into the hands of a strong intermediating power, a power so strong that it will be impossible to argue with her, and for this reason will she gain *trusteeship* (the most beneficial) over the liberated Slavic tribes. And, most important, that Russia be alone here, and that there be nothing to involve Germany.

NB. Include article on Constantinople *without fail* (always interesting.)

England's cause, speaking *à la longue* is in any case a desperate one: for the Slavs, although much favored by England, will still be drawn to us, there, they will say, are our roots and our center. So England will only preserve them for us: *Union* of the Slavs with us is a matter determined by history. And Constantinople?

If the Greeks are to give up Constantinople, a huge schism in Orthodoxy will set in, owing to the separation not only of the Bulgarians, but of all the Slavs from the universal *unifying* patriarchate because of the political conflicts with the Greeks, who control Constantinople.

1) and we are losing the Slavs, 2) since we do not want to separate from the universal church, 3) we should by no means allow quarrels between the Greeks and the Slavs; we must be reconciled, so as to take Constantinople and put it in our pocket.

Begin the article thus: The question of Constantinople is considered untimely, dreamy, but in it lies understanding (the essence) of the solution of the whole East/ern/ ques/tion/, etc.

Gave himself airs, bought a cow, Russicism, more Russian, but does not even speak Russian. In Petersburg from generation to generation, children grow up, gentlemen of the bedchamber, but our future rulers do not go to Russia. Catch Peter at dawn.[178]

Sit a pig down at the table, etc. Russian character. Overstep the bounds. Photius.[179] Platon Zubov is surely a Pugachov. In our day, lawyers, writers, etc.

Catch Peter at dawn, etc. I.e., everything in good time, art either just like that, or a heartfelt instinct to seize just the instant, hit the nail on the head, not to be overdue and not to anticipate, neither early nor late. That is the sort of decision we announced (i.e., the loftiest words, etc.). And our delight did not wear thin and was not disappointed and we poured cold water on the enemy at just the right moment. Still later, —and they would certainly have begun to despise us for our weakness: such a huge colossus, and [so weak] such clay feet, so weak. (The clay feet the Russian people.) The bankers, they say, have already set unworthy conditions for loans of money to Russia (*The New Time*, No. 249, November 6).

96

And now right on the head. [Catch. Catch Peter at dawn, but he has dall] Had we been overdue, Russia's delight would have worn thin and Europe looked at our menacing (but tardy) step as the desperate trick of a man driven to the wall. A genuinely higher principle of life: *seize the instant*. Catch Peter at dawn, etc.

Novel[180]
November 6, 76 //

Dreamer.

But in the soul there is always, eternally the question (and it was there before) through a dream: to be upright and honest, daring to be upright and true. Daring to accept the *truth* with all its consequences.

He recognized, finally, that a dream (like the woman's *dream* in *Pugachevsty*)[181] —only saved him from despair and from the rigorousness of questions.

At first only the shame of living with the wife without being a husband, *on a salary*, tormented him.

NB. The woman is tormented by the question: is he really convinced that she lived with a lover? NB. She *did not*, but hides it from him and pretends that she did.

Shake off the paralysis of reverie and become a man. (Tongue stuck out, refusal to duel, 100 r. stolen).

He saved himself from this through the dream, in the dream he was a paragon of nobility.

When he got together with his wife later (i.e., in secret, furtive conversations), he suddenly became her friend, and since he had sort of lost touch with the world, even tells her: how he dreamed of becoming a hero in her eyes, of making her fall in love with him.

He tells her *this*: from this arise graceful, amicable relations full of love. The wife is surprised—(story of Karl Ivanov/ich/ and the girl who jumped out).

I lie and live in a dream world, I want the real one.

Forces himself to become the savior of a child. At first he forces himself and later he began to love ingenuously, and he is glad that he can begin life anew. But he immediately dreams again (even about the child) with embellishments.

He is a dreamer, but not an idealist, rather with full scepticism.

If you knew what a sceptic I am.

He does not know if he is religious, but invented a heaven and believes *in it*— and he uses this to *console* himself for his lack of faith.

Tells how he dreamed of being Christ's minister: thus saith the Lord. //

Existence itself is a delight, the only one (but existence is not eternal, I avoid this question and stop up my ears with dreams).

An artistic nature (his wife says to him), but does not write anything. His playful and graceful explanation why he does not write.

Meanwhile relations between his wife and him become more and more secure. She loves him terribly.

And real life runs parallel (NB. devise) and absorbs both him and her. He *spoils* everything, any sort of reality, with dreams.

But he does not *spoil* it, rather creates it, and what is more, like no other man but having finished, does not become attached to it, but as if to say well, that's over with, leave me in peace and—dream.

Passion for his wife. The wife deceives him with a sham love affair to arouse jealousy. He experiences suffering, but lets her go. Wants to kill himself.

She confides everything to him, her love, *that she was faithful,* and accepts him as he is.

But he kills himself (solely from *mal du siècle*). //

Flourishes. Flourishes are worn out lies. (Combine with sit a pig down at the table). Zubov, Pugachev (sat on the throne).

Skobelev, who punished with the knout (same *New Time, Russian Antiquity*), *Scharnhorts, Nabokov*[182] and the water-tower—Rostovtsev behind the door, etc.

NB. Combine this with bought a cow.

On Kornilova. I visited her out of *curiosity.*

Bought a cow—combine with Kokodos, who was preparing to enter the St/ate/ Council (process of estrangement from Russia, in Petersburg where more and more, from generation to generation they do not know Russia).

On Meshchersky and his sketches.[183]

NB. Woods and woodless tracts—inquire about the text of the law of Nik. Petr. *Semenov.*[184]

The socialists honor Christianity in the ideal. (Although they abuse it, develop. NB. They said nothing beyond Christ in a moral sense.) But they do not honor it in action, active. For if all were actively Christians, not a single social question would be brought up. Economic, kitchen questions would be brought up, for example there being no woods and no expanses. Communism against one's will, disappearance of the family, etc. If there were Christians, they would settle everything. But it is *impossible* for the present for everyone to be a Christian, only individual cases are possible. (Perhaps these individual cases *secretly* lead and preserve the people.) It is impossible, perhaps, also by laws of some sort, by laws of human nature, f/or/ ex/ample/ war every 25 years.

Lead Article. November. On autocracy as the reason for all of Russia's *liberties.* NB. This is the difference in the views of the Russian-aliens and the Russian-

Russians: according to the aliens—tyranny, according to the Russians—the source of all liberties. Thus, if the government (if this were even conceivable) grew just a tiny bit afraid of its *subjects*, it would immediately become un-Russian and not national. From the position of the head of the government this is impossible, and that's why there are all these liberties. //

Take the enthusiasm constantly surrounding the Tsar and the Tsar's word. *The Russians themselves will not allow* disorder either to take root or even to appear *in the event of the most absolute liberties.* In this event Russia could be the most liberated of nations. [to this point] That is the Russian understanding of autocracy.[185]

War, Prudhon, mankind does not want war and yet every 25 years.[186] (The bourgeoisie, wants peace, the workers. Mankind is so poorly organized that it cannot but *support* its own poor edifice with the sword). Magnanimity in war, in peace—cruelty.

Spiritism. Absurdity of the theories and irrefutable facts. Scientific investigation is the most usual path, but we need different investigators: ours are *uneducated*. This same Mendeleev, for example, or investigating, will not have the power to deny *fact*, and then in the event of conscientiousness and *not commonness*, will certainly approach spiritism from its very worst side, not stop at the threshold.
Because they are uneducated.

Our specialists may be *men of science*, but they are uneducated (I dismiss all personalities, the Mendeleevs, etc.).

These men are not Fausts or Humboldts—erudite in universal thought and universal generalization; they are little technicians and hacks.

For general tranquillity it is necessary to turn the system of the great powers into a system of two forces; for the other three forces are mirage.

MacIver.[187] Unusually noble tone. Military straightforwardness. Lofty, valiant spirit. Excerpt on the torture of our prisoners. Tore out their tongues with strings. How must it be for Russian mothers of the missing. Charred old woman. Our Turkophile newspapers. If they had worked for money, they could not have betrayed us better. But how much money would they have gotten?
England is rich. To dampen our enthusiasm—that is what their aim was. After the failure of the business they fell on Chernyaev. They deceived him with telegrams. Most important, it is a stupid aim to divert society's enthusiasm *now* and after the Tsar's words. Yes, even for money, they could never have earned more pounds sterling. *But we do not know their aims.* But although their zeal is worthy

of *payment*, they displayed remarkably little wit. And it is the sort of newspapers that are printed in 15,000 copies. Strange and surprising.

I do not believe that they accepted money, but if money is dearest of all to them, then of course they let a chance slip. //

On the fact that all England waged war with us all summer, sent fleets, etc. While we, despite the Tsar's undoubted good heart, did not send a penny from the Treasury to those martyrs dying of hunger. Even farsighted Austria wasted quantities of money from the Treasury and *sowed her guldens well*: the Slavs will remember her aid. Why should we not even now send the Slavs a couple of million? Well spent. After all, it is stated in the manifesto, etc. (on the heroic war for a holy cause, etc.) //

To Ratynsky *N/otes/ from the House of the D/ead/*.

Storylet. A Gentle Spirit.[188] *Intimidated (sic)*.
With severe surprise. —Size of a small cupped hand. —*All* of this will grow (i.e., the impression in the future).

While she is here it's still all right: I walk up and look every ten minutes, but they'll carry her off tomorrow, and—how shall I remain alone? I'm used to her sitting here and before, I was used to her song, how can I live without her?

I call Natalya, she is crying, what did she say, wasn't she complaining.
I walk-walk-walk—how shall I live?

NB. This is already at the time of the song, as if in passing; I knew that I had lost her then (forever) (in the scene with the revolver).
I was sure that I had lost her.
I did not want acquaintances: a fixed time a month to the theater, etc. (she had no mother). There was a female cousin—one ruble.

White coffin, flowers (it was I who ordered flowers brought. Natalya brought a bouquet.

A Gentle Spirit. Became terribly silent and asked to go nowhere. Song. Youth.
She spoke with him a bit just before the murder very tenderly (and even somewhat playfully), but shortly.
She stood, resting her hand against her forehead, and sort of smiled (a long smile).

She rejected my love. Intimidated her.

After the revolver, over tea, she looked at me glancingly (convulsively) and suddenly for an instant quickly smiled, as if she were *mistaken*, and suddenly a quick cold shudder passed through her body and over her face.

Served as an officer, pawn shop, revolver.

Paid every morning, clean linen on Saturdays (no sooner).

Made her give out loans and record them, she did not want to, the officer started coming.

I was offended by people (*in passing*: I left the regiment by verdict of the officers, because I did not accept a challenge). I wanted to acquire very, very little, thirty thousand, buy an estate or go abroad.

I spied out an orphan whom they were *marrying off*.

I wandered around Petersburg, living hand to mouth, spent the night in flophouses. The desire for decency seized me, when suddenly I received six thousand.

Here is how the petty tyrant arose.

She did not know that I held the pawn shop. I said an office. Having learned about the pawn, she was at first not very surprised, but later. //
Revolver. She was staggered. She respected me.
Holding the revolver, I took vengeance for everything in my dismal past, the officers, including me, and the disgrace of wandering and everything.
I understood this several days later, after the scene with the revolver. I understood this for a long time. I purposely extended my understanding for a year, in order to enjoy it, and I did enjoy it.

I was guilty—yes, but they drove me to it, they drove me to it. (He says this in the middle.)

I waited for the shot, but it seemed to me that if I decided, there wouldn't be a shot (i.e., overpower).

I led her by the hand, she sat down and looked challengingly at me, but she was afraid, she was afraid.

She was *intimidated* even at home. She married me as a liberator. But I received her coldly. False calculation! (NB. They wanted to sell her.) I received her *coldly, but I myself* was hunting: now I'll be in the clover.
    NB. The whole catastrophe from wedding to revolver occurred quickly, in 5 months.

"Severe surprise." And only then in this severe surprise, *for the first time (!)* I grasped that complete and long-standing estrangement of her from me! But then I, imagine, I still thought that she loved me and suffered from love of me and pangs of conscience. *Like a despot, I delighted in this idea for a whole year and ½.* (NB. This is stressed to himself and in passing.)

All that I did not understand.

In passing. My suit, old coat, but cleanliness (linen for example).

I waited for the shot (and was taking vengeance on everyone, both for my hand and for my expulsion).

There was none of this (i.e., in my thoughts), but it all rested in the sense of that instant.

At the very end, afterwards: I walk-walk-walk: I do not know whether she despised me or not! I do not think she despised me, it is not possible that she despised me after the revolver!

Terribly strange: why did it not once enter my head in all that time that she despised me. I was convinced to the greatest extent of the opposite until the very minute she looked at // me then with *severe surprise.* Then I immediately understood even the disdain, [understood] that irrevocably, that she had despised me all the time, always. Oh, so what, so what! So she despised me, but how did she end up alone? So what if she despised me. Just lately [she was alive] walked, talked... [But I do not understand] I do not understand at all. She *threw herself* out the window. I know that, now she is dead. That is also right. Well what if she had stood up and spoken. If only a single word, if she had looked at me and said something. One single, one single... [My whole life for this.] I called Lukerya again. Now I will not let Lukerya go... [not for anything]. She talked with her a lot. It is 6 hours now I have wanted to do it and still cannot get the point of my thoughts.

Now she is in the coffin, in the hall. I am still walking. I want to understand this, that is the way it was. —I am simply telling it, telling it as I understand it myself. I am far from being a literary man and do not give a damn. The horrible thing is that I understand everything.

The problem is, if you want to know, i.e., if we are to start from the beginning...

...She came to me to place something to be published in *The Voice*, about, it said, a governess so-and-so willing to travel or to give lessons in the home, —a governess, it said, to travel. —

She brought an ikon.

That I had been expelled for the duel, —she learned all about that.

The song, once a week, weaker and weaker. I suddenly noticed it. Stood, went out, (wanted to go out), but only reached the end of the lane. On the street

102

I stopped and stared—a dog, a horse or talked with someone, started to suffocate, returned, walked around the room, sat down, took her by the hand: "Tell me something" (something stupid because it took my breath away). Suddenly with severe surprise (I was terribly surprised), but suddenly it all passed, and I just collapsed at her feet, kissed her feet— [She had an at]   I apparently did not say much, I merely told her frankly that I would take her to Boulogne, to swim in the sea. I melted with love for her. *She had an attack*.

Richard Moleyer. Oh, I have loved the poets, from childhood, from childhood. I was left alone at school, on the holidays (never before about school), with my comrades I was not a comrade, they despised me. They had just sent me 3 silver rubles, and I immediately ran off to buy Guber's *Faust* which I had never read.

I am evil which does good. In the evening I bought some sweets, but I was ashamed, —then I talked all the time, —she was silent (in passing still), i.e., I tell you she did not turn away from me at all. It was hard for her with me, it is true. I saw that. Oh yes! but I thought that she had stood it all! But she did not turn away at all. And it was like that for three weeks. And most important, the last day I made her laugh, made her laugh as I left.

She rejected my love. Let her! Let her, but let her revive, let her love even that officer, while from behind, from the other sidewalk, I will be watching.

When I married, I brought her home, proud of my superiority.

The portrait of the Pope, in the Hermitage. //

Let her come up to me and fall before me in silence, and then we would embrace, also in silence.

I saw that she had begun to love me. But it was as if she had forgotten my existence.

She just *forgot* about my existence.

Why did I not tell her the story of my life? But I was ashamed. I am very chaste. And *proud*. N-o-o-o! That is something else, but I am not chaste and not proud. However, not by reputation, I simply did not tell her and did wrong.

She kissed me (I thought, through strength).

You see she was getting ready, she was packing her suitcase.

I liked the idea that here I was already forty-one years old, while she was barely sixteen, I liked that idea. Because she was not yet 16.

Bought Shakespeare. She asked me: what is compromise? I answered.

That time she again slept on the couch, dressed, and two days more, but then without saying anything I bought an iron bed and screens and put them in the other room.

At first she went out to give out (pledges). But she gave it free to one lady. Argument.
She asked me about the duel.

I would get up at night and ring my hands over her and weeping in happiness say: "Still she is alive... here... [she] I'll do it, I'll do everything, and she will see that there is still time." She was sleeping and did not suspect that I was standing there. Her little bed, small, iron, cheap, I paid 3 silver rubles for the lot at the second hand market.

Now I will not let Lukerya go, *she will tell me everything.*

Fleeting phrases without fail at the end. "I wanted to reeducate her character." *Last phrase: "No, but how am I to live now."*

Adopt an offended tone? Adopt it or not? Or an arrogantly calm one?
Even my thoughts flitted past. Why did they flit past, they had always been near me.

The more she reproached me, the more I was purposely severe with the pawners.

After the shot. I stood the victor, I was proud, that was bad: (to be proud). But then I am good, I am good, but sort of unbalanced. I wanted to take vengeance upon her. —Did I want to or not? There was that idea.

All this when my soul was in the *depths of humiliation*, all this arose in me in order to take vengeance... on any such sort of creature, i.e., not to take vengeance (I am good), but just so, to let her know (*I told her this after the explanations*). NB.

When she wants to say something clever, she suddenly *too naively* shows by her expression that she wants to say something clever. Too hurriedly. So it is evident that she both values intelligence terribly and believes in many things terribly much, which is unshakeable. Youth. (I told her this *after the explanation*).

You know I am afraid of your intelligentsia, i.e. I always suspected the intelligentsia, sure all this time, but occupied with this nonsense, while now. //

The arshin is dear. Fattened piglets.

Donations declined, but then the government should have given two million. Spend it.

After MacIver and Kraevsky.

The New Time on the Fr/ench/ language,[189] No. 254. Thursday, November 11. From *The R/ussian/ Archive* on the French language (bought a cow).

Russian serves the principles of magnanimity, disinterestedness and philanthropy. What do we see in Europe. And so humanity has divided in two parts.

The New Time from the 12th and 13th and *The Russian World*—on Chernyaev.

In any case neither Mr. Poletika nor Mr. Kraevsky is possessed of a significant intellect. [or] Or even simply an intellect. This was finally [be] [explained] became so clear that now it is even possible to declare it affirmatively.. Now it is even possible to say it affirmatively.

Andrei Alex/androvich's/ (attacks on Chernyaev) I want to believe they are not from a malicious heart, but [for] to give the newspaper originality. Another of them (Poletika) might really have envied him; why did not he, with his wealth, free Serbia!

The Mosc/ow/ New/s/ and *The Russian World*—November 13.
The Mosc/ow/ News/, 12th.[190] I foretold all of this about the slaughter of Bulgaria and about the English, who will seize Constantinpole and *will start* to lead the Slavs astray. It was confirmed.

Amuses Bożić. Sunday, March 14. 2 million from the government to the hungry. And that is what they allowed in Bulgaria.

The New Time, November 14, No. 257. On the freedom of the straits and Constantinople not being needed. What is *freedom of the straits?* When it is necessary, they will block them up, how are they secured? //

Memento memento. The Russian World, The New Time, from November 14.[191] On *privateering*, on [the levy] the double guild duties as a sacrifice to the fatherland.
Cruising is permissible, privateering is not.[192] Nonsense—not only privateer-

ing, but the bombardment of Odessa is impermissible. Precisely the same *bashibazouks.* The Turks have exploding shells. Certainly there will be. Should we too use them. No, it is shameful, dishonorable, better we should pay with temporary suffering, but on the other hand our *duty* is then a human one to accept guarantees and measures so that in future *a country like Turkey not make war*, with anyone, at any time, because this country does not understand: why exploding shells are forbidden.

And France would do better to prepare not for the exhibition,[193] but in general (NB. *The New Time*, No. 258, November 15).

In the same issue *The New Time* on theft among the gentry, etc.[194]

The history of the Eastern question is the history [of the quest] of our self-awareness.[195] In the article in *The N/ew/ Tim/e/*, 16th, No. 259 (in a satirical article) they say that if one were to point out their own interests there would be much more animation among the common people. What interest, for whom? In our country it is precisely the common people who are interested in the lofty idea of helping their brothers—above interests, and this is not at all an idea, as you say in European languages. It is an ideal in Europe, because there is not one people there which would place the interest of their *brothers* above their own advantage, and that is the reason it is an ideal there, while in our country it is a reality.
  The last jumble of Europeaneering. Our ideas will gain the upper hand.

The history of the question (again the same *New Time*). Sort out the verbiage, the reasons why we are bound to the Eastern question—from altruism or *our own defense.* Our people always want *to be animated by a higher idea. Loftus* republ/i/c—well let them.
  I to Polonsk/y/.
  In our country, in their wisdom, the Tsars wish to arbitrate together with the common people. *L*—they even crossed [the str] //
  It was impossible for us not to declare war (Lev Polonsky, not from altruism). That is true. //

The affair dragged on, the eruption of words began 1) the higher idea of altruism always in this. But our people will scarcely arise for advantage, the high/er/ feel/ing/ of altruism and Tsargrad.
  2) What is Tsargrad. A new word to the world of the Slavs, etc. //
  Loftus, republic well let them, there is none stronger than our republic—the common people in union with the Tsar. Lev Polonsk/y/. "Altruism is useful for us too,"—but that was always well known, good always bears good fruit and even a hundredfold, and it is no use wasting paper and ink on these senile remarks. I said to seize Constantinople.

But every people has *its own:* ours will not march for an advantage which is still floating in the sky, make war on the Bosphorus, but they will march for the sake of the Slavs. —They do not demand reward, they die (according to Meshchersky—they meet the volunteers in silence and what'll you give?) (The English have direct interests, and they will march). They have trade, we have something else. You think that they will become merchants, change, grow wiser. God forbid. We have a different idea. They have goods, we have other things. We will have our say. Then something really national and popular was manifested.

You are sick of it.

The New Time, No. 260, all talk is about how Russia's moral interests in the milit/ary/ question outweighed the material ones.[196]

Once again. About the fact that one should not agree to anything with Turkey—take under trusteeship.

To yield trusteeship to England is to destroy 4 centuries of our policy.

Yukevich's letter.[197] From a shaken family, so he would certainly consider his parents better. But they did not even inspire him to endure long and much, following the example of all men who endure, for others and for their neighbors.

These are not balls: *these balls* did not lead to this before.
They are still hanging themselves, but if he were a grown-up: Eh, a real scoundrel, I am! To be good, it seems is worse, they did not listen to me, he says, faint-heartedness; now he will demand a reward. //

The same with any moral duty, you can instantly find a moral loophole, to free yourself.
Boors in the same prison with their mentor. —But they're off to the common people. Our convictions, they say, are wrong, you feel like simply swearing from boredom, and they free themselves from all constraint.
I do not reproach only those going to the common people, but the whole tribe, for the sins of their fathers. And not even of the fathers. Something older was destroyed, *modus in rebus.* Now it is necessary to create something else. Any way out is fine. /.../ They will come of themselves, respecting themselves, and will make others respect themselves. And for this reason the war is not for a thief, but for the most apropos altruism, for here is something to respect them for (and here turn to L. Polonsky).

For this being (the high-school student) everything ends every minute. It is easy for him to die, because he leaves something of too little value.

Now (with the humanities) base people have the right to live, i.e., the sickly of average strength remain alive *(mens sana)*. And even if the sickly are perhaps heroic and magnanimous (personally), do not worry, for on the other hand they are so irritable, touchy, that in succeeding generations they give birth to scoundrels. True, for a long period the breed will make a recovery to something higher. But then all the weaklings will increase again and again, etc. for a very long time, [for many centuries] in the course of many centuries.

"Domestic Conversation." Notice: this language. I call this firmness. Thus speaks a *man* firmly convinced of his power and his success. Diplomacy should imitate such language, to prevaricate. However, with Russia that is almost exactly how they do speak (See. Wednesday, 17, *The Russ/ian/ World*. Notice on "Domestic Conversation").

Strepito belli propelentur artis.
Letters to me: Find me a position. //

Chapter one.
A Gentle Spirit. A fantastic story.[198]

From the author.
1) Who was I and who was she?
2) Marriage proposal.
3) The most noble of men, but I do not even believe [him] myself.
4) Only plans and more plans.
5) The gentle spirit revolts.
6) Dreadful memory.
Chapter two.
1) Proud dream.
2) The scales [will fall] suddenly fell.
3) I understand too much!
4) Late [in all] by only five minutes.
[She killed not herself, but me.]

Explanation

The Mosc/ow/ New/s/, No. 296. Book on the use of Christian blood by Jews.[199] Price 2 r. *On Sadovaya at Korablev's*.

The New Time on Salisbury Novem/ber/ 19, No. 262.
The Marquis of Salisbury, his trip (v. sup. Russia good-naturedly yields, Saltykov, clever, clever).[200]

The Mosc/ow/ News, No. 296, on privateering.
Ibid. K.M.'s Letter from Paris on the French mood *against* us.

However they display Russia's disinterestedness and the Tsar's words and promises, through the natural logic of things, the affair is rushing to a head and war with Europe is inevitable. Here what is important is neither the Tsar nor Beaconsfield, nor even whether we seized it or did not seize it this time. Here we have the Eastern question as a whole and in future, and consequently Russia's reinforcement by the Slavs as well, but Europe will allow that only in the last resort. It would still be good medicine at the present moment, again, for the hundredth time to avoid a resolution, to resolve the matter through compromise, but that is terribly disadvantageous for Russia, since we injure the whole in the East/ern/ question, i.e., give up our idea, cede our age-old right, etc.

War is more advantageous, more advantageous to end it at once and for good.

Our Tsar has been determined by fate to mend our neglected influence on the East. The task is very easy now, since 2/3 of it has already been done through the logic of things itself. It is clear now that it is impossible for the Slavs to live with the Turks and no *hatti humayuns* will help. It is necessary, in any case, to devise a new combination. But I repeat, England will devise one of her own. She will liberate the Slavs, but alone, and will not let us even get near. So let us go stick our hands in our pockets. They always hate a benefactor. And the Slavs, beneficiaries of England, will reach out toward us, but if we confer benefits, then, on the contrary they will reach out toward England.

The New Time, No. 263. Gladstone's opinion that England, and not Russia, should confer benefits upon the Slavs.[201] Telegrams. //

December
Here important (*The N/ew/ T/ime*, No./ 263 from *The St.-P/etersburg/ New/s/*. Girs's on how our brother Slavs take clothes away from Russians.[202] Put this alongside Meshchersky's report on taking away the wounded. "What'll you give?"
Embourgeoisinated trash, *except the common people*, such a glorious future.

We are above those trashy nobodies. Shchedrin's general, with his flashes of spleen, is above his base modern son, although he himself is to blame for him.

December 5. Concerning Baimakov's bankruptcy.[203] Only as much as can be made of the most charming bankruptcies and still lump everything on the government: "well," he says, "they declare war, securities fell, and now I'm a bankrupt."

The New Time, Decemb/er/ 4. Ordinary reader (excerpt) on Demert. All these souls are worn pennies before they've even lived, all these Demerts, Pomyalovskys, Shchapovs, Kurochkins.[204] Don't you see, they drank and fought while drunk. And so acquired their liberal valor. What innocence. While others suffer, they drink, i.e., enjoy it, since vinous vapors oppress their brains and they imagine themselves generals—certainly generals, if not in epaulettes then at very least destroying, humiliating, punishing. Cheap and vulgar. Trash generation. It's old—from the 60's . Now they are all completely drunk, and nothing came of them. They produced nothing and no one. But long live contemporary youth.

December 6. Lermontov's tale of Kalashnikov.[205] Belinsky, towards the end completely devoid of Russian feeling (the most talented of the Westernizers), thought in the words of Ivan the Terrible: I order the axe whetted, sharpened— see only the taunts, the tiger's cruel gibes at his victim, while in the words of Ivan the Terrible, these very words signify mercy.

You deserve death—go, but I like you too, and so I will do you honor, whatever honor I can now, but do not grumble—death! This lion was talking to another lion and he knew it.

You do not believe it? Shall I amaze you even further? Then know that Kalashnikov too was [even] satisfied with this mercy, and he considered the sentence of death of itself just. That is not in Lermontov, but it is so. //

December 6... "We will *be* something," "Something will come of us." That is what haunts and moves the part of our people capable of action. Of their prophets and poets our society demands passions and ideas. (We shall be pure.) We thirst to understand and know the great idea of which we are capable.

On Panteleev (*The St.—P/etersburg/ New/s/*, No. 336. Sun/day/, satirical article). Burenin on Panteleev.[206]NB. We were all raised in the most fantastic inactivity and in a two-hundred-year-old unaccustomedness to any sort of occupation. Bureaucratic activities have been the formula for inactivity. It was suggested and permitted only that one be engaged in dissipation. Society, which was untaught and forbidden any sort of *self-initiative* on the part of a citizen, not only did not become integrated, but disintegrated into the pests infecting it of even lower levels. Nothing was developed. Completely fantastic characters were developed [appeared] (Panteleev).

Thought turned into dreaminess, into conjecture. (There is nothing surprising in the fact that the socialists appeared more zealous than the Westernizers, the government itself schooled them in it.) Nor is there anything surprising in the fact that these socialists were advocates of serfdom, as in the middle ages, for they had lost all vestiges of a sense of duty and civic spirit. Only ideas and esthetic sense had their day, while deed obeyed the coarsest egoist. Fantastic events, like December 14. The fantastic disputes between the Westernizers and Slavophiles, which started after both of them had ceased to be Russians. The new era of the Tsar-Liberator, but for now, disorder.

Answer: Pensée universelle. Before any questions about what will come of us, or what we will be, it is necessary quite simply to become Russians. It is easy for us, for if we vanished the Russian people would remain. They are all safe and healthy! Hurrah! Let the rotten rot and the healthy live. Hurry. Catch Peter at dawn, he is dallying in the place, so he stinks of it. That is what the great reformer thought, looking at Russia as a large-scale and industrious landowner would (transforming all Russia [into a single] into something like a single huge landowner's farm).

December 6. In the diary I wanted to talk about the fact that it is necessary to be independent and Russian people. December 6. Lashed rams. //

Decemb/er/ 7—*The Mosc/ow/ News*, No. 314, December 6, Monday.
In the article from everywhere: On the novel *What is to be Done?* in the critique of *Revue des deux Mondes.*[207]

December 7. Communism! Nonsense! Why, do you think that a man would agree to go along with a society in which not only all personality, but even the possibility of initiating a good deed had been taken from him. At the same time they would take away or torment with gibes even the slightest sense of gratitude in your heart, something without which a man cannot and should not live.
/.../[208]
Communism could have appeared only at the end of the last reign, during which the Petrine reforms were crowned and when the Russian intellectual had come to a point where for want of occupation [at] he began to clutch at all the ravings of the West and, not having *experience* of life for a critical check, immediately applied Frenchery to himself, annoyed with the Russians, because it is impossible to make anything of them. The proletarians in France. Apropos, is it true that in our country the question of communal farming has been raised again?

The N/ew/ Tim/e/, Tuesday, December 7, No. 280.
Destroy the commune in Russia, and the common people will immediately be corrupted in a single generation and in a single generation they will supply material for advocating of socialism and communism on their own accord. For example, in the most thoughtless manner we advocate the destruction of the commune, one of the strongest, most original and vital distinctions of the essence of the common people.[209]

NB. They will destroy the commune—the last bonds of order will snap. If order was torn asunder in high society, and a new one not given, at least there was the consolation that the common people were all in order. *Any sort at all,* but in order, for there remains this bond, a most strong one: communal landownership. But they will break this bond too—and what then? There is no new one yet, nothing has come up (was there even a sowing?), but out with the old, root and all, —and what will be left? We will die like flies. Going to the people now is absurd and even pitiful, well, then it won't be absurd to be acquainted with the commune. /.../[210] //

The New Time, No. 281.
On *The Inspector General*, not understood at all by Boborykin, and on Kraevsky,[211] expelled from the Slav/ic/ Phil/anthropic/ Committee, review of *The Stock-exchange /News/*, tell them without fail.

Several distorted opinions (18 cent. prod. of the West).

Panteleev, daughter, from Sokha Andreevna.
The most important pedagogy is the paternal home.
Burenin—demands contemporary types in literature, greater investigation of life (Panteleev). At the same time in *The Voice* there is a series of articles on criticism and art. But the splendid work of art which just appeared, my story, about that not a word.[212]

Our journals are monsters, a Western form, the sheets are filled mechanically. And political opinion was not to be found. Meanwhile—here are the facts—all this is thrown around. Classify; economic facts, moral facts, illuminate, sort out, not fantasizing and not philosophizing cunningly, but on the basis of the facts, ancient chronicler, etc. Everything is done in a servile manner, we are slaves, we have not learned to be independent. There is no independence. Note that our liberalism and even our *redness* is characterized precisely by the fact that it victimizes any conception of independence in Russia. And this since the very beginning of our liberalism, since Belinsky, since Herzen. They are only shallow liberalizers, but in the main they are really the most frightful conservatives. *Status quo*—the reds deny everything, but are servilely unoriginal. Denial of everything—because // it comes cheap, not requiring the slightest learning, two or three sciences, atheism and communism (for in our country there has never been socialism, they simply resolved it through the formula of communism and the example of the international commune) does not require any science or school. The uneducated doesn't even have to read, he can hear from a comrade and then (sincerely and candidly) despise everyone. Around them is the servile silence of both sympathizers and non-sympathizers. The latter are worse, because it is servile and cowardly silence (here for the youth).

Add vagrancy and the crowd, but even this is without initiative, and it is too old.

NB. I have always been supported not by the critics, but by the public, who among the critics knows the end of *The Idiot*—a scene of great power that has not been repeated in literature. Well the public knows it... etc.

Burenin, investigating Grigorovich and Potekhin (*The N/ew/ T/ime/*, No. 283), turned to Reshetnikov concerning national novels.[213] But *Notes from the House of the Dead*, where there is a mass of national scenes—not a word. Among the critics *N/otes/ from the House of the D/ead/* means that Dostoevsky exposed the jails, but now it has become obsolete. That is how they talked in the book shop, suggesting another, more immediate *exposé* of the jails.

NB. The rotten tribe that cannot live without slaps in the face, is miserable without slaps in the face, and even if you do oblige them, they will then be very grieved and start giving slaps in the face to their friends and stalwarts.

NB. The essence of their satire lies in finding the scoundrel behind any good action. They content themselves with that, they have done their duty.

One of the most characteristic traits of Russian liberalism is the terrible contempt for the common people and as a result, the terrible aristocratism before the common people. (And who are they? Some seminarists.) Not for anything in the world will they forgive the common people their desire to be themselves. (NB. All progress through the schools is intended to break the common people of being themselves.) All the traits of the common people are ridiculed and put to shame. They say, the benighted kingdom is ridiculed. But that is just the point, that together with the benighted kingdom, everything radiant is ridiculed too. So the radiant too is disgusting: faith, meekness, submission to the will of God. Our democrats love an [abstract] ideal common people, [toward wh] in regard to whom they are all the sooner ready to do their duty since they never existed and never will exist.
Our independent mold, independent cast of the conc/e/pt of power. //

Anna P/etrovna/ Boreisha. The aristocrats of the movement who called the women warders animals.

NB. *The Mosc/o/w News*, No. 316 (lead article). All our journals, the conference[214] had scarcely begun when they start grumbling and complaining that, "See," they say, "they still don't believe Russia, but Russia announced that she doesn't want acquisitions," etc. It is absurd to be surprised at Europe's behavior, it is absurd to grumble, but it is most absurd of all to reproach Europe in this case. And no matter what Russia said here, in this kind of case no one would take her at her word. For Russia still wants to occupy Bulgaria, and even if she stood there three years and seized nothing (Europe would not believe that), she would influence the Slavs with her might, —and for Europe that is worse than victory and conquest. The Slavs will see that Russia is stronger, insisted on having her own way and tore to pieces the *inner essence* of the Paris treaty, —and so in the future she will have acquired a moral force in the Balkan peninsula, when the East/ern/ question comes to an end. And England knows that it will come to an end sometime. Indeed, this really is not necessary for Europe, it is just jealousy, it is just hatred, and then there is that ridiculous project of the Belgian occupation. —But then it is *all* unnatural: Russia cannot renounce herself.

Ergo: Result: Russia must rely on her sword, and not on Europe's friendship and on occupation to insist by force, declaring and continuing to declare that she needs nothing, except a guarantee of reforms for the Slavs, no conquests for herself.

Germany's refusal to the Paris Exhibition: what terrible animosity, significant animosity.

Oh, better I had not told them.
Oh, better I had kept it to myself.
Kept it to myself, I myself do not know what.

Note also, that this society (Muscovite, Griboedovian) is no better, no worse than any other and that such societies always *exist* everywhere (we are not saying must exist).
The Inspector General—Cuvier.[215] //

That swarthy thing, he is a Turk or a Greek.[216] The whole outlook, all the feelings of this petty-peevish man comes to that.
Natalya Dmitrievna—(whom Karlov killed).[217]

In contrast with Aleko.[218]

NB. Aleko killed. The realization that he himself is not worthy of his ideal, which torments his soul. That is crime and punishment. (That is satire!)

Pushkin screams about Chatsky: "But whom does he tell all this, it is unpardonable!"[219] On the contrary, on the contrary, he could not do otherwise, it is artistic, and he entirely believes himself. In his little world. All in all only the tail in front. Only Griboedov made out Chatsky favorably, while it should have been negatively.

Chatsky is satisfied with little. *The legend is fresh, but I find it hard to believe,*[220] —i.e., he does not notice that now it is exactly the same. Not in that form, not in that uniform—that is what the difference is for him. Lacks depth. Does not understand the basic essence of evil.

But Aleko killed, do you think, he's going to shout, I'll go looking all over the world. Get me a coach, a coach![221] He says, men are guilty, *not I.* Or, better, Moscow is guilty. No, Aleko stays.

The latest satire is fruitless, ambiguous and even harmful, in that it cannot or will not say what it wants.[222] On the contrary, it makes fun of everything contrary to the evil it denounces and reduces it to the same common denominator. Why does it do it? *It is afraid of anything more red than itself.*

December 13. Mon/day/. *Program of the Decem/ber/ Diary.*[223]
1) Year over. On the purpose of publication.
2) Satire, Chatsky, *The Inspector General*, Aleko—Shchedrin.
3) Three sciences: atheism, socialism and communism, academic house.
4) On Kornilova.
5) On the little girl.

Satire in our country. In our country literature has provided the positive rather than the satirical. Our satirists do not have a positive ideal on the inside. Gogol's ideal is strange; in the inside there is his Christianity, but his Christianity is not Christianity.
The latest satire is inept, they fear the reds. //

The Mosc/o/w New/s/, No. 318, Saturday. *The Mosc/ow/ New/s's/* most remarkable article on the autumn demonstration December 6.[224] They are right: it is very possible that someone has to threaten Europe with communism, coming from Russia and stir up Europe into a frenzy against Russia. Article in *Journal des Débats.* Really, a strange coincidence.
The Turk is brave against a sheep but against the brave, a sheep himself.[225]

NB. Chatsky's witticisms are not witticisms, but impertinence. And that is the way it should be: he pursues not the essence of the matter, but merely individuals, quarrels with them and makes personal remarks.

NB. In Ostrovsky[226] the positive sides of life have somehow begun to blend with satire. This resulted only in general bewilderment and lack of recognition of Ostrovsky by the critics even now.

NB. *He,* by whose will the great works of Gogol [app] could appear in Russian. (Like Cuvier.) From the little town to the most elevated institutions of Petersburg.

This naiveté, unnoticed by Griboedov, i.e., by Griboedov together with Chatsky, considered (by both) merit or virute. Oh, it would be another matter if Griboedov had portrayed this precious trait of a petty character as an artist, himself conscious of its pettiness and comedy, but portraying it as the real truth... But then everything positive in the type of Chatsky would have had to disappear, and Griboedov would have portrayed directly the solemnly positive type of a man suffering not because of himself, but because of society, almost the ideal of the man who ought to have been (or at least of a young man). Let us consider what sort of positiveness this is.

In our country satire is afraid to provide the positive. Ostrovsky wanted to. Gogol is frightening, but Griboedov gave it. All of Chatsky (and the ugliness of comedy). After that, Aleko, and then the *new satire*, they are afraid to say what they want (implied vileness *Jour/nal des/ Débats*). Almost true. This is the positive side of Russian independence that we wanted to convey in our publications. They hailed the year's advance, the liberals, the old men were silent.

Independent origins (of the war). Commune.

—What should Russia say about the war?

[Det] The war will determine a change of direction.

—After that, on the matter of youth.[227] Remarks on *intrigue* in *The Mosc/ow/ New/s/* and on lashed rams. But enthusiasm. It is this enthusiasm that needs an outlet.

—Kornilova—

—and the little girl.

Our satire, having spoken out positively, is afraid of losing its charm, is afraid that people will say, "So that's what you've got in your inside, not much."

NB. Gogol in strength and depth of laughter is *first in the world* (not excluding Molière) (a spontaneous, instinctive laughter, and we Russians should note that).

NB. This boasting of Gogol's and manufactured humility is that of a clown.

NB. The Polish aristocrat who divided blood into dogs' and gentlemen's. /.../

In general liberalism and satire: "Oh, if we wanted we would create such an ideal that the whole world would shine and I would be radiant with light, but... they do not let us speak, and for this reason we only scoff."

NB. *Aleko.* Of course, it is not a satire but a tragedy. But should there really not be any tragedy in satire? On the contrary, in the inside of satire there should always be tragedy. Tragedy and satire are two sisters and walk side by side, and the name for them both, taken together is: *truth.*

Ostrovsky would have grasped this, but he had no strength of talent, he was cold, prolix (tales in his roles) and not sufficiently cheerful, or rather, comical, has no command of laughter.

Ostrovsky was not successful with form. [Compar] Although Ostrovsky is a great phenomenon in comparison with Gogol, this phenomenon is a rather slight

116

one, though he did have something *new to say:* realism, truth, and was not entirely afraid of a positive inside.

That insignificant, blind-from-birth nothing of our lives (the one who killed Karlov).

NB. —Gogol. And alongside the aureole of genius, that extraordinarily offensive figure poked its head out.

Earlier satire could not and did not know how to indicate its positive ideal, and modern satire, although it does not know how either, *does not even want to.* On the contrary, if it knew how and could, it would be unhappy. //

The Mosc/ow/ News, No. 321. Tuesday. Lashed rams. Pest newspaper. Irrefutably proven political intrigue in the demonstration December 6.[228]

Program
—Kornilova.
—Little girl.
—A year has passed.[229] On the idea and purpose of publishing. —Independence, for everything independent is subject to doubt, let us take the current Eastern question, it is strongest of all because it gets into national principles.
—We live in a savage time. December 6.
—The beautiful and the sublime.
—Panteleev, set aside characters, there is no author, there was a story.

They are surprised that Europe does not believe Russia, but why sort it out? A higher idea (Scottish professor), for if it had been stated in Russia, these words would have been subject to abasement. The commune (a few brief words). Communism. December 6.
Panteleev—there is no author, —but the liberals deny the positive interpretation of the Panteleevs. Interpretation is our non-independence. But the liberals want non-independence and despise the common people. Europeaneering (a colossal slap in the face).
Satire (not candid).

I want to finish about literature. Positive [types] experiments rather than satire. *A Nest of Gentlefolk*—experiments scarcely identified, but ones which yielded much. Our literature has provided more positive types than negative, since satire—has no inside.

However we do have the brilliant Gogol.

And yet, we have a satirist like Gogol. What is the reason that society remained dissatisfied?

It is that satire cannot portray a positive type.

Moreover: satire herself has none (does not know how to say it) and because of this generated dreadful confusion in society (for *Dead Souls*[230] was a most popular thing), a controversy arose.

Contemporary satire does not want slaps in the face, [scoundrel's] supposition of the scoundrel.

Ostrovsky, —but he said too little.

They started to point to Griboedov. Yes.

That naive time said everything, —Chatsky a positive type. Aleko. —I want to do a critique, I shall analyze *Woe from Wit.* //

The New Time, No. 289. Remarks on architectural studies for women.

O, and Gogol thought that concepts depend on people (the retribution of the future law), but since the very appearance of *The Inspector General* it has somehow seemed to everyone, if only vaguely, that the trouble here is not with people, not with individuals, that a virtuous town governor in Skvoznik's place would change nothing. Moreover, there could not be a virtuous Skvoznik.

In *Woe from Wit* the brilliance was captivating, the satire on Moscow, but no depth at all.

NB. Chatsky: *What do you want to know for?* It is impossible to imagine anything more stupid.

NB. The psychological justification of Sofia's love for Molchalin is not brought out, she did not dream up his qualities.

They write that we have cooled toward the East/ern/ question. That is untrue: the common people have not cooled, sincere addresses, etc. The intellectuals have cooled, or rather, the reactionaries.

It's a simple matter: are we to consider the Slavic cause organically Russian in the political sense, for example, equivalent to being cut off from the seas, the 1812 borders, Kiev, Smolensk, Petersburg, the Crimea and the Caucasus, *or* merely a Russian amusement. The very formulation of the question of nations and nationalities, the question of the East, of the Eastern Christians, merged in the commonfolk's understanding not only with philanthropy and not only with our political mission (as happened for the most part in the minds of our intelligentsia), but for the most part and above all it was a *question* of the fate of Eastern Christianity, i.e., the question of the fate of Orthodoxy, i.e., the question of Christ and of serving Him, of the glory of serving Him. —That is what I emphasize and point out. It is my idea, no one pointed it out, but it is so, and it is the truth. And knowing this, we should recognize that the Eastern question is primarily Russian, national, it concerns the common folk and is *always popular*. Among the common people the idea has arisen that Russia only exists in order to protect Christendom. Investigate it thoroughly, in this question one glimpses traits such that the Old Believers immediately join the Russians in their desire to sacrifice, while knowing perfectly well that all of these Slavs are heretics. The key to all solutions. //

In poetry you need passion, you need *your idea*, and certainly the pointing finger passionately raised. Indifference and true reproduction of reality are worth absolutely nothing, and most important—do not even mean anything. Such artistry is absurd: the simple but only slightly observant glance notices much more in reality.

The Mosc/ow/ New/s/, No. 322. In the lead article: hateful opinions of the Russians in *Débats* and *Liberté*.

Divers/io/n. Feed, and sleep, and defecate and sit soft.

Write serious things for you—you don't understand anything, and it's impossible to write artistically for you either, one must do it talentlessly and with flourishes. For in an artistic exposition thought and purpose are revealed firmly, clearly and intelligibly. And what is clear and intelligible, is of course scorned by the crowd, it is a different matter with flourishes and obscurity. But we don't understand this, so it must be profound. (NB. The story *The Queen of Spades*—the height of artistic perfection—and Marlinsky's *Caucasian Stories* appeared at almost the same time, and what happened—all too few understood the height of Pushkin's great artistic work, the majority probably preferred Marlinsky.)[231]

Nowadays all forces are cast-iron (their convictions are probably cast-iron too).

The responsibility to know no higher purpose or eternal life, but to replace it with love for humanity, conveyed by this unhappy woman with the completely unexplained quest/io/n: why should I love humanity? etc.

It is impossible to use love of humanity to make up for the absence of God, because man will immediately ask: why should I love humanity?

Others may have not only convictions but something even more cast-iron.

We are just as much Russian as European, universality and commonality of all mankind—that is Russia's significance.
Real/ly/, we bear in our seed a kind of essence of the common man, and this

119

will be so in the future too, and the people which develop will be so. And the more strongly we develop in the national Russian spirit, the more strongly will we respond to the European spirit, take its elements into our own and become related to it spiritually, for this is the commonality of all mankind, and... and, perhaps, we would even be helpful to them, to the Europeans, having told them our special Russian word, whi/ch/, violently separated into sects /?/, they still have not heard. Our language ability, our understanding of all European ideas, our emotional and spiritual mastery of it—all this in order to unite in harmony and concord the uncoordinated, individual national units, and this is Russia's appointed task. You will say this is a dream, ravings: *good, leave me* these ravings and this dream.

I proclaim—*as yet without proof*, that love for mankind is inconceivable, [completely] incomprehensible and *completely impossible* without accompanying belief in the immortality of the human soul. Though our sages shrug their shoulders, this [axiom] truth is wiser than their wisdom, and, I believe, [in future] shall certainly sometime become an axiom among all mankind.

The Englishman strives above all to be [and to remain] an Englishman and retain the form of an Englishman, and love mankind not otherwise than in the form of an Englishman.

There are somehow not enough of those bonds which unite man with life, he becomes somehow weaker and more insignificant.

The sentence—they will accept it as positive instruction, which had to be so. Perhaps it could happen that he will simply comply with it.

Incidentally (and, we assume, *mal à propos*) I declare that they are ceasing to understand humor and jokes. This is a very bad sign—a sign of a decline in the mental abilities of the generation, we must await everything from the young people, hope is in them.

Just look at the Great Russian, he rules, but does he look like a ruler, to what German or Pole is he not obliged to yield. He [in] is a servant. But all the same, in this—in his endurance, expansiveness, his feeling, he *is* a ruler. His ideal is the type of the Great Russian Ilya Muromets.[232] //

The boy who hanged himself... Of course imitative. But something deeply egoistic, nervously proud, rushing horribly toward disunion is developing in the next generation. The bonds prove to be weaker and weaker, unable to bear the pressure. *Isolation*, those who isolate themselves—so what, that is the way it has to be. We, it seems, have reached the very highest stage of disunion with the common people. —Example December 6.

Liberalism, satire play hide-and-seek.

We have been assimilated, become part of its body (Europe).

Burenin.[233] The first will not understand. One should not judge without elucidating the idea, but they will not understand the idea, because they don't want to. Panteleev is so clear. Abstractness. Now the accumulation of practical skill has only begun. But the fruits are still far off, and society has not matured fully enough to elucidate itself to itself. And the elucidators will not be heard.

In this sense, the fate of our satire is exceedingly remarkable. There is no inside. Abstract liberalism became aristocratism, became undemocratic and the more time passes, the more it breaks with the common people. In satire the supposition of a scoundrel. *Débats.* Apropos: editor's words.

Great word. Points of contact with Europe no longer remain. And why do they fear Slavism, nationality? We shall become related to Europe to a higher degree precisely when we become national and stop wandering around Europe like international mediocrities with no respect.

Herze/n/.

And even love, according to them, is advantage,[234] I do good for my own interest out of self-preservation (in the higher sense, it is as if this disproved something about the independent existence of the idea of love). I love in the last resort because one loves me. But how does one inspire love for all mankind, as for one person. Out of calculation, out of advantage? Strange. Why should I love mankind? But once I suddenly find a different sort of calculation. They will say it is false. But I say, what business is it of yours—// I know myself what is false, but only false, in general, on the whole, and meanwhile I may very, very well seem peculiar for personality, for sport, according to my personal feelings. Napoleon I seemed that way, but probably nothing of love for mankind lay in the idea. However, the idea will arouse controversy, and I leave it to be elucidated in the future, here I will say only that the idea of love of mankind is one of the incomprehensible ideas for man as an idea. There was revealed to us only the great ideal in the form of a feeling. The possibility was clear: the ideal was and is. But it is no easier for that. And most important, with the absence of the idea of immortality.

One of the most incomprehensible ideas for man as an idea was revealed but once in the form of God incarnate, in an objective image—unexplained (but having engendered) and strengthening only a feeling.

December 6. *These would* with disdain. Aren't the families to blame? "We have no family," —I recalled the words of one of our [sati] most talented satirists, who told me this.[235]

Decemb/er/ 6. I had a project for them, and, if only circumstances permit, I

121

[sometime] (certainly) will set it forth.

Lib/eralism/. Satire. And if they were permitted to say everything, they would, perhaps, be terribly distressed.

Our satire, f/or/ example, it is not silent, it writes, and writes beautifully, but— as if it itself does not know what to answer you.[236]

You will find those more liberal than I. True, this argument is only a temporary one, but while it was concentrated on the pursuit of any independence for Russia, it turned in this way into aristocratism.

Our liberalistic Europeaneering.[237] Breaking off from the common people. Disdain for the common people (it is the democrats). They go among the common people, the common people beat them, and now they are enemies of the common people and despise them. They are, they say, incapable of anything. They do not want to learn the national truth. There are thousands of examples, tens of thousands, and they are terrifying in their prevalence. [With] [and their own]. //

Just the other day Boborykin declared in his lecture on Ostrovsky[238] that there could be no historical drama in our country for there were no historical characters. (Undistinguished lectures. The author said, for example, that faithfulness to history is demanded of the dramatist, whereas he had an example and cited it himself, that in Shakespeare there was no faithfulness to history, but only faithfulness *to poetic truth.* Through faithfulness to poetic truth incomparably more of our history can be conveyed than through faithfulness *only* to history.) And then what, another journal, which had until now called Boborykin's lectures shallow, immediately started praising them, how he spoke about the fact that there can be no drama in Russia (a different matter, he says, in England). Konrady, etc., etc. applaud (v. *The New Time*, No. 293, December 20). Thus, they themselves do not notice that, detached farther and farther from the common people, they will become aristocrats and form a caste, and not just in thought, but in action! For, severed completely from the convictions and spirit of the common people, they clearly form a *status in statu* with disdain for those below them, for the uneducated mob, for the vulgar herd. "Yokel's faith." Then they will want to preserve their schism, their caste, will want to keep their precedence, their power in the government. [Compel.] The educated will not want to meet with the peasant, because they are of different outlooks and education. They will want to guarantee, protect themselves, and do they really not understand that it really comes to that, leads to that? //

All this will come to pass little by little, now more than before, because before they diverged only in thought and spirit, while now they are already clashing in a practical sense. And these will come to hate the others. It arises like a new feudal law. And these are the ones who consider themselves liberals, democrats!

The New Time, No. 293, December 20. *The Mosc/ow/ New/s/.* Futile surprise about the fact that, how strange, they say, Turkey commands and everyone listens. Idle chatter.

But that is why our satire leaves only bewilderment and [ev] further, even pro-
motes instability of thought, and not that it asserts it.
An air as if, having spoken positively, it were afraid of losing its ch/a/rm. Satire is not defin/e/d. Obliged to smell of its inside.

[I am not speaking of the higher satirists. Among the lower ones] Besides,
there might even simply be a little liberal calculation in this—he says, if I tell my
idea, some clique in our liberal camp will find it too moderate and conciliatory
and they will hiss me off the stage. Notwithstanding, it is good if the hissers are
smart. Moreover, if the hissers too would speak their thoughts, the same thing
would happen to them.

In our country all the valor of our volunteers is forgotten, and men, disgraceful men, stricken, but enriched, in whose hearts there has never been a single burst
of passion, yell only about their drunkenness and disgraceful behavior.[239] (Fleeting slaps in the face, [themselves] the sweetness of self-abasement.) /.../

Others (*The Voice*) entered [in] (buried themselves) in this position false to
Russia, without knowing themselves why, from some sort of confusion, others
(*The Stock-exchange /News/*) are simply angry about contemporary positions (stag-
nation), putting forward the ideal of wealth and wealthy pigs. But even a pig needs
self-esteem. At least in some cases, despite the fact that this is incredible. Without
a certain self-esteem you won't even be wealthy. Loss [of honor, cyn.] of national
honor leads to the loss of personal honor, money for boots, and it will be a kingdom of rogues. Demean ourselves before Turkey, whatever the price, that only
there be peace. //

If the absence of higher sense in eternity, it is civic. They have become corrupted. Scarcely fit to recover.

The whole Orthodox East must belong to an Orthodox tsar, and we must not
divide it (in future between Slavs and Greeks).

In the Slavic question, neither Slavdom, nor Slavism is the essence, but Orthodoxy. //

December[240]
Chapter one
1) Again on a simple but abstruse matter.
2) Belated moralizing.
3) Unfounded allegations.

4) Something on [youths] the youth.
5) On suicides and arrogance.

Chapter two
1) Anecdote from children's life
2) Explanation of my participation in the publication of the coming journal *The World.*
3) At what point is the matter now.
4) Regarding a certain proverb. A word on "dallying Peter." //

Commune
1) Bewilderment (December). First explanation of the bewilderment [Europ.] Our national principle is universality.
2? The Stundists, our democracy, will turn into excessive Khlystism.
2. Foma Danilov [Great idea. Great whores] hero and every Russian.
3. The soldier and Martha.

On communication of the great idea. Great whores.
There is no movement among the common people. And are these movements really in character for our people.

Crit. 4. Idealists and realists. Flowers with an understanding of nature are better than an exposé of bribe-taking.

Calculation. Litke.
4. *A Gentle Spirit. The New Time.*

Socialism, destruction, and the next day.

January 1877 //
The Diary of a Writer

Wretches and the commune.

The commune and Europeanism. Europeanism is turning against [national] European principles. [supports the commune] Persecution of the national party.

NB. The commune keeps a man on the land. In our country a passion for vagrancy and adventure. Separate everyone to their own plot and they will pawn everything and sell it /.../ (Removed the grove.) Give them power—you will not manage. It is better to keep them in check, in the commune. With self-government there could be changes made.

Bewilderment. Axiom (last line of the Decem/ber/ issue). Europeaneers. Russians are Europeans from birth. It is their nationality. That is the first explanation of the bewilderment.

The New Time, December 31. *Among the newspapers and j/ournals/* from *The Russian World* on the sale of *The Voice* to the Turkish embassy.

The New Time, December 31. Friday. *On Foma Danilov*, non-commissioned officer, tormented for his faith by the Kipchaks.

NB. On how a great idea is communicated to such souls, whom, apparently, it is impossible even to suspect of being occupied with the higher ideas of life: Foma the Martyr, Vlas, Jean Valjean.

The basic mistake of our critics. It is 30 years now we have simply been set on the very lowest level of understanding the matter in the eyes of Europe and genuine enlightenment. Our conservatives have had no objections. Kirghizi, they themselves thought it was not so good that way. Tendency, labels, ruin an author. Good feelings, useful for mankind, but then it is decided *a priori* what is good and what useful. A description of a flower with love of nature contains much more civic feeling than an exposé of bribe-takers, // for it contains some contact with nature, with love of nature. Anyone who does not love nature, does not love man. He is not a citizen, etc. —This in the form of a supplement to criticism.

Corneille and revolution.

The Mosc/o/w N/e/ws, December 31, '76. Lead article, letter of Catherine II to Zimmermann and the talk of the foreign press on Russian revolutionary movements (*valet rouge*—Knaves of Hearts). Anecdote about the Englishman who shot at the Russian volunteers.

Injury to the mind, but not the heart, Kirillovs[241] [Kir] God-man, Man-God, uneducatedness from donothingism. Misunderstanding of contemporary man. *Virgin Soil.*

The New Time, Sat/urday/, January 8 (No. 310?), —Stasov's satirical article on the Ideal and Realism.[242] Love of mankind. He sees the ideal in the word, that is more important. Repins are fools, Stasov is worse.

NB. Consciousness and love, which, perhaps are one and the same, because you are not conscious of anything without love, and with love you are conscious of a great deal (the painted apple) —etc.

But then conventionalism; Artemieva, Dickens.

NB. Tirade on the fact that the more national we are, the more we shall be Europeans (Every-Men). Then, perhaps, a type will be created for the first time which does not exist now and which is only in the dreams of all Russians even of the most antithetical movements (Slavophiles, Nationalist, Reds, etc.). It is time to stop being ashamed of one's convictions, it is necessary to express them.

NB. Error of mind, not of heart, etc.
Satire (Shchedrin) destroying their own Europeanism. //

NB. Idea. Infect the soul with one's influence. Vlas. Victor Hugo.

NB. Let the Slavs be fed by us or by the Europeans, it is all the same, only let them be fed. Otherwise chauvinism. It is absolutely untrue, and there is no chauvinism, for if I wanted the Slavs to be fed and be beneficiaries only of the Russians, it is not at all chauvinism, for I wish this neither for the advantage nor the vanity of Russia, but for the advantage of the Slavs. Any sort of reconquest, if only there is food for the Slavs, with Europe against us, it will be to their detriment. And there is [animal] corporeal bread and spiritual bread. —The Slav-Europeans are the Poles, the Czechs, the Serbs, of the higher intelligentsia.
To want to feed the Slavs is, of course, good, —to turn to Europe is also not bad, etc. What another schoolboy wants—(artlessness).

Orest Miller, who combined in himself Slavophilism and Europeaneering.

Christianity is proof of the fact that God can be contained in man. This is the greatest idea and the greatest glory of man, to which he could attain.

Apple. Loving an apple, it is possible to love man. The French, without taste, *roman /?/, Victor Hugo*. Realism, photography. Photography is like nothing else—etc.[243]

Art. Stasov. Repin.
Litke, calculation (Moltke). Lack of faith in the national movement. Cynicism has begun. Our people do not shout, do not demonstrate (stood at Anichkov Palace). Cynicism has begun. Failures, parasites. The blood is good. Satirists.

92nd page of *Virgin Soil.*[244]
Our democracy is as ancient as Russia herself, but those from '89 (Meshchersky's idea). Answer to the author of *Virgin Soil.*

Stundism. Precious vessel. It will turn into excessive Khlystism.[245] //

The soldier, tortured for his faith,[246] on the other hand, the soldier with his

126

daughter.

Depravity. What will swallow up whom?

With the destruction of the commune.

Depravity of the upper classes. Stundism. They deny the national movement. Broke with the common people. Redstock. Europeaneers joined him. Towards despotism. We have been free since the beginning of the Russian land. The Europeaneers want /.../ depravity. But there already is a str/o/ng nucleus of the *conscious*. [Satir] Although the Europeaneers have literature. Satire. No inside. There would not be anything to say. *Virgin Soil*—that is the author's secret idea. That's Potugin for you! That is what the inside of Potugin's satire is. There is no reason for us to be disturbed by revolution, for we have been free these 1000 years.

Everyman. Russia a new word. In that is her nationality.

Speech of the Scottish rector.

High society has gone to pieces and become stupid. And what pleasures it has: *comtesse* so-and-so (while behind their backs they call each other fools). Played dirty tricks on so-and-so.

That they wrote me regarding the immortality of the soul. And in general they write with questions. No higher convictions, goals.

Idealism and realism.

Knaves of Hearts, etc. Excerpt from the October Diary on how *cynicism* triumphs.

They deny the movement. Why didn't the common people shout? Consequently there was no movement.

The press treated non-commissioned officer Maximov's exploit coldly. Not our world, they say: what, defend Christendom (Granovsk/y/. The Crusades. Universal. But Christianity is not universal. Oh, the pigs). The honesty and strength of spirit alone should have struck their hearts: this *non-commissioned officer is the incarnation of the common people*, with the unshakability of his convictions, and on the other side our corrupt society.

January

—Say Christ, Lord, say it!

—Well Christ my Lord.

—Even if you don't believe it it, even if you say it with a smile (only a good one), Christ will forgive you—both you and me. He Himself said: I will forgive insults against me, only insults of the Spirit are not forgiven.

—And what is the Spirit?

—The Spirit is what is now between us and why your face has become kinder, and why you would like to cry, for your lips were quivering, —not true, don't be proud, they were quivering, I saw them, and the Spirit is what led you from America that day to remember the Christmas tree in your parents' home. That's what the Spirit is.

—Well, all right.

—Only it doesn't exist, that's the problem.

—You know, father, you're a fine fellow, yes, sir! //

To Nekrasov

—Live with me in friendship.

—It's difficult to get along with you, really.

—Even your wife didn't get along with you. (NB. Begrudges his wife's attachment to the arbitrator.)

Woman. What are you talking about, Savelich, you fool.

—He's an angel, an angel!

That's how I speak to him, Kharitovna, just like to an angel.

But an angel would hit me in the mug for that. //

Neatness can be an inborn, an inherited quality. But most often it is acquired through experience and long years as a necessity in the struggle for existence. //

Words and proverbs.

The lady dreamer.

The smallest thoughtlet.

Molchalin is not a scoundrel. Molchalin is really a saint. Touching type.

Being only is, [in] when non-being threatens it. Being only begins to be when non-being threatens it.

You acquired much learning not through intellect, so because of a lack of intellect you do not know how to deal with this learning.

He looks as though he does not understand what he's thinking about (idiot).

Assimilation (co-incarnation) (fop). Au/gust/. Yazykov (volunteers, *balničari*, dispose to slumber). Belles-lettres—belletristics.

Such matters must be done completely, not for ornament (i.e., for altruism).

Each of them is better-looking than the next, but not one is really pretty.

We love and desire new women most of all in an elevated human form, and not in a form which has lost all sense of the human, in the form of something rushing about and gone mad (from Meshchersky in his letter on Serbia, the Cossack woman—the printer's signature and the woman bombarding me with letters).

The early bird gets the worm.

What is the difference between demon and man? In Goethe, Mephistopheles says [I am part] in answer to Faust's question: who are you: I am part of that part of the whole which wishes evil but does good. Alas! man could answer, speaking conversely of himself: "I am part of that part of the whole which eternally desires, thirsts, hungers for good, but as a result of his actions there is only evil." //

Critical remarks. *Zola.*

I have not time to be fastidious, so I'll take the first I come across, so here in *Le ventre de Paris.*[247]

Le ventre de Paris, p. 30 on cabbage and carrots (forced ecstasy).

(That is not art; he starts and does not know what to say.)

P. 34. *Florent* is a man who was fleeing from Cayenne, and apparently became so muddled in five streets among the vegetables brought in by cart that he did not find the road or passage. It is all nonsense, it is all exaggerated pictures (there, he says, that's how I describe cabbage!) —Foolishness!

Painter *Claude.* He is not a man. The eternal ecstasy is ridiculous. These are the ecstatic figures in Kukolnik's dramas, like [art] *Domenikino*[248] the fanfaron, the blatherskite. Only they spoke of Raphael, these, of cabbage.

Florent dies of hunger and proudly spurned the help of an honest woman. *Zola* considers this a heroic deed, but in his heart there is no brotherhood, what sort of republican is he? Accept her help and render it to others out of the fullness of a noble heart, —that will be paradise on earth.

The main thing: all of this is incorrect, all of this is exaggerated, and for that reason far from *réalité,* and for that reason you cannot (should not) spit on George Sand.

Sign. He will describe every nail in the heel, a quarter hour later, when the sun rises, he will again describe that nail in a different light. That is not art. Give me a single word (Pushkin), but make it the most necessary word. Otherwise it rushes off in all directions and drags in 10,000 words, [but] and still cannot express itself, and this with the most complete self-satisfaction, but spare me.

Overture to *Tannhäuser.*

That, they say, is love of nature. No, that is love of one's own chatter and confidence in one's literary perfections.

But still the day proaches, i.e., approaches.

If not a beaming, then an unctuously joyful look (from the Maikovs).

And looked at him with severe surprise.

Ladies? Well the ladies, of course, are each one better-looking than the next, but no really pretty ones! Well, are there any really pretty ones? No, not a single really pretty one!

G. A/vseenko/—the most obtuse literary creature of all those who people Russian literature.

Women are terribly ticklish? Did you try tickling them?
The wretches are riff-raff, shoemakers ruined through drink, workmen, etc.

Tout Paris pour Chimène a les yeux de Rodrigue.

N.N. S/trakhov/.[249] As a critic, very like that matchmaker in Pushkin in the ballad "The Bridegroom," of whom it is said:

> She sits over piroshki
> And beats around the bush.

Our critic greatly loved the *piroshki* of life and now holds two prominent positions in respect to literature, while in his articles he *beats around the bush, ad hoc,* circled around, not touching on the core. His literary career gave him 4 readers, no more I think and a thi/r/st for glory. He is sitting soft, loves to dine on turkey, and not his own, at others' tables. In old age, having gained their two places, these men of letters, who have done so much nothing, suddenly begin to dream of their glory and for that reason become unusually touchy. This then adds a completely idiotic air, and a bit later, they are entirely recast as idiots—and remain so their whole lives. The main thing is that this self-esteem comes not only from the role of man of letters, of author of three or four rather dull little pamphlets and a whole series of circumlocutious, *ad hoc* critiques, published somewhere and sometime, but from the role of the 2 public posts. It is absurd, but true. A purely seminarian trait. You can't hide the origin anywhere. No civic feeling or duty, no indignation over any sort of dirty tricks, on the contrary, he plays dirty tricks himself; despite his severely moral air, he is secretly a voluptuary, and for some gross, coarsely voluptuous filth he is ready to sell everyone and everything, civic duty which he does not feel, work to which he is indifferent, the ideal which he does not have, and not because he does not believe in the ideal, but because of the thick layer of fat due to which he cannot feel anything. I will speak a little more later about these literary types of ours, they must be exposed tirelessly. *i/*

—The locksmith will come, have a bit of tea, and the colonel will go and sit there at cards and lose.

—Fool.

—I heard it from a fool.

—That's all you know how to do, you heard from others.

—And you're speaking against the authorities, who keep us here out of charity.

—The colonel will be late, and the locksmith will come early.

—And you said that God is just, but you see he isn't.

—Yet sometime he'll press him down (the colonel), for he's the one played him a prank.

—But then, maybe he'll be in paradise, but not the colonel. He'll be in hell.

—That's because he hired a carriage.

—What paradise is that in.

—Oh, you, stupid, me they'll let in because I don't believe by faith, and you because: well, you believe, but don't you have any coffee?
[What do you want that for?] [I for you]

—But it's me that had to suffer for you. But I'll be in heaven.

—[So you'll be in heaven?] That's for the coffee. —I will, to spite you I will. Is that for my not having had any coffee? Yes, because you didn't have any.

—You'll be back again, but now just sit without coffee. —Though it is true that we're without coffee, still don't you make me mad, Prokhorovna, leave me alone, evil human tongue.

Fool, heard it from fools.

—Oh you, granny, you should submit to your guest, put on a new one. Only the blue heavens. Everyone found out about it.

Lukeryushka, *I understood* it that way.

—You're below, in hell, and I'll look down at you from above.

All this is one conversation.

He at least wrote so that it was possible to read him, but the other one, to introduce the tiniest thoughtlet, he'll bring in a whole load of hay.

And as regards style, many of our writers have grown fond of writing with [a cert] [the most] a certain almost [lavish] arrogant verbosity. What do I have to do with the public, I am introducing an idea. In the old days at least they wrote so that it was possible to read them, —well, Belinsky, for example, but now some-one else—to introduce the very tiniest thoughtlet, [at first] he'll bring in a whole load of hay at the beginning. //

Words and sayings

131

It's time for the bones to be in place.

You think he drowned: *do you have to soon?*

Or, if they were not unlucky, they were not lucky either.

Seminarist, son of a priest, who formed a *status in statu*, is now a renegade from society, but it would seem that it should be the other way around. The priest cleans out the common people, is distinguished from other classes by his clothes, and has not communicated with them in sermons for a long time. His son, a seminarist (lay), broke with the priesthood, but did not join any other class, despite his desires. He is educated, but in his own university (the Religious Academy). Because of his education [eats through] he is eaten up with self-esteem and natural hatred for the other classes, which he would like to crush because they are unlike him. In civic life there are many things he does not understand intrinsically, vitally, because neither he nor his brood participated in this life, so that in general he understands civic life distortedly, merely intellectually, but most important, abstractly. It wasn't hard for Speransky to plan the creation of classes in our country on the pattern of the English,[250] lords, bourgeoisie, etc. With the destruction of the landowners, the seminarist would in an instant come to reign and do a lot of damage with his abstract understanding and interpretation of things and current affairs.

You probably wanted to say one thing and said something else. Don't be angry, it happens... [onl] even with very great thinkers.

And even without that (NB, i.e., without a French education) [The Russian] the Russian intellectual in a huge number of cases is nothing more than *an intellectual proletarian, who arrived through nurses and governors in the wind* from Europe. Something without land under it, without soil or root, just being blown along. One can say: blessed are the poor in spirit, but it is impossible to say blessed are the proletarianized in spirit. And this French education, even under the very best circumstances, i.e., if he actually thinks about something, and reads something, he is, it turns out, nothing more than high society's *international* mediocrity. You meet him often. He is an impeccably gloved young man, etc., who gulped down a few stylish *ouvrages*... some *argent*, but whose mind wanders in eternal *ténèbres*, yet for all that, terrible impertinence. That's all the good we'll get from them. All of them, of course, are preparing (hope to) to rule the state.[251]

The mamas of high society can take comfort in their young men. //

How can new ideas be disseminated when they ridicule your idea from the very first. We will not worry about that. The Areopagus will ridicule you and hiss, but somewhere there is always, in an unseen corner, a woman by the name of Phamar and Dionysius, member of the Areopagus,[252] and the idea does not die (it gets into circulation), grows and multiplies and conquers the world...and the sages fall silent.

Piccola bestia.

Baptiste, tout de suite ce mot à son adresse.
Tout de suite? Madam ignore peut-être le temps qu'il fait, c'est à ne pas
mettre un chien dehors.
Mais, Baptiste, vous n'êtes pas un chien.

The Sultan granted [amnesty] complete amnesty to all the Bulgarian in-
surgents, excluding the chiefs and ring-leaders, and all who [actively] participated actively in the insurrection. One wonders, to whom did he grant amnesty? To all
who did not participate in the insurrection?

[To Nekrasov IV,V] *Contemporary man.* He avenges all the injuries which
no one did him, nor thinks of doing him.

[To Nekrasov] I am a fool, and so by birth, but you... etc.
And that one's making a show of his abundance of love.
Abundance of love is a good thing, but then it is possible to override a jade.
Journal des Débats. Oh, how it pains them that Constantinople will be ours.
They are complaining, *Journal des Débats.*

Their first and main characteristic, their essence, their main trait—is that what
exists now will continue eternally. Their minds are timid. Oh, he does a little
free-thinking, he'd have the commune in a minute, but in reality he considers all
these chamberlains an unshakeable wall. There's lots of servility here.

How can it not seem to him that here are *des pentureaux.*

Life is beautiful, and it is necessary to do something so that eveyone on
earth might confirm this. //

Women. —Who are manifest even in our unsteady ideals. Tatyana—and friend.

Was at the kneeling (i.e., she prayed).

That was the nature of the Russian priest in the true sense, i.e., material advantage in the forefront and beyond that—evasiveness and caution.

What difference does it make that he bought a cow—Prachkov.

Except Mashenka. Opposite the Mikh/ailovsky/ Theater.

In France the proletarians are without land, and the owners are ravishers /?/

of the land. There is no brotherhood, no serenity in possessing the land, no silent joy. And [re] as a result you get owners of the land of France, and not her children.

It would be more likely to have no 1st of the month than no *Messenger of Europe.* If *The M/essenger/ of E/uro/pe* did not come out, there was no 1st of the month. Or:
The Messenger of Europe did not come out—so there (won't be) wasn't a first of the month.

Russia's only possible word on Constantinople: Yes, it is neutral, but this neutrality is under *my* protection.

Hollow man.

No, really, in what language *will I understand* Latin and Greek?

He is a gentleman who has the air of a non-gentleman.

Won't be without kopek and ruble.

The Voice has the air of a fool given voice. //

Order: Kazan and O/ur/ Lady of Kaz/an/.
Ivan the Terrible. Young men looking for work.
Our gallery of old men; we must stir them up.
The factory worker who killed his wife (wherever it was), and the cabby (skewbald horse) in Moscow on his deceased wife, etc.

Prince, I do not believe your appearance, I always consider that your appearance is a physical defect in you, not a moral one: in appearance you are no gentleman, but in spirit you are.

The Russian people haven't composed any malicious songs. For example, they sing "Barynya," but with gaiety, not indignation. (In "Barynya" there is more gaiety than indignation.)

We have left them behind. But I was no match for you.

Grovellingly liberal publication (Stasyulevich).

NB. Christ is God as far as Earth could show God.

And stingy as a kopek.

You were just born of the bathhouse damp, as the deceased from the House of the Dead said, cursing (after all half are probably deceased now), when they wanted to designate some disgraceful geneaology.

The farther you move from "factism" the better.
A rich man, and in uniform, but still he is late, while the locksmith is rather poor, but comes again and again.

And you said that God is just, but you see he isn't—the rich man always gets rich first.

Oh, Prokhorovna, why, maybe he's rushed off to his ruin, while the other, even if he's fallen, maybe that's how God has kept him honest.
But still he's played that prank.
And for that he'll land in heaven. //

Account of Attacks
For 1873

—April 20
—June 4
—August 1
—November 3 and 19
—December 27

1874	1875
—January 28	—January 4
—April 16	—January 19
—May 13	—April 8
—June 27	—July 4
—July 15	
—October 8	
—October 18	
—December 28	

Attacks

1875, September 29, strong (but not one of the strongest), at night, towards morning, between 5 and 6 o'clock in the morning, *after a 3-month interval.* Full moon. Tightness. Light t/hroa/t bleeding. Very strong rush of blood to the head. Irritability.
October 13. Morning, in my sleep, at 7 o'clock, not so strong.
1876. *January 26.* Monday morning, in my sleep, at 7 o'clock, rather strong,

135

1st quarter of the moon.

   April 30, on Friday, morning, in my sleep, at 7 o'clock, rather strong. Rush of blood to the head. Melancholy and hypochondria. Last ¼ of the moon. Before this I had greatly upset my nerves through long work and many other things.

   May 7, at 9 o'clock in the morning, rather strong, but weaker than the preceding. Did not regain consciousness for a very long time. A few raised spots. Head not hit so hard as the back and legs. /.../253

   May 14, morning, in my sleep, between 6 and 7 o'clock. Rather strong. Little blood seeped out, legs hurt more, partly the small of the back too. Head // hurts too. /.../ —Great irritability.

   June 6, average, morning, in my sleep, small of the back hurt.

   June 13, morning, between 8 and 9 o'clock, in my sleep, average, head hurts. /.../ NB. As yet unprecedented increase in the frequency of the attacks.

   August 11, morning, in the Znamensky Hotel, after [journey] journey on arrival from Ems, average.
   August 19, morning, average, severely hurt my limbs.
   October 10, morning, between 9 and 10 o'clock, in my sleep, rather strong. Irritability. Day clear and frosty. 1st day cold.

   November 15, at 10 o'clock, morning, in my sleep. Day clear and frosty. Very fatigued state. Understanding very hard, [eac] rather strong.

   February 1, in my sleep, between 9 and 10 o'clock in the morning. Day clear, and frost *set in*. Very fatigued state. Fantasy. Fuzzy, mistaken impressions, legs and arms hurt. Rather strong. /.../
   February 19 rather significant attack.

   February 26 rather significant attack.

   March 17 significant attack. Violent change in the weather. Beginning of the wane of the moon. //

Words and sayings
   Your tongue is not a trowel, it knows what's sweet.
   A penny's worth of ammunition, a ruble's worth of ambition=Chatsky.
   Like a flea himself, he is drawn like a plow.
   Foot-shambler.
   International mediocrity.
   An impeccably gloved young man, who gulped down a quantity of fashion-

able *ouvrages*, but whose mind [continues to roam] wanders in eternal *ténèbres*, while all his life his heart craves only *argent*. But in what *ténèbres* did his mind not roam.

Both phrases pertain to two of our critics (Druzhinin and Avseenko). With a passion for *argent*. He is dying before he does anything, because of the notion that, as he says, my life is short, it's all the same if I don't manage to do anything. A mistaken notion, and it is apparent that the man had lost touch, lost touch with mankind. What is this, how can you begin something and not finish it. Others will finish it for you, even Peter did not finish his business, except, except that he started it.

Do your business as though you were about to live a century, but pray as though you were about to die right now.

There is no end to it.
(In our country, one can say: everything liberal is rotten, fatal.)
But instead of a heart you have (Laroche)[254]—some little pecuniary piece (a little piece of something pecuniary) (something pecuniary) etc. *L.*
An evil people, evil with all their might.
—But you're evil, you're evil with all your might. //
—But they think that it was for boots I hid (i.e., stole) (the money).

...To serve as a connecting idea, round which all would unite.

Man does not live by bread alone. That is, a man, if only he be a man, will not rest content even having eaten his full, but feed a cow and she will be as serene as any liberal who had finally bought, for his liberalism, his own house. G. Blagosvetlov (who attained his house).

A limited man (Belinsky) who was not able to discern in the guilty, the not guilty, or in the righteous, the guilty. For according to him, anyone he deemed righteous was always righteous, and the scoundrel always a scoundrel. Books and women—books.

He is kind of dull? Yes, kind of unfortunate.

Applies to our intellectual proletariat. One can say—Blessed are the poor in spirit, but it is difficult to say blessed are the proletarians in spirit.

And how they thundered and [glittered] glittered then (i.e., were celebrated).
We do not have sciences, but even now only "scientifics,"—as a certain editor, publisher of a monthly journal used to say in the old days, when there were still sections and headings, one of them under the title "Science and Art":[255] "Here's a storylet for you, what // criticules, why "scientifics" too—quite a little number

137

we put together—he-he-he..."

Many of our writers on the common people continue to be taught about the Russian peasant by foreigners.

You, gentlemen, you are all great figures, earnest and self-satisfied. In comparison with you, I am a reed wavering in the wind, and how could I be self-satisfied!

And how much strength of spirit this revealed, which he, a straw man, will never have.

Well, I didn't invent it, so I must have heard it from someone.

To Orest Miller. Let's assume abundance of love is not a bad thing, but then it's possible to override a jade. Always [lov] the same old thing—it will grow sweeter, not love that is, but abundance of love.

That sated cow, resting content like Mr. Blagosvetlov, sated by his business, and having attained his own home (on the corner of Nadezhdinskaya and Manezhnaya) on the corner of Blagonadezhnaya and Manezhnaya.

NB. Variant on Blagosvetlov.[256] [All of these coul] You must be honest and have the charm of honor in public, without this you will not manage to have decent influence with any amount of talent. [All of these] And really: look at those trading in liberalism, *he* summoned up his strength and risked starting a newspaper. Now he isn't fooling many. Now only a fool wouldn't know that as soon as he puts on weight, all the ardor will disappear and the sated cow will finally rest content, like Mr. Blagosvetlov, sated with his *Business,* etc., and come back to his house.

or variant... and rest content like a sated cow, which, if you give it something to eat will rest content, as Mr. Blagosvetlov does, etc. //

"Cannot help become almost Russian power" (question mark set here). But how not a power? They are surprised at that! Pushkin and *Prisoner of the Caucasus,*[257] isn't that power, Zhukovsky and Schiller's influence with him—isn't that power, incipient socialism and Belinsky—is it really possible that even Belinsky is not power? All of this is power and one awesome in its manifestations even.
What strange doubts, what a strange question mark.

You are one of those Europeans who wander around the world, but in the most noble sense of the word, and by world one must figure not world at all, and I do not at all believe that you borrowed a hundred francs from that skinflint Victor Hugo.

138

In our country, criticism is off-hand, by whim. Someone reads several novels, so he goes and starts writing the criticism section. That is why there is so much lack of content. With a great talent it is possible to express many feelings (Belinsky), but still not be a critic. But a study (scholarly!) of what influence writers (Schiller, George Sand) had on Russia, and how much, would be an extraordinary and serious work. But we'll have to wait a long while for that. History of the transformation of ideas from one to another.

The realists are mistaken, for man is a whole only in the future, and certainly has not entirely exhausted his possibilities by the present.

Only in realism is there no truth.

Photography and the artist.

Zola overlooked the poetry and *beauty* in G. Sand (in the first stories), which is much more real than leaving mankind with only the filth of the present.[258]

With only "the living truth" ([as far as I am concerned] truth in Zola's opinion), from which it is impossible to extract any thought.

Realism is the figure of Hermann (although in appearance, what could be more fantastic),[259] and not Balzac. Grandet is a figure which means nothing.[260] //

Gustave Droz[261] *Monsieur, madame et bébé* 74 editions. *Entre nous* —34 editions. *Le colier bleu* 27 ed/itions/ *Babolain.* 22 editions, *Autour d'une source* 18 ed/itions/. *Une femme gênante* 17 editions. Stendhal *De l'amour* in 17 years— 11 cop/ies/.

Kekhribardzhi. 7.40, for mail 4 r. 40 k.

Failure of the office of Baimakov[262]
Baimakov and Luri
Grew in Harmony
Together grew both plots
Two bankruptcies—there'll be three!
There'll be three and five and eight
There'll be an awful lot of failures
Both in summer and toward fall
And the critic Strakhov writes.
In three articles on spiritism
(of which two are superfluous)
(on the universal nonsense)

139

All on extra dimes.

Only Strakhov prophesies
and only critic Strakhov
In three articles on spiritism
Finding in that nonsense
Two or three dimes extra.

Addition

Dostoevsky

He is right: Without children, neither marriage, nor family, nor life. —They crave a noble exploit which neither God nor fate will send, but the children let even a man incapable of a noble exploit do something noble. —Children ennoble. And without nobility you can't survive, besides, there might still be doubts: is what I'm doing noble. But the exploit of motherhood excludes any doubt.

No family. Shchedrin caressing a child.

The boy's suicide.
(economic reasons)

I suck you in
May 3 evening
  —valuables   —137
  —money   —303
                       ————
                 440 r.

Account May 29
May 3 [money] left in all   440 r.
from May 3, come in for *Diary*   258
    And for books   66

                   Total   764 r.
                           526

                           238 r.
             And Trishin   400

                   Total   638
             Come in   254

		And for books	15—60

Borrowed by me	30 r.		June 6	907 r. 60
Move, purchase of clothes	60 r.		Outlay	168
Nurse, flat, purchases	52		Total	739 r.

Expenses	142	I. G.	250

	989
[A.N.]	50

	1039
Things	175
From Raspopov	25

	1239
	+3 from subscib/ers/

Total, June 16	1242
	142

	1100

July 3, in Petersburg, after general account in total 714 r.
Of this I take myself 50 r.
Slav/ic/ P/hilanthropic/ Com/mittee/ 25

			715
Pic/ture/	76		151

	151	Total	564 r.

Letter to Anna.
Sunday July 18/30
Herb *Yanthium spinosum* for hydrophobia,
Kiddies cost one dear, / Anna Grigorievna, yes, / Lilya and [both] those little boys./
—That's our misfortune!
NB. In sight of.
Ann/a/ Grigoriev/na's/ outlay and for deed and income from Mamocht. and Nadein.

Were (with outlay for deed)	—514 r.
And income (from July 3 through August 17)	— 77 r.

August 17 total	591 r.
	256

Total:	335 r.

August 17	−335
	113
Paw/n/	12
	————
	462
	221
	————
Sept/ember/ 3	241

Sept/ember 18	481 + 5 r. = 486
Pechatkin	240
Ap/artmen/t	76
Trish/in/	30
Bed	5
	————
	351

NB. NB. NB.

December 16. All /subscribers/	−*133*
Of them—renewing	− 59
Completely new	− 74

Account December 5

Our debts	Rough/ly/ *complete*
Pleshcheev towards 750 r. Prepared	250
Pechatkin on promissory note. Due December 24	110 r.
Vargunin remainder of debt	156 r.
NB. (Alonkin 425)	
Mu/tual/ Lo/an/ Co/mpany/ January 20	500 r.
Trishin	540
Pawns	260
Pechatkin	262
To Obolensky (through November issue *not* inclusive)	144
	————

	Debts	1972 r.
	Outlays	320
		————
		2292 outlays
For advertisements		325
		————
		2617 r.

Proposed purchases

For myself [100]	50 r.
For purchase of lam/p/,	120
mir/ror/, tabl/e/,	
tableclo/th/, kniv/es/	
for An/na/ Grig/orievna/.	
Teeth or purchases	150
	————
	320

142

For advert/isement/ in *The N/ew/ T/ime/*	−75
in *The R/ussian/ W/orld/*	−60
S/aint-Petersburg/ N/ews/	−30
The Gov/ernment/ Me/ssenger/	−50
The Voice 7 ad/vertisements/	−50
The Stock/-exchange/ New/s/ 5 ad/vertisements/	−60 r.

325

Reduced debts		
Pechatkin		162 r.
Obolen/sky/		144
Pawns	[260]	100
Advertisements		325
Purchases		320

1061	1061
440	440

Total	1501 r.	[Total 1461 r.] //

December 5.   10 o'clock pm.—

in total	1390 r.
If received from Isakov	9—90
From subscriber	6—90
From Nikolich and Kuzmin	89

1495 r.—80 k.

December 10 after various expenditures total sum remaining	165 r.
And planned from pawn	150 r.
December 20—after accounts remains	13 r.
Still to spend	100 r.

Total	113 r.

NB. (Things not pawned)

December 31	148 r. 70 k.
Cash	611 r. 50 k.
148-70	
611-50	

In all 720 20 k.

January 9 77 taking another 100 rubles from cash, in all with receipt and expenditures in balance   65 rub.

—And cash   900 r. 60 k.

NB. Things *not* pawned.

143

NOTEBOOK XI

(1880-1881)

Addresses

Ct. Tolstaya Bolshaya Millionnaya, Lobanov house, 30, diagonal from the Hermitage.

E. A. Shtakenshneider, Znamenskaya St., 22.

Demidovsky alms-house for laborers, No. 106, on the Moika near Litovsky Castle. *Yakovlev.*

Gorbunov Iv. F-ch, Fontanka, 113.
Aksakov—Nevsky Prospekt, No. 6.

Anna Nikolaevna Engelhardt. Sadovaya, Nikolsky Market, Nikolsky Bridge, No. 124 (Ton's), in Ton's rooms.

Bestuzhev-Ryumin, Basseinaya, No. 33.

Saburovs (Andrei Alexandr/ovich/ and Elisaveta Vladimirovna). Kirochnaya, opposite Nadezhdinskaya, Kavos house.

Tikhomirov (Osip Timofeevich), merchant of Pavlovsky district. Bogorodsk. Moscow province, Nizhegorodsky railroad. Pavlovo station.

Savelev, Alexander Ivanovich, Furshtadtskaya, No. 30, apt. No. 2.

Orest Fedorovich Miller, Ertelev Lane, house No. 2 (?).

Ivan Sergeevich Aksakov, Moscow, Spiridonovka, at Nikitsky Gate, Rozanov house.

Countess Anna Egorovna Komarovskaya, Marble Palace.

Nikolai Savich Abaza—Troitsky Lane, hse. No. 38. Tuesday between 4 and 5 o'clock.

Countess Alexandra Andreevna Tolstaya, Winter Palace. //

Yuferov, Alexander Nikolaevich, Znamenskaya, 29 No. Corner of Basseinaya. //

—Current things.
—Answer Anichkovaya.
—Answer question about Faust. //

Diary 1881.

Schools for the commonfolk. Two levels of schools for the commonfolk, in the first only reading, *some basic* writing (they will learn something, they will be clerks, quite a few will forget) and three prayers. And then the other level of schools, also for peasants, but higher. There are very few of the second level as yet, but once you have the first level, that means you have *given birth to a force.* Whoever is educated has already begun moving, has already started on his way, is already equipped. And you will see how within a few years in your country schools for peasants *at a higher level* will already begin to appear *of their own accord:* demand will grow, desire will be born, and the schools themselves will result. But here in our country everything comes suddenly.

Everything suddenly and with classicism (my thoughts concerning classicism). Gradualness has not been observed at all. NB. Foreigners have a *feeling of duty,* in our families there is decay... and so forth.

Classical reform. Carried out the classical reform in the abstract. The main thing, forget that we are not Europe.

For planting the grand idea thanks goes to Katkov and the deceased Leontiev, but for applying the idea no praise can be given. They were brought in by the cudgel. The Czechs. German boy (duty) and Russian boy (decaying family). The number of hours gradually rising from year to year. History, natural sciences, Russian language. Let there be no ideas. They will accumulate their own, that would be worse.

Our history should have given us spiritual ideas. The spiritual ideas of a German boy are different: his system, his way of life, his nationality. But in our families we have only decay. History should have saved us from decay and directed the mind of the youth, if only to the historical world, from *abstract gibberish* and *junk,* which make up the spiritual world of our society. In a word, we did not act according to our nationality. (Our young Russian boy is more developed than the German.) If only the teachers of literacy could be regulated, so they did not teach liberal absurdities. It would come of its own accord. There is no culture, an empty place. There is no culture in the past, and what the indication is for the future, i.e., Europe with a consciousness of its supreme Russian destiny—you spit on this. Precisely because of its Russian destiny. You have become ashamed to acknowledge Russian independence. I

145

thought this up not out of my fantasy but in the spirit of Orthodoxy.

Ah, you threshold, my home's threshold. Analysis of the song. It is full of passion. It just entertained one/.../ The old man is stern. /I for/ But it is still not intended to entertain. A father's only son, like a plea. The poet is not beneath Pushkin.

Boat my little boat. Along the meadows. Floating down the mother river. Bandits.

You may be ashamed, or may not, but I am not ashamed and do not want to be, a father's only son.

Eyes watery blue with the light (clear and bright). //

Drunkenness. Let those rejoice in it who say: the worse it is, the better it is. There are many like that now. But we cannot without feeling bitter see the roots of the commonfolk's strength [poi] poisoned. And for what reason? To parade our politics in front of Western Europeanism, to support the various Kumans, etc.
    Honesty. Thefts /?/. "Honesty is as much a fiction as is religion, for frightening little children." Bring out the *connection* of the decline of honesty and of honor (in our society with the decline of the ideas of religion, family, morality, and so forth).

"Orthodox Survey." Leskov. Turkish costume. That would be someone to put your trust in. And they would work on it. But put Yanyshev above everyone else and a priest with a star (Vasiliev).

Leskov. Specialist and expert on Orthodoxy.[1]

Vereshchagin and the artist.[2] Unevenness of artistic remuneration. Vereshchagin and the novel being written for three years.

Shchedrin—His whole flock of Glebovs, Mikhailovskys, Eliseevs.[3]

N/otes/ of the Fath/erland/. All of the literature makes you tremble, especially that of the satirical elder.[4] No one would dare to go against him: a liberal, they would say, [through and through] liberalism through and through. —No, you are playing at being liberal, *when it is not advantageous,* that is when I should take a look at you.
    You push your way through with rehashed thoughts.

Everyman.[5] Elucidate in *Diary. The Country* and *The Messenger of*

Europe[6] on my speech. (Garland.)

He was worried about the eternal, rather than the temporary-utilitarian (for grand basic reforms). *The New Time,* No. 1664 and 1665. Bring in tallow, rye and wool.[7]

Mir tax collections. *Without fail. The New Time.* Article *"Mir Tax Collections."*[8] No. 1671. Wednesday, 22 October. *Also:* Look at No. of *Russia* from 21 October.

Into article on finances. Just like the Varangians arriving by invitation. Our land is great and rich, they went away and left the land in disorder. I am not speaking for the advocates of serfdom and I do not bemoan the status of serfdom, as they will not hesitate to ascribe to me. I bemoan disorder and anarchy. This anarchy and absence of lawfulness is a corrupting element no less than drunkenness. It will lead to despair, to rebellion. Kulaks. NB. The unfinished peasant reform. They will be brought to despair, they will bring up the question of allotments. The kulaks too will start to agitate, stir up, and excite the commonfolk about new golden // tsarist decrees and they will begin to do that in order to distract the commonfolk's attention away from the kulaks' own offenses. And what is being done in the courts? A mother is badly beaten, a bribe is paid, and they give the mother a flogging for committing slander and so forth.

/.../ *Reconciliation with the Poles.*[9] France, destroying herself completely in Catholicism, for if it were not for Catholicism, they would have to accept socialism immediately. But they want neither one nor the other. [Wil] The only thing left is the bourgeois [lib] liberal with his immortal principles of '89. Meagre sustenance.

Shchedrin. Sketches.[10] *Abroad. Not/es/ of the Fath/erland/.* September and October '80. "They will take them off to the police station." What that means is they do not take them to the police station at all. That is where the satire should be. Insult to a woman (at Palkin's). Theft and personal insult, shooting at Loris-Melikov, but they just simply salute. —Once, forty years ago, they took Shchedrin off to the police station and so he became frightened. But that was to a prosecutor's post. He almost wrote "Prison and Exile."[11] The conversations with counselors Dyba and Udavoi are the height of stupidity and servility. About the Berlin officer. Don't you yourself stick out your *chest* at home? Don't present yourself as a hero. [Pr] NB. They praise Shchedrin because they are in awe of liberalism and even of *Notes of the Fatherland.*

Children. About children's jobs in factories. And as soon as possible. For the article on roots and finances.

Belinsky. Uncommon striving toward the perception of new ideas with extraordinary desire, each time, with the perception of the new, trampling everything old, with hatred, with vilification, with contempt. As though a thirst for vengeance against the old, and I burned up everything I used to honor.

This never [Th] used to happen with Belinsky. Just exactly like people nowadays, i.e., the average, which means the commonplace, the street.

France. *The New Time*, No. 1667, 28 October '80. Tuesday. Prophecy of Baron Hübner about the approaching social/ist/ movement in France and in Europe. Russia is invited to the union[12] (*Russia must not. She must look after her interests. Socialism will collapse at her feet*). But in France it looks inevitable; all the Jesuits and all the Catholics who were driven out of Paris by the stupidity of Gambetta will side with socialism, the Legitimists, all the Bonapartists will side with it. Granted, conservative France is still strong, despite the stupidity of the rulers and the stupidity of the republic. But this is the beginning of the end. The end of the peace is coming. The end of the century will bring forth an upheaval such as there has never been before. Russia must be prepared, not budge, watch and wait, if only Russia were not enticed into the union. Oh, horror! Then that would be the end of her, the complete end. We have no socialism, none at all. There are only a few fledglings of Peter's nest. The healthy part of Russia, though, will not budge, and this part is innumerable.

Gambetta, behind him a gilded halo. NB. Correspondents. Molchanov, 29 October. About monks. All of them and who is for them—lache, lache, and lache. And if they start talking about Felix Piat and the puffing *Gambetta, who has a gilded halo behind him,* every line and comma exudes respect.[13]

Finances. The basic ideas ahead of the current ones. There is nothing new in this idea except perhaps that this one has never been applied (has not been put into practice). //

The execution of Kvyatovsky, Presnyakov, and the pardon of the rest.[14] NB! How the government—it could not pardon them (except the will of the monarch). What is execution?—In government—sacrifice for an idea. But if the church—there is no execution. The church and the government, the two must not be confused. That the two are confused is a good sign, for it means that it bows to the church. In England and in France they would not even think of hanging—church and monarch at the head. My conversation with Sidoratskaya about the university. Her exclamation.
Seize upon this point and ask: did murders and crimes stop. Did Loris-

Melikov destroy evil will? (Goldenberg.)[15] The quantity is not what is important, but the mood and the persistence of criminals unheard of anywhere up
to this time (Felix Piat praised), sincerity. *Easy work.* Women—the brutality
of their service. *The women's issue.*

Overstrained... On these worn-out, rehashed, overstrained themes.

Shchedrin. The theme of Shchedrin's satires is a policeman hidden somewhere who overhears him and informs against him; but Mr. Shchedrin cannot
make a living from this.[16]
    NB. Instead of the policeman, about how none of our public figures, in
any field, *really knows what he wants.*

The New Time about Finland, No. 1691. Friday, 14 November. On Finland's claims.

Felix *Piat.* Felix Piat says it, Rochefort confirms it. Is it possible that we
will upset their expectations.

The newspaper *Order.*[17] But disorder is what it is, at least in its
thoughts./.../

Economics article. In the economics article on the *general system* in our
ministry of finance add a few words about the fate of Russian agriculture. The
capital has gone into the railroads. Ruined agriculture has been abandoned by
everyone since the emancipation of the peasants. While the *axiom* is: that
there is prosperity and sound finance where agriculture stands firm. France
in '90. They ask heaven knows what from the Russians, but everything, even
industry and agriculture, depend on the population density. In our country
the earlier agriculture was destroyed by emancipation. No law exists on workers or even on the definition of property ownership. The peasant brings shame
and disgrace to the soil, kills livestock with lack of food, with drunkenness,
and is unable (at least not in the foreseeable future) to rise above the minimum that the land gives to him. On the other hand, individual land ownership // stands as a separate element—*as an oprichnik*—from the commonfolk,
from the land. Manifestoes around the churches. "In due course, it will come."
Unsolvable question. Will the commonfolk want to be convinced that not all
the land is theirs and that the oprichniki should not exist? But what if it is to
be left *up to them*—will they do it and what do they have the strength to do
to raise the minimum? (Grove of trees removed, 5 kop. for a log.) Unsolvable
problems, posing a threat in the future. But for the time being, if there is no
agriculture, there will be no sound finance either (salt tax, attitude of the
workers toward the proprietors, great freedom for the resettlements and so

forth).

Aristocrat. Aristocratism of the Russian muzhik's bearing. //

Free R/ussian/ Academy of Sciences. Plan of Russian Free Academy of Sciences.

Concerning the rejected Mendeleev, why don't our Russian scientists set up their own Free Academy of Sciences (donations).[18]

The New Time. Article by V. P. on Mendeleev.

The Messenger of Europe. The M/essenger/ of Europe "is useful for the mind." This was said a long time ago. But bearing in mind such an excellent goal, it could, I think, refrain from serving /the oth/er goal so literally.

It could, it seems, disregard this other goal, at least not pursue it with such literalness.

All nihilists. Nihilism appeared in our country because we are *all nihilists.* What frightened us was only the new, original form of its manifestation. (All are Fedor Pavloviches right down to the last man.) Aksakov's word about Gorbunov. On the contrary, at Suvorin's they applauded the stupidity of commonfolk and of soldiers.[19]

It was comical to see the commotion and the trouble our wise men took to discover: where did these nihilists come from? But you see, they did not come from anywhere, they were all among us, within us, and part of us *(The Devils).* No, how can it be, the wise men reason, we are not nihilists, we simply want to save Russia by rejecting her (i.e., form *a layer* of aristocrats above the commonfolk, raising the commonfolk up to our own // nothingness). (Pobedonostsev's speech in the Kiev Ecclesiastical Academy.) Comparison of nihilism with the schism (Umanets). But the schism brought much benefit.

Continuous complaints that the society is not livening up (comical).

Goncharov. It is impossible to remember everything. Now, for example, at the Pushkin celebration in Moscow, it seems, all his virtues had already been recounted, everything the monument had been put up for had been brought out, but still they had forgotten one virtue, nearly the most important one, i.e. that he was the teacher of our Goncharov, Ivan Alexandrovich. And if Ivan Alexandrovich himself had not reminded us of this in a letter, published everywhere later, to the Society of the Lovers of Russian Literature, no one would have remembered this virtue of Pushkin.

150

The New Time Si/../li, No. 1712, Tuesday, 2nd December. Telegram from Paris that in the Théâtre des nations socialists in the galleries /.../ed on the audience.[20] As if to say, we are poor and you are rich, so take that. The point is not that only some 2000 people listen to Rochefort and Felix Piat, but that the mood of the nation's fourth estate is against the rich (the stories of Anna Nikolaevna). That is the element from which everything will emerge. What can this pseudoclassical republic manage to save? (They started flinging garbage, i.e., it is not hard to imagine what that was.)

To Kavelin.[21] But when will they finally stop, these lords (on the commonfolk from above).

You yourselves say that this is an old story, that it does not exist now, and as soon as any mention is made of the debate, you start in again on the same old story. i.e., you deny the spiritual nature of the Russian commonfolk.

You have never seen the red flower, but I am going to tell you about it.

I say: Alexei is a man of God—the ideal of the commonfolk, but now you will say: but a kulak.

The peasants did not massacre you at emancipation, and now they are getting along with you, but in France the poor people s/.../t onto the rich from the loge. //

The church, churchliness.

Peace mediators of the first call-up. Now what significance would they have had if they had not encountered the trustfulness of the commonfolk.

You hand it all to the mediators, but the commonfolk you have forgotten.

All groups of commonfolk are that way in their youth—how frivolous this is, how stupid.

That means you do not even understand what you are talking about here.

All the elements are identical, but the distribution is different.

From that various things, objects and personalities come.

The saintly separated themselves from the world not from loathing but for the sake of achieving moral perfection. In fact the ancient hermits almost lived in the public square. Hermit Parfeny.

And simply to bear the thirst for spiritual enlightenment is in itself spiritual enlightenment.

You would say that in the West the image of the Savior has grown dim? No, I would not say such a stupid thing. (P. 447.)

P. 448. For goodness' sake, if I [want—] according to my convictions, am I really a moral person.[22] I blow up the Winter Palace, surely this is not moral.

Conscience without God is a horror, it can deviate to the most immoral things.

It is not enough to define morality as being true to one's convictions. One must also constantly raise the question: are my convictions true? There is only one way to test them—Christ. But that is not philosophy, but faith, and faith is the red flower.

People of dubious morality are usually only shrewd operators. But where did you get all of this? (Mammon).

I cannot recognize a burner of heretics as a moral person for I do not recognize your thesis that morality is being in harmony with internal convictions. This is only *honesty* (the Russian language is rich), but not morality. For me there is only one moral model and ideal, Christ. I ask: would he have burned heretics—no. So that means that the burning of heretics is an immoral act.

Conscience, the conscience of the Marquis de Sade! —that is absurd.

Is the act of the journal *The Messenger of Europe*, which slandered me, moral. //

The inquisitor is so singularly immoral that in his heart, in his conscience, the idea of the necessity of burning people could be accommodated. Orsini also. Konrad Wallenrod also.[23]

Good is what is useful, evil is what is not useful. No, what we love. All of Christ's ideas can be debated by the human mind and seem impossible to fulfill. To turn the other cheek, to love more than yourself. For goodness' sake, now why should that be? I am here for an instant, there is no immortality, I will live in my [I/.../]. The unthrifty (The English minister). What, may I ask, is thrifty and what is not.

The government is created for the average. When this government was being created, it said: I am created for the average. You will say that history did that. No, it used to be that the elite always led. For you come before these men. And right after these men, this is true, the middle actually formed its middle-minded codex based on the ideas of the superior people. But a great or original person would always come and shake the codex. Now you, it seems, recognize the government as something absolute. Believe me, we have never even seen a more or less fully developed government, much less an absolute one. All embryos.

Societies banded together as a result of the need to get along. This is not true, it was always as a result of a great idea.

They do not run into the desert (away from the French governors of the past century).

152

The church is all the people—this was recognized by the Eastern patriarchs very recently in '48, in answer to Pope Pius IX.[24]

Turn the other cheek, love more than yourself—not because it is useful, but because it is pleasing, to the point of a burning feeling, to the point of passion. Christ made mistakes—it has been proved! This burning feeling says: it is better for me to stay with a mistake, with Christ, than with you.

You say: Now you know Europe has done much that was Christian besides Popism and Protestantism. How true, Christianity has died there but not all of a sudden, it died very slowly and left its traces. Yes, even now there are Christians there, but then too there is so terribly much perversion in the interpretation of Christianity. //

The act is moral, but not the idea.

Moral is only what coincides with your feeling of beauty and with the ideal in which you embody beauty.

His behavior (and that is only general), let us suppose, is honest, but the act is not moral. The reason is that what is *moral* is not completely decided by the simple concept of consistency with one's convictions—because sometimes it is more moral not to follow one's convictions, and the convinced person himself, keeping his conviction intact, stops because of some feeling and does not complete the act. He curses himself and feels contempt in his mind, but in his feeling, which means in his conscience, he cannot complete it and he stops (and knows, finally, that it was not cowardice that stopped him). [That which] This is the only reason he stopped, that he recognized that stopping and not following his conviction was an act more moral than if he had followed it. Zasulich—"It is hard to raise a hand to shed blood"—this vacillation was more moral than the shedding of blood would have been.

Turbid wave. Is this what I am after the Karamazovs, a turbid wave? And you, I take it, are clear and unclouded? Ah, if I had some anecdote for you. To resort to sullying things around the edges. The president stole an apple.

Vital life has flown away from you, only formulas and categories remain, and it is almost as though you were happy about this. More peace and quiet, you might say (laziness). //

And you get angry, oh, you get angry, sit there and get angry.

"To make a mindless man seem wise." The mindless man is you, but the truth must be revealed.

"Slavophiles and Westernizers do not exist *as parties.* This is untrue. Recently they have indeed been formed as parties. —Slavophilism just barely, to be sure, but Westernism is a fully armed party, prepared for the battle against the commonfolk, and certainly political. It stood over the commonfolk like a watchful guardian-intelligentsia, it denies the commonfolk, it, like you, asks what is so remarkable about them, and like you, it denies them any independent characteristic feature, maintaining condescendingly that these features are found in all infantile groups of commonfolk. The party stands above the issues of the commonfolk: above the zemstvo [above], since the common-folk want and recognize it; the party hinders them, wanting to control them by bureaucracy, it abhors the ideas of the organic spiritual solidarity of the commonfolk with the tsar and talks about a foolish old European woman [who] *(This foolish old woman we)* and, of course, invites this old woman only for the party's sake as the crowning touch, in order to be like the Euro-peans, *but we'll again fetter the commonfolk.* For if the commonfolk do not want an old woman intermediary between themselves and the tsar, but con-tinue to believe as before, that they are children, literally children, and the tsar is the father, then all that can be done is to fetter the commonfolk again.

> This foolish old woman we
> From Europe....
> Will bring in... for the answer,
> But we'll again fetter the commonfolk.

So there are your ideals! What do you mean, you are not a party? Surely you have in you a definite power. And whom do you hand your work over to—has this entered your mind, Mr. Kavelin?

In 1st No. The ideal of human beauty is the Russian commonfolk. Dis-playing this beauty unceasingly, the aristocratic type and so forth. You feel the equality unwittingly; a little later you will feel that the commonfolk are above you.

Serfdom! The scornful attitude toward the commonfolk in our liberals (and in all) in Kavelin, f/or/ exam/ple/, and the extolling of the intellectual layer—[its re] there are traces and remnants of serfdom (in Kavelin too, for example), even in those people who did not have serfs.

The machine is more important than goodness. The governmental ad-ministrative machine—*this is all that we have left.* It cannot be changed, there is no way to replace it without cracking the foundation. It is better for us to make ourselves better, the functionaries say. The official procedure for over-seeing and managing Russia, even though it may be fatal, is still better than goodness.

The bird in the hand and the two in the bush. //

Too little intellect. We have too little intellect. Cultural. There is no cul-ture—everything as if in the dark. Something happens—see how everyone far and wide judges it. But there is a culture—a negative one. Monasteries are not necessary. Science is above the commonfolk. All—the Kavelins, the Gradov-skys, they all agree. As they agree about me. The dignity and the grande monde of the peasant.

The New Time, No. 1721, 14 December, Sun/day/. Beketov's letter to the editor of *Minutes* (police).[25] After this why should they be afraid to grant freedom of the press. We ourselves will be the ones who tie it up and lead it right to the border. In every liberal there is a functionary and a trampler of the freedom of the commonfolk. In this very No. in a feuilleton there is a stupid letter from a student about the division of the medical and law faculties of the Russian and the hist/orical/-philological faculties. "What do they have in common?" he says. The reason they need to be kept together is that the medics and the lawyers are only specialties and that they have in them so little of the spirit of science, education, culture. If there were a spiritual unity of students, the higher sense of science would enter both the medics and the lawyers. At least the issue would be brought up. But you want to separate them even more and do it through *uneducated* specialties. Vivat the future functionary.

Rus, No. 5. On the student history. Both the good and the vulgar.

No culture. We have no culture, for two hundred years an empty place. Explanation to the reader of what culture is. Neither science, nor development, nor honor, nor the best people (14 classes, légion d'honneur). We knock our heads together in a dark place, whatever issue you want, and we are lost immediately. Schools, nihilism, students, crowning touch or hopes placed in the commonfolk—we fight over everything, but resolve nothing. There are the seminarians—they appeared with// a wolf's pedigree, with avarice. There are the good natured—Kavelin. The Polish issue. The women's issue.

Gradovsky, St. Isaac's Cathedral—fathers. Now where will they come from, the fathers. Now they have decided—a constitution! There will be institutions, there will be a constitution, there will be everything. Peacefully. But where will it all come from, if there is nothing (except those petty aristocrats towering over the commonfolk and the nation).
Beketov and the student—knocking heads together.

Kavelin—advocate of serfdom—(the first part of his answer).

Introductory. General poverty. Nothing is bought. The merchants complain. The factory owners cut down. Shirts. Restaurant. Books. Redemption money for pawned items all spent [pov.]. Now they are still chopping down the woods but soon one and all will turn into swindlers, the urge, the appetite of Captain Kopeikin.[26] Landowners squawk, there is no labor. Without labor. The hungry ones are the upper classes, not the lower classes, and the upper classes turn into swindlers. It has a political effect. Thirst for external change. Tabula rasa. Everyone says, still it will be better than it is now. Finances, Abaza, etc.

(All hope lies in the commonfolk, so do not undermine the roots of the commonfolk.) —Someone else for the crowning touch.

Kopeikin, the honor of nobility, the sword of nobility, instituted by Peter—away with everything. And there the Westernizers stopped, with only external change. They mechanistically expect the external forms to be the salvation. This is the last word of the Westernizers. //

Study Russia. In our country it has come to the point that we need to study Russia, to learn it like a science because we have lost a direct understanding of her. Not in everyone, of course, and blessed is he who has not lost the direct understanding of her. But there are very few of them. They did understand, though, that the situation was bad, they knocked their heads together. They are not selling out, they became embittered. Everyone is like that, no longer a Westernizer and no longer a party.

To Kavelin. You are a nihilist, all the more comic and pathetic.

We cannot even maintain an ambassador properly, so they say, except perhaps only among the highest nobility, so take a consul instead. //

Article by N.B. in *Rus*, No. 5. Yes, there is a culture, but it was born by denying the whole and turning to only the smallest minority of the people. The rest are negatively acculturated. (By the way: why did Peter find it necessary to enslave the commonfolk in order to produce an educated class?) They freed the peasants abstractly, not only not understanding the Russian peasant, but also denying him, pitying him and sympathizing with him as a slave, but denying him individuality, independence, his entire spirit. (Kavelin.)

Plan.[27] As far as I am concerned, I am *almost* certain that his project will not be accepted, despite the fact that beyond absurdity he also has within him unquestionable virtues, for example slyness and gaiety.

Peasant. Like a fly in the syrup. This is not so much disorder as the despair of disorder. //

Plan. And so the aristocratic lady who has returned and is nagging her husband will unwittingly help swing the game of the Eastern issue to our favor.

Bearing in mind only the gaiety of Europe.

To roll Gambetta out as an ally.

Young members of the embassy who can dance.

Rus. In answer to *A Word:* we call for acknowledgement. And this is such a damned affair, that *everything* must be acknowledged, not just some small part of it. For the essence of the matter lies precisely in the fundamental character of the Russian commonfolk. And if you bring this up—everything must be known. Or else you will just reach Gambetta's conclusion in his conversation with Mr. Molchanov, the correspondent of *The N/ew/ Time,* in that same conversation which ends with Mr. Molchanov's cry: Vive Gambetta!

Molch/anov/.

Gambetta.

So our entire Westernizer party is [sho] saying the same thing as Gambetta: you cannot escape the common path, for all groups of commonfolk... are the same. —Well, isn't that what Mr. Kavelin is saying?

Introductory. —But what about the sins of the zemstvo! You do not get sound finance from them. The muzhik, drunkenness, shamelessness: it is a lost cause, I might as well be a kulak too. There is no truth. The East. Asia. Railroads, we live for Europe. The economy, 4 instead of 40; pretend to be poor, sit on the roadside. Peter the Great would have done it.

The minister of finance, internal affairs, foreign affairs—and... and... Westernism.

There is no culture. N.B. There is a culture, but one that negates yours— don't confuse the two. It is drawing nigh. It has started to speak.

No, there is no culture. They were looking for the nihilists. Gradovsky, the pulpit of St. Isaac's Cathedral.

Now where can you get the fathers?

Kavelin, unfortunately, turned up. //

Kavelin. Oh, not such a nihilist that he has to be hung. Kavelin's analysis: there is no Russian independence, he says. The red flower, Aksakov; to read the proclamation in the classroom; and if the issues of honor, of expedience have gotten confused.

Before me stood a high school student. To stab his father or to save a child is all the same thing. Plague, Yazykov: Oh, and what if they all died! Everything has gotten confused and it is more serious than you think, for they are more honest than their fathers and they get right to the point. You read a proclamation in the classroom concerning honor, duty, and he asks you (Aksakov) what is honor, what is duty. It's a very good thing that he asks at all because otherwise he will keep quiet about it. —Why is everything like this in our country? And so there is no culture. *There* even the revolutionary is cultured: Lassalle. Kavelin will answer: moral ideas do not exist. The inquisitor is an incendiary, philosophically so. [But ab] Categories are not life, but more about this later. Unclear, unclear, they will say all around, unclear

A. D. Gradovsky will say. I will explain at the first opportunity (do you hear, at the first opportunity, this still needs to be explained later) —I will explain by classical upbringing (we still know nothing about what is going on nowadays, i.e., will the hen be on top of the eggs as usual or is it up to the eggs to teach the hen) —but why it did not take root.

There is no culture.

There is no culture: the classical system.

Plan
Wet snow.

Plan. Russia is looking only for gaiety.
The satisfied aristocratic lady, returning home, nagging her husband, etc.

Plan. To amuse Europe ourselves—this is such a nice little idea. Instead of almost as far back as the battle of Poltava "threatening the West with the whip."

Formula. The Russian commonfolk is entirely within Orthodoxy and its idea. There is nothing else in them or for them—and in fact they need nothing else because Orthodoxy is everything. —Orthodoxy is the church, and the church is the crowning touch and is forever. What the church is—from Kholmyakov.[28] You think I will start explaining now; not in the least, not at all. All this will be done later and painstakingly. But meanwhile I will only offer this formula, and I will also add another one to it: he who does not understand Orthodoxy will never understand anything in the commonfolk. Not only that: he cannot even love the Russian commonfolk, but will love them only as he would want them to be. Conversely, the commonfolk will not accept such a person as their own: if you do not love what I love, do not believe in what I believe in, and do not honor what I hold sacred, then I do not honor you as being one of us. Oh, they will not insult him, will not eat him, will not beat him, will not rob him, and will not even say a word to him. Expansive, solid, tolerant in their beliefs. [He who loves] the commonfolk as [se] a person would wish them to be, will be heard out if he is intelligent and reasonable, they will even thank him for the advice, for the science, not only that, they will [even] make use of the advice (for the Russian commonfolk is expansive and knows how to make abstractions), but they will not honor him as their own, will not offer to shake hands, will not give their hearts over to him. And our intelligentsia from the Finnish bogs passed right by. They get angry when they are told that they do not know the commonfolk.

That is not how you should try to get along with them. On your own terms. No, our intelligentsia has a long way to go before it gets along with the commonfolk and a long way to go before it understands them. I am the only one who came, said something, peas. /?/ and other points. Vodka, drinking away tax money. But for the time being, the spirit of the commonfolk will be consoled with the truth. They are searching, but they are not even allowed to budge. (the fly in the syrup). The authorities. The courts, for their own, flesh of their flesh, trustfulness. Ask the commonfolk. Let the court be flesh of my flesh. Call them together, ask them directly, what about it, is it really possible to recount everything, am I really up to portraying it. Have the court—the truth, let them come to believe in the truth. Trust. The tsar-father asks, the force is adamant. The church is in a sort of paralysis, and has been for some time. They do not know Orthodoxy—you cannot really be angry with them for they understand nothing, and in essence the commonfolk is honest, and if they do curse a great deal, they can be forgiven, and other than a few scoundrels and connivers from the borderlands—they stand up for everything they hold most precious.

Constitution. So you will be representing the interests of our society, but not by any means those of the commonfolk. You will enslave them again! You will keep asking to have them kept under the gun! And as for the press—you will send the press to Siberia, the moment it is not to your liking! It will not be allowed to speak out against you or even to breathe in your presence. //

The New Time, No. 1733, Koyalovich. De Robert's speech in Tver and the address of the Tver zemstvo to Loris-Melikov. Koyalovich on Poland.[29] Reconciliation of the Poles and the Russians on ethnographic Poland (Warsaw). But you must understand that such an idea, an idea of Latinism and of Western civilization, is an idea which the Poles will not yield to you for their ethnographic Poland. This is similar to when Italy was knocking on Rome's door, and the Pope in the face of the obvious and inevitable loss of his miniscule earthly state—that was precisely when he proclaimed the idea of Rome, that the pontiff is the sovereign of all the earth and that without an earthly kingdom (without the third temptation of the devil) Christ would not prevail. What if the Poles are weak now politically. They are strong in ideas while you are weak in ideas, Mr. Koyalovich, since for their idea, for sovereignty over the Slavs (all of them) in the name of Latinism and Western civilization—in the name of this idea, you yourself, with your own hands laid the first stone for the foundation of this Polish idea. The slyest Pole, disguised with good intentions, would have written no more slyly than you, Mr. Koyalovich.

Innocent Petersburg. They think all of this up, of course, in Petersburg the people are totally innocent (while the boyar's wife is looking but does not catch on), but all business is handled from below by the kulaks and the functionaries.

The voice of Vasily the Great. Reforming the liturgy: 10 million criticized on the Tekin Turkmen expedition.

159

Krylov "The Pig under the Oak Tree."[30] Krylov has a delightful fable. A pig, etc.

Now we would certainly not want to be like this portrait. //

Culture. School. The German child: because we are a culture. That is why we are smarter and stronger than everyone else (just in case the German begins to boast), it was not the army that defeated France, but the school teacher. In the opinion of the father and the son—the secondary school is something holy. //

To Yurev. Pray to God that He will give you more Russian thoughts. [I kn.] God will surely hear your prayer.

Organ. An organ of disorderly thought. There, whether you pray or not—nothing will come of it, and least of all, order.

Express/ions/. Cursers. Why do you speak to me that way? Whoever you are, you can be sure that such words are beneath you, for they are slander.

Economic. I am not speaking in favor of this idea having anything at all new in it. The only thing new in it (absolutely new), would be if they actually wanted to put it into practice. //

Europe believes only in money, and when it sees such serious expenditures for pursuing the goal of gaiety—it will be morally disarmed and will forgive us.

Plan. Nightingales' tongues, cigars at 130 r. a hundred from Feiko's (Feiko's has such cigars).

But there is some kind of idea here. There was actually something he wanted to say. Nevertheless it cannot be understood as something whole and finished, but only as an embryo which could actually be made into something. Take the idea, at least.

Cocottish ladies.

Singers, Patti...

Astronomers, academicians resting from their labors. This vessel could be named after [some] ac/ademician/ Veselovsky (someone who is one of our most inactive academicians).[31]

--somebody who is one of the most inactive (resting) of our Russian academicians.

Economic. Besides the fact that there is [no] thing to keep the layers in place (two birds in the bush)—besides that the privy counselor will not want to.

Plan. It is sailing in the open sea, steamships, little steamships, lifeboats, in case anything happens, well just anything.
Attack of the corsairs, with blank cartridges, broadside, a squeal, a shout, and suddenly the Turks turn out to be young cavaliers with flowers, news, gossip. //

Administrat/ion/. It is impossible without the best people, the fact is that the best people cannot be created, appointed or certified that way.

Plan. I am almost sure that it will not be accepted, at least in the present form.
coquettish ladies [cocotte] thus cocottish ladies (but with virtues, for exam/ple/ loving art or politics). But let the cocotte be, surely this is no secret, at "Livadia."

Perhaps a vessel with a social coloration, like our journals for socialists and communards, to soften their severity with gaiety. There could be donattions, young girls, and so forth.

Plan. No, not that, but some tiny village from Eastern Rum/?/ and they attach it to the Bulgarian kingdom, in five years through the village, and Russia's goal will be reached in that way.
But the main thing, to succeed through gaiety, innocence, and flocks of nightingales.

Plan. Now the idea is not a new one: the type of idea was given in the Livadia and in the round ironclad ships, so that Europe, at least, remained convinced that they were launched for the pursuit of the goal of gaiety, while we, of course, built them in utter seriousness.

The New Time, No. 1737. On the zemstvos (excerpt from *St. P/etersburg/ News). //*

Plan. In five years through the little village, with compensation to Austria by the kingd/om/ for each little village/this way, therefore, the goals of Russia are also achieved.

NB. *Finances.* To pretend to be poor, sit on the roadway, put the hat out in front, ask for half-kopeks, now why send the embassy secretaries to Europe this way.

Krylov has a delightful fable about a pig.

Plan. Rest, for four months of the year, *la Russie se reccuisse.* And rest is essential so as not to be bored by continuity, as little at a time of a good thing, as they say.

Finances. Now /eve/ who does not have any stars (?) (does not have two stars).

Finances. Functionaries. But you see this is two birds in the bush. No, it is better to keep the bird in the hand. And they do keep the bird in the hand.

It must not be opened up (administration), there are principles here. Outside elements must not be admitted.

Why do the zemstvo institutions turn into administrative institutions by their very nature and disgust the commonfolk?

Plan. But the main thing, the main thing, is that our ruble will grow. For Europe, seeing our innocence, will feel trust toward us, and trust will make the ruble rise immediately.

3 points. 1) A completely different attitude of the administration toward the land than existed up to this time.
2) A completely different view toward Russia, as not only a European power but as an independent and Asiatic one.
3) A completely different view toward administration itself and reforms in it.
That to bear this too in mind, on the contrary to bear nothing but this in mind. //

Asia. That Russia is not only in Europe, but in Asia as well, and that perhaps more of our hopes lie in Asia than in Europe.

Title. "The Pig." To one suitable pig.

Finances. How to do it? I do not know. Peter the Great would have done it. The principle is what is important. That is just the point, that we have no idea at all how to go about it. What we have is this, based on a deficit of 50 million for the current year, they immediately proposed reducing the army by 50,000 men.[32] Precisely, precisely, they hit the nail on the head: our country is wasting real money (how can our country not waste it), so that it is gone before you know it, but nonetheless it is the army that will no longer have fifty thousand of its soldiers nonetheless.

162

Others even recommended reducing the army by one-half all at once (go on! go ahead! seeing as how it is liberal!). Now why only in half, wouldn't it be better to reduce it all the way, // and to set up in its place a national guard, seeing as how our country has never had this liberal European institution (already obsolete even in Europe). Why not even set up a mobilized unit. The editors of the liber/al/ journals will become colonels and division commanders—wonderful! [Not] The point is that we have no idea how to economize. Reduce not the soldiers by a full 50,000 men, but the swindling in the management of the soldiers and so forth (Administration. But this is the principle.)

In the extreme case not just 50,000 soldiers, but even one hundred thousand could be reduced for a while, in view of the quite indisputable benefit from this economizing, but where then will all this money go, that is the question. There are plenty of empty or half-empty pockets just waiting for it to go into their bottomless pits.

Rus. And so forth. In our country it is more liberal (than the crowning touch). We should ask the commonfolk first of all and only the commonfolk.
They will tell everything to their father, but over there...etc.

Plan. Openness, directness, and such pure, supreme innocence. Through this will you be victorious. //

Finances. Emancipation, land ownership. 20,000 versts of railroads, the workers' issue, the issue of the lands, will parallel property be able to get along with the commune—all these are questions and require more finances. Now, capital loves external and internal tranquility, if not it goes into hiding. Now we did not know how to be capitalists by any means: all we knew was how to run a pawnshop. But now suddenly there is an additional 20,000 /versts/ of railroads—which in Europe were built in half a century, but in our country all of a sudden. What kind of tranquility do we have, what kind of movement of capital do we have. We must bide our time. But they are pushing Russia: it is all because we are not Europeans, all because we lack the crowning touch, all kinds of shouting.

And that is why the financier must stand, so to speak, outside of time and space and grasp the eternal and unshakeable idea... (as the roots).

Finances. Birds in the bush. Well, what is your zemstvo anyway, when we ourselves do not know what it should be, the commonfolk's zemstvo or the functionaries'? You find it amusing, but what if they suddenly decide and proclaim, quite firmly and inalterably, that it is to be a commonfolk's zemstvo, of their own accord, they unbind its wings and then what if suddenly this zemstvo truly of the commonfolk all on its own, absolutely without any

163

pressure from higher up, wishes to become a zemstvo of the functionaries and begins to pull toward that itself. Not [that] without reason did it take two whole centuries for taste to develop, and you would want us to exchange something firm and longstanding for these riddles, for these charades, for these birds in the bush. No, it would be better for us to reform ourselves, etc. A bird in the hand.

Plan. Ces dames... Under the veil of their beauty and innocence. (The sea air, digestion.)

Plan. And Russia will meet [them] her enemies like *ces dames* under the veil of their [poverty and] innocence, innocence and poverty. Now why then will they come to destroy // the thatch-roofed huts, oh, enough of that, they are Europeans, you see, they are educated. For one of our professors has said that the Russian cannot be magnanimous or have noble feelings because he is uneducated. And so, how can I help concluding conversely that Europe and Europeans cannot fail to be magnanimous or fail to have lofty feelings because they are educated?

Well what about Poland then? [Well how about th] And the borderlands?

Well how about that then, with all that innocence?

Here you are throwing yourself at each trivial thing! The Polish issue might not even exist then. All these borderlands of ours, all of this is trivial—you should keep track of the main thing, the main and vital thing.

Hm. The main thing, there is some truth, perhaps, in what he says. I.e., I would not say, God forbid, and what a stupid, ridiculous plan, but.... there is something in it... something sly and practical.

I am *almost* sure that they will not take to it anywhere and will laugh at it everywhere, if they even favor it with laughter, but into consideration—oh, perhaps they will take it into consideration. The goals of gaiety are what were pursued, when everything is so gloomy and dismal.

The borderlands, this is all absurd, this is all trivial and the other way around, all trivial. /.../ Russia is Europe, so it goes, and we are Europeans, and we will pursue the goals of gaiety. And never again and nothing more, that is all there is to it.

I am sure that he will think better of it, that he will renounce his stupid words about the borderlands. When he was formulating the plan he simply forgot about the borderlands and became flustered when they caught him unawares, but still there is something in his idea, and etc., i.e., of course, his plan is absurd, but how funny.

In the gaiety there is an idea and in the innocence there is an idea, and in everything together there is an idea. //

164

But... the idea of gaiety and the idea of innocence are, so to speak, really an indication or even a prophecy of some higher political system. Of course, his way of saying it is stupid and he could not express anything, but... I am sure that his plan, etc. I am almost sure...

Finances. "The Country." To teach the commonfolk their rights and duties. They are the ones who will teach the commonfolk their rights and duties! Oh, such youngsters! (Cynicism, despair, there is no truth, drunkenness--what would become of the commonfolk if they had no religion? What would become of them? Someone would then start teaching them their rights and duties. Why, the commonfolk would hang themselves!)

Finances. Revive this root--the soul of the commonfolk. This is a great root. This root is the source for everything.

Keep driving Russia on: why is it that she is not Europe! now how is it that she is not Europe? It has been decided, at last, and the question is settled: it is because the crowning touch is missing. And so every last one of them shouts about the crowning touch. Mechanistic consolations are always [styl] easy and pleasant. Because the crowning touch is missing, that is why Russia is not Europe, but that means there is nothing to brood over and nothing to be alarmed about: put on the crowning touch and Russia this very minute will take her place in Europe. The main thing and the pleasant thing in these mechanistic consolations is that there is no need to [worry about] think about anything:

> We, no doubt, will soon agree,
> If you just sit down with me,[33]

as the magpie Yakova put it aptly. But what if you are not really fit to be a musician? You *are* fit to accuse, to deny, saying whatever you please. But just give yourself something to do and good heavens, what would happen! There would be only idle chatter, there is no doubt about that. But the only thing produced from the white waistcoats is this idle chatter, and still there would be no action, here they are shouting about the reduct/ion/ of 50,000. The chatterbox type has been produced.[34] For example, a dignitary comes out and speaks to his assembled subordinates: good heavens, what he says sometimes! Some other prominent and leading person sits down in front of you and also begins to speak: without end, without beginning, like some drug. For an hour and a half he speaks. This type has been produced. This type which has come into being has barely been touched on. There are many things that our serious literature has not yet touched on and has overlooked. It has fallen terribly behind. All are types of the thirties, forties (and many, many [of the sixt] of the early sixties).

Finances. Only when the spirit of the commonfolk is consoled in the truth and seeing the truth.

Plan. Now sooner or later it must come to that, i.e., to gaiety and innocence, otherwise we will be devoured. Europe sees us not as Europeans but as Tatars. Let Bismarck undertake a war with us... —Bismarck? Never: he needs us for France.

--Oh, how absurd! Well, let us just suppose, it is nonsense, let Bismarck declare war on us: who would be his first ally? That same Gambetta, that same France... [If] I assure you.

Finances. And... turn to revitalizing the roots, plant money in that, fertilize that. Otherwise...

Now what is new about that? (they will laugh at it). Now it may be that there is nothing new in this, except perhaps for one thing, but I will speak about that at the end of the article... But now to the point.

Where are the roots, then? Well, for example, the commonfolk themselves and their soul.

That is the root, the first and most precious.

Give them freedom of movement and you will instill into their souls, the idea that there is truth in the Russian land and that her banner stands high... and many things, even things you do not expect, do not envision, and do not intend, will be accomplished, and your finances will be as smooth as butter...

God and the Tsar support it. Do not shield the Tsar from the commonfolk. //

Finances. How they read to them... If they do read it, that means there will be something.

False ideas: we will take them for nothing.

The only thing that will appear is commissions for reducing the commissions.

Let the ruble become valuable to ourselves [val] —and you will see how it will immediately become valuable on the European market as well and its price will rise in an instant, and without a single external loan.

The system of taxation (changes). All of these are supposedly very useful medicines, but they are mechanistic, it is time to start on something else, something superior.

Russia is entirely for her own self and not for Europe.

Although Russia is in Europe, Russia is also Asia, and this is the main thing, the main thing.

Drastic measures, drastic solutions. A gloomy economy.

Now the Eastern issue will resolve itself. Essentially the Eastern issue does not even exist for us now. We will solve it suddenly, at some future date, we will choose a moment in Europe similar to the Franco-Prussian War, and when it does come, Austria will start to fall apart on her own. Because there too everything will solve itself, all the considerations and all the Bismarcks notwithstanding. If only we would not get involved, oh, if only we would not get involved, i.e., to save the existing order and so forth. Go ahead and let yourself fall apart, lie around doing nothing—and meanwhile we will stand firm and will stop the wave simply because we do stand firm. We just keep standing. And simply because of this, that we are standing, that we exist, we will save European humanity! But we will further explain this little fable subsequently. That radical medicine is required here.[35]

[But] They themselves will start asking the functionaries for this and will begin to pull in that direction.

And who are you? Aren't you the children of functionaries and the grandchildren of them? //

Finances. Towards the revitalization of the roots—they can look into this, and even allocate a million-odd a year for it—arrange an official audit of it, form a commission to study methods for revitalizing the roots and a subcommission to gather information, but to give it all up and think only about the roots, no, that is impossible. —For now there is at least something, but then we would be heading straight into nothing.

Plan. No, you have no idea how much they hate us. No, that is not the right civilization, we are not Europe to them, not Europeans, we bother them, we smell bad... No, they foresee an idea, a future, independent Russian idea, and although this idea has not even been born yet in our country, but the land is terribly pregnant with it and amid fearful pangs is getting ready to give birth to it, still we only disbelieve and laugh. Well, but they do foresee it. They foresee more than we ourselves do, the intellectual, i.e., the Russian. Well, enough of this idea, we are smothered by it, we [all] exist, they say, for Europe and for her amusement, everything for Europe, all and everything— and for our innocence.
They will come to believe it then. Of course they will not believe it the first year, they will only be astonished, but then later they will believe it, later they will believe. With money, with expenditures, we will win them over. They will believe in money. Within seven years or ten years they will believe... (sooner or later we will get there).

Plan. His plan, obviously, is stupid, it is some sort of frenzy, not a plan.

Asia. *Plan.* To the devil with Asia, in our Russia everything is in disarray, while here they are still dreaming about Asias. To ban the Nordenskjölds.[36]

Plan. The Turgenevs, the Lev Tolstois, to compel them, order them. Here creativity is needed, here artistry. Here a person must understand art.

And here Grigorovich is the only one who can do it. A galaxy, a galaxy to order around. Now, you are too gloomy, we do not need you (that he is telling me).

Now, Ostrovsky is not suitable, not that genre, it will not do, Pisemsky too, we do not need you either, you are too gloomy. But the young ones, the young ones. //

We will invent the type of philosopher, a real dandy, who will go out and start to give philosophical lectures [about] on the theme of gaiety and innocence and whom all the ladies at once will fall in love with. Poets, the theater. The newspaper in which there is not a single word of truth, deliberately so, but only all the gayest things—whimsy. We will establish an entire new academy of sciences to be concerned henceforth only with whimsy for the amusement of the ladies.

Plan. I thought also the Livadia with the little cocottes so pure though fallen from grace. But no, no, we must hold high the banner of virtue. Of virtue and innocence. It is quite a different matter beneath the surface, the papal curate and the repentant sinners. Be converted, the converts and so forth. Well and s/o/ on. That is how it can be.
--Well, now all of Russia's income will be used up on this.
—Almost all. But all the better. Everyone will see how harmless we are, how innocent we are and how firmly we stand by our idea.
—And where do we get a billion for the railroad?
—Well, what is an extra billion. A loan and that's it!
—But the borderlands, the borderlands? And Poland...

—But a loan, a loan, an all-European loan on everyman's market. And what is an extra billion? An extra billion is nothing.

But reduce the army, as a measure to establish confidence and reduce it to the minimum, to nothingness. The money will be found. Well, what are you afraid of? Didn't I read that now they are already writing that it can be reduced by half and that there will be nothing left—this is right now, now, when everyone wants to devour us and each one is nursing some grudge. //

Plan. A large amount of money will start going—there is nothing we can do, it must be held securely. Flocks of houris, nightingales' tongues, and how many silk stockings will be worn out, how many slippers—[gay] by gay secretaries and by all of this officialdom. Braid, gloves. Three, four pairs of gloves a day for each one. And the larger expenditures?

--But the land, how will the land exist, without any money, the Russian land?

—Somehow or other. Now why should you be worried about the Russian land? Everything will be superb. The main thing is the *mir*, and everything else comes after that.

Everything will appear, money will appear and so will taxes, they will increase even more!

Plan. One comes in, another goes out, one or two hundred thousand a season we will make feel more gay. Two hundred thousand gay minds we give to Europe a season, now that is marvelous, that is what is known as results!

They can roll out the Jesuits and the highest Catholics.
Oh, the Jesuit is quite something, but all the rest are a mere nothing.
The Jesuit is a person of importance.[37]

Everything is permitted and everything is concealed that way.

For you see this is very much the same thing that our prominent Russian minds are leading us toward in the papers. They simply cannot see beyond their own noses, and for that reason they cannot foresee what they might come to. And following behind them, we will come right to this too, i.e., to [indic] gaiety and innocence.

Asia. Finances and plan. In the past we made them stronger, and now they are stronger than we are, and who if not we ourselves made that possible. We revived France, Germany, etc.

Plan. The fathers of the Jesuits, of the Capuchins, of the Bernardines, and so forth, expelled from France.

Bared breasts, tears of repentance... All of this is photographed and painted right on the spot. But all of this is magnificent in the higher sense as well. Even aristocratic ladies could have made visits for the purpose of contemplation, and that there would have been nothing, nothing at all like that. Now of course // there, in other sections, some of these corridors... However, I will not persist, I will not persist. You know I cannot stand it myself. I only meant to be gay.

Plan. Obviously, all of his square vessels all this is absurd and stupid; it did not turn out for him. But gaiety and innocence, generally speaking, as they say—oh, perhaps this is what higher politics is nowadays. This paltry little idea. Even a full-fledged idea.

Finances. Even without this, everyone is a boss to the poor and downtrodden, but now they have another twenty official bosses.

NB! *Plan.* Now Gambetta will come out on Bismarck's side, although certainly knowing that Bismarck sooner or later will turn France into a nonentity, and beyond that, certainly knowing that if anyone in the whole world would take pity on France and not let her be turned into a nonentity, that would be Russia, and still she will go with Bismarck against Russia (foresight that Russia is the bearer of some new idea).

Plan. Territorial rights to Siberia and all of Asia handed out to the Jews, the Americans, the English, they can even be guaranteed a five per cent return. The island of Novaya Zemlya bestowed upon Nordenskjöld because he discovered Siberia for the Swedes 300 years after Ermak.[38]

Plan. It stands to reason that our European embassies should invite people onto the vessels, but in order to do that, strengthen their staff with particularly brilliant young secretaries. Train the secretaries in Petersburg, and in order to do that, establish in Petersburg two or three more lycées with French and English, with dancing and fencing and so forth. Set up a department of moderate liberalism and so forth. But the main thing is money, money, and money. Get it from the commonfolk.

/.../ Break all the best into pieces and give them out as territorial rights, or if no one will give us anything for them, simply give them away for exploitation // with a guarantee of 5 per cent. Let all sacrifices be made, if we can just get rid of this trash.

Finances. If only the truth were guaranteed to them (the commonfolk). [From] And they would give you more. It is incomparable. And, you know, they would even drink more. Two shots a day (in the days of temperance societies). You laugh.

To revitalize. This is the main root. To teach the rights and duties. Ah, such youngsters.
Asia.
The point is not so much to set out to revitalize the roots, but to take this on as our unique task.
Severe, gloomy economy...

Let there be a deficit, let there even be bankruptcy.
If this is serious, then the army could even be reduced, granted not more than by 1/10th. But it will not have to be reduced. They will come to enlist in greater force.
The point is not the economizing itself, but the principle of economizing.

How everything is bookish, haughy. They are unable to write ingenuously. They are very proud of themselves, they use the wrong tone. They
patronize, teach, watch like guardians, they close themselves off in the cloud
of their own [imp] glory.

Finances. How can I be compared with our financiers (NB. Now if only
they do not consider themselves, from my words, real financiers.)

If only they would come to believe in their courts, if only they would
come to believe in their justice of the peace system and would recognize it as
their own, [as v] as flesh of their flesh and as bone of their bone. How can
this be done? The know-it-alls write: the commonfolk must be taught their
rights and duties (Oh, the rascals, oh, such youngsters! These are the ones who
are going to teach the commonfolk their rights and in particular their duties).
Learn from the commonfolk first, my lords, ask their opinions, and they
themselves will point out what they need.

Plan. Plan of a dreamer, a *lunatic.* //

Plan. The main thing.
--Your plan is a satire.
--What do you mean satire? I am in earnest.
--But the best satires do come out "in earnest."
--Is that what you think, they will take this for satire?
--That may well be.
--On whom? On what? Oh, if only they knew how sincere I am.
Plan (At the beginning) —Women, women, the main thing is women, be-
cause women handle everything. Nowadays it is the women's era everywhere.
The women's era, I tell you. And so, first of all, in all of Europe the first wo-
man is already, of course, the aristocratic ladya.
—Who is that?
—The ladya, the ladya! The English ladya. Others pronounce it lady, but
I pronounce it ladyá. And even with the stress on the ya. It suits the Russian
language better. Well, in one word, I want it that way. And so, ladya...

Finances. Asia. The Eastern issue. No matter how we get involved there,
still with Austria we, while she is together with Germany, will do nothing, despite all of their insolence. It may be, they are just waiting for us to get angry.

A program of finances.
—Revitalization of the commonfolk.
--Russia — Asia.
—Economy.
—Elimination of aristocratism, of the Petersburg view toward the com-

171

monfolk and toward Russia and humility before her.

Plan. Nightingale's tongues, which must be something awful that just flashed into my mind, but I said tongues, so let it be tongues. You can also get tongues from sparrows and crows to assure that these are nightingales' tongues. //

Plan. They add on a little Bulgarian village, that way our goals are fulfilled.

For we have no other goals in the Eastern issue. We certainly do not intend [in our country] to conquer Constantinople!

Finances. Finale. Reduction of 50,000 of the army. You will not acquire, slip right through your fingers. But we need an army, and how we need one, no matter what the *very* intelligent people say now, well then more on this topic later.

Whatever money we get will slip right through our fingers, and we never will see it again, while the fifty thousand we will never acquire again, once we cross them off (with those same principles), this is a dangerous road to take. That is, do you see, it might be possible, it really might be possible, but only if it were known for certain that the money will not slip through our fingers. But how can this be known for certain? We will find out for certain only when we mount a program of decisive "severe, gloomy economy, economy in the spirit and force of Peter if he had wanted to be economical." //

Petersburg is nothing, and the commonfolk is everything.

Finances. They are even drinking up more vodka, but you see I want to look at it only from the financial point now. Ask the commonfolk about their needs and do it first and foremost with no interference from the intelligentsia whatsoever. Oh, it is impossible to eliminate the intelligentsia, they will say many wise things, but let them say it later. For they are children, with tears, delight, and love.

Finances. The peasant... That in freedom he has truth, that in the courts he has truth, in the zemstvo. That they love truth and honor the bosses and so forth.

NB. *Enlightenment.*

Finances. Besides the 3 thousand more as much as you like. —Now what do you mean? Now this is not only the minister of finances but also of intern/-al/ and also of extern/al affairs/ —all of them together cannot do a thing, even if they felt like checking into the rubbish you mentioned. We have here a fully developed reality, we have here two centuries of history, they cannot be broken. Now what you are proposing is no financial measure at all.

—I know this, that it is not a financial measure, but you do not expect finances. There is nothing new in my article except that it has not been applied.

The pig.

And how much might get to the commonfolk.

Revitalization of the roots, [besides that] the size of the military forces, there are nothing but expenditures in it which could have been used for the revitalization of the roots.

Asia. This does not at all mean forsaking enlightenment and following a regressive path (not poking ourselves *so much* into Europe, for this poking in has cost our finances dearly. We freed [Fr.] Europe from Napoleon, the wars, we built up the forces there, while we now maintain a million troops against them. And what they even forgot about Russia).

Saved the tsars.

Asia. We will do even more for Europe later. Namely, we will come in handy to her at the most decisive moment for her. But now what: we will fall in love to the point that we are for the Pope, or to save the tsars. //

However, this topic (about the commonfolk) is so vast that how can I cover the whole thing. I will be glad if I said just one droplet of something comprehensible about this first and main point of the revitalization of Russia.

Finances. Functionaries: You think we are decayed, you will see how sturdy we are. No, we will still stand our ground. The building will stay standing with us, it will stay standing through the simple mechanics of inertia. Now, we will collapse, and the fall will be great [but the shock might co] . But meanwhile we are standing. And what can you offer us in place of this. We are something, but you are nothing. But you model of Europe, your passionate desire and love for the commonfolk, the love you talk so much about and God knows whether you still have? But then how can you yourselves start asking the functionaries for this?

Savalev.

For the Mar. No.

Extremely incoherent article of *The New Time* about Gambetta and the stability of the republic.

No. 1748, 9 January, Friday.

Remarkab/le/ No. of *The New Time*.

Asia. Asia, a mistake in the beginning, the mistake has continued for too long.

Krylov. This is a very good fable, and is it possible, is it really possible that any of us would want to resemble this portrait?

Kavelin. He is an old man already and he is *fading* with the most complete ignorance about the Russian commonfolk and with scorn toward them.

Finances. Economy. They do not even fear bankruptcy; no sooner will we start being independent, than our creditors themselves will feel respect for us and they will not declare our bankruptcy, but will wait and hope. They will even come to us with their services and will offer capital. But we will not take it from them, enough. //
About Europe, about our politics in Europe, we lived for Europe and not for ourselves. The East/ern/ issue. The factor, as entering into the Franco-Prussian war.

The New Time, No. 1751. 12 January '81. Monday, Letter from student A.F. (in *Novo/rossiisk/ Telegraph*) on the rights of students. *Into consideration.*

The Moscow News, 1881, No. 9, Friday, 9 January. Lead article on schools and on the opinions of *The Messenger of Europe.*

Finances! This is what the 14 classes will say "taken as such," speaking in philosophical language. //

Fin/ances/. No, let us rather become somehow virtuous and ease things up a little in accordance with the spirit of the times, but in doing so we should not let anything slip by.
To Kavelin. Imitativeness is the same among all groups of commonfolk (and they give you nothing but a bunch of fifteen-kopek pieces in change, so you get angry, while now the groups of commonfolk are identical). By this you simply proved that you have lived a long time but perceived very little. //
To Kavelin. You say that it is moral merely to act according to one's convictions. But where in the world did you get this from? I simply cannot believe you and say to the contrary, that it is immoral to act according to one's convictions. And you, of course, have no way of proving me wrong.
You do not consider shedding blood moral, but shedding blood by conviction you do consider moral. But why, may I ask, is it immoral to shed blood?
If we do not find our authority in faith and in Christ, then we will lose our way in everything.
Moral ideas do exist. They arise from religious feelings, but can never be justified by logic alone.
It would become impossible to live.
A play on words: a Jesuit lies, convinced that the lying is useful for a

174

good purpose. You praise him for being true to his conviction, i.e., he lies and this is bad, but since he lies according to his conviction, then this is good. In one instance his lying is good, and in the other instance his lying is bad. What a marvel.

To Kavelin. As long as you stand your ground you will always be downcast. You will no longer be downcast when you accept the fact that moral ideas *do exist* (from feelings, from Christ), though to prove they are moral is impossible (coming in contact with the other world).

To Kavelin. This is very regressive of you, Mr. Kavelin. How is it that you were so careless and went so wide of the mark. Now what will Princess Maria Alexeevna say.

To Kavelin... Of course, this is not scientific, although why shouldn't it be: the tremendous fact of the appearance on earth of Jesus and all that came after that demand, in my opinion, scientific elaboration. But at the same time, science cannot reject the meaning that religion does have for humanity, if only as an historical fact that is staggering in its continuity and tenacity. The conviction that humanity has about *coming in contact with the other world*, persistent and permanent, is also very significant, you know. And you see it cannot be resolved with one scribble of the pen [since] , the way you resolved the question about Russia, i.e., all infantile groups of commonfolk have and s/o/ on.

To Kavelin. I.e. all groups of commonfolk in an infantile condition, as you put it, have and so forth and so forth. This would be a much too facile type of science.

Now this is Petersburg science, Russo-European...

To Kavelin. The inquisitor and the chapter about children. In view of these chapters you could at least regard me although scientifically, not so arrogantly in the area of philosophy, even though philosophy may not be my specialty. Even in Europe such force of atheistic *expression* does not now exist *nor did it ever.* Accordingly, it is not like a child that I believe in Christ and profess faith in him, but rather, my *hosanna* has come through the great *crucible of doubt,* as the devil says in that same novel of mine. Now, perhaps you have not read "Karamazov"—that is another matter entirely, and in that case I beg your pardon.

Finances. Economy. Resolutely, as the former lords-landowners, we set the tone penniless, we carry on drunkenly through Europe. Here, look at how rich and splendid we are and how we can throw money out the window. //

However, I am not fit to write purely philosophical articles, in the future I will not.

Portrait of a pig.

We already have at our disposal solid data from recent times, that people

175

in our country do not want to resemble this portrait. So away with it, this portrait, we were tired of it even before this.

And what kind of enlightenment? In your souls there is darkness, not enlightenment. In your souls there are such depths of darkness that no ray of light can illumine. Whom do you think you can enlighten, whom?
Now it is quite clear: because you yourselves are not enlightened, your souls are as insipid as an egg, you are mediocre, you are rubbish, you are much too blatant...

A conspiracy. Learn from the bast sandals how to behave, telling the tsar the truth, then as now... *in a conspiracy against the commonfolk* (your crowning touch will be brought about).
Not new... now it is done unconsciously, but later it will turn out that way simply through historical necessity.

Finale (if there is room), without being afraid, I said it, a citizen's concern. I am not receiving any reward nor will I receive any. Two *parties* in *battle*, in an actual, organized battle. It is false if they say there are no parties.

Your crowning touch. which the commonfolk heard about and immediately termed "Overlordship." //

Asia. For only because of our contempt for Asia did we fail to notice up to now how necessary Asia is for us.

39, 50, 49, 48, 46, 41, 38, 31.
Finale. I know myself that it is not an article on economics.
I stand for the principle that the revitalization of the roots comes before mere worries [from] of current concern. But then, whatever you wish.

Kavelin.
—Moral ideas do not exist.
—Mistaken expression.
—To prove them intellectually is impossible, this is true.
—But that they nevertheless exist—this, however, is unquestionable. //

Ideas.
22 Sept/ember/.
Society for the dissemination of the holy books of the Old and N/ew/ Testaments. Translation of the Chet/y/ Minei Saints' Calendar into Engl/ish/ (at the first opportunity a selection).

NB. Self-restraint and bodily abstinence for spiritual freedom, in direct contrast to the material manifestation, continuous and unlimited, leading to the slavery of the spirit.

Attacks '79-80.
10 October '78.
28 April '79.
13 September '79.
9 February '80.
14 March '80.
7 September '80. One of the rather strong ones, at a quarter to 9 o'clock, disruption of thoughts, transfer to other years, dreaminess, pensiveness, guilt dislocated the small bones in the spine or damaged a muscle.

6th November '80. In the morning at 7 o'clock, right after falling asleep, but the diseased condition was endured with great difficulty and continued almost a week. The more time goes by, the weaker the organism becomes in enduring the attacks and the stronger their effect becomes.

Starting 6th February /?/ a thaw began very soon which lasted a very long time, almost two weeks. After a too early winter, the penultimate attack of 6th September also corresponded to an abupt change in weather after a long and gentle summer, to cold and rain.

Words, special words and expressions

17 August '80.

You have become an outright liar and you keep pounding away at it.

But you cannot answer Gradovsky.

Gr. Gradovsk. is the same Gradovsky, but in a scattered form.

If you were to take a feuilleton by A. Gradovsky, cut out all of its sentences separately, put them into a basket and spill them out from a roof somewhere onto the pavement, what comes out is a feuilleton by G. Gradovsky.

Grig. Gradovsky was the *first* to rush out and speak up for A. Gradovsky. In their sharing the same last name there is something ridiculous. (Did G. Gradovsky think that all Gradovskys must defend themselves if one of them is insulted?)

Both Gradovskys are the two Ajaxes of Russian literature. *The Voice* said I should be ashamed [that] for praising *The Shore*. We will leave *The Shore* alone, but your praise, unquestionably, I would consider a disgrace to me. Your enmity does me honor.

One Gradovsky immediately dashed off on the other Gradovsky's behalf.

But you cannot answer every Gradovsky.

Rigid, potatoey and always cheerfully complacent German wit.

The product of a dulled and debased Westernism.

This poletics has appeared as a result of moral uncleanness, just as a louse comes from physical uncleanness, and body lice come from sensuous uncleanness.

To what extent man has *worshipped* himself (Lev Tolstoi).

If an end existed in the world, then there would be an end to the whole world. The parallelism of lines, /the triangle/, merging in infinity, one quadrillionth is still insignificance next to infinity. In infinity, though, /parallel/ lines must come together. For all of these apexes /of triangle/s nevertheless in finite space, and the rule—that the more infinite, the closer to /parallel/— must remain. In infinity /parallel/ lines must merge, but—this infinity will never come. If it were to come, there would be an end of infinity, which is absurd. If /parallel/ lines came together, there would be an end to the world and to geometric law and to God, which is absurd, but only for the human mind.

The real (created) world is finite, while the nonsubstantial world is infinite. If /parallel/ lines came together the law of this world would come to an end. But in infinity they do come together, and infinity is unquestionable. For if there were no infinity, there would also be no finiteness, it would be inconceivable. And if infinity does exist, then God and the other world exist, based on laws other than the real (created) world. //

He stole—Well, all right then, they did not find the person? How could they, he did not leave his name, you know.

So that is how they preserve their souls. They do not preserve their soul.

A perturbed, but not logical head.

Satan. Your idea was, of course, dressed up more attractively, but I took it in its nakedness.

Our deacon reads so sonorously and eloquently and it comes out of him sounding so good and so *literate*.

Allow me to send for your answer *within a few days.* Allow me to send *within a few days for your answer.*

The *seminarian.* What he is like. Damned seminarian, worthless atheist. The Russian liberal: damned aristocrat, worthless atheist. He flaunts his two-bit enlightenment over the commonfolk.

Threw it out with heart and mind.

We are not always sinful, on the contrary, we are usually even saintly [Otherwise] And who would be able to live if it were otherwise.

Appealing. And to write something so original and *appealing* that it will be hard to put the book down.

Wet grief. Women's wet grief (i.e. tears).

Woe from Wit (Goncharov).[39] Griboedov's comedy is brilliant but inconsistent. //

> Driving up outside Geneva,
> At the foot of the cross adored,
> There *he met* the Holy Virgin,
> Blessed Mother of Christ the Lord.[40]

FOOTNOTES TO NOTEBOOK X

1. Much of the material in Notebook X concerns the "Eastern question," and much of it is paralleled by Dostoevsky's issues of the *Diary of a Writer*. Where these parallels are of some importance they are pointed out in these notes, and the English reader can use the Brasol translation (see Note 4, Notebook VI) for comparison. —The first entry in Notebook X refers to the day when Baron Rodic's (1813-1890) speech directed to the leaders of the Herzegovinan uprising was published in the papers, Rodic being the Austrian Stadthalter. See Boris Brasol, trans., *Diary of a Writer*, pp. 293 ff.

2. See Brasol, pp. 281-83.

3. See Brasol, pp. 275-81.

4. "The Tale of the Adventures of the English Milord George and the Brandenburg Countess Fredericka Louisa," published by Matvey Komarov in 1782, and republished almost annually in large printings up until the 1917 Revolution, popular reading.

5. This refers to a polemic between a "zemstvo" official named Ofrosimov and a leader of the local Ryazan nobles over the latter's complaint about immorality and atheism in a local seminary.

6. See Brasol, pp. 286 ff.

7. The Russian paper had summarized an article from a Latvian Lutheran paper complaining about the new German law (January 1, 1876) making civil and church marriages equal, and also equating various other civil acts with church ones (registration of births, deaths, etc.).

8. See Brasol, pp. 286 ff.

9. In the first part of the April *Diary of a Writer* (Brasol, pp. 273-75) Dostoevsky indignantly quotes Avseenko (praised in *The Voice* April 14th, not 13th), who wrote: "The point of the matter is that our commonfolk have failed to give us the ideal of an active personality. All that is beautiful, in our observation of them, and which our literature, to its great honor, accustomed us to love in them, appears merely on the plane of elemental existence, of a secluded, idyllic mode of living, or of a passive life. Just as soon as an active, energetic personality emerges from the midst of the commonfolk, its fascination usually disappears, and more often than not the individuality assumes the unattractive features of a peasants' bloodsucker, a kulak, a stupidly-willful person."

10. Neither the first nor last parts of this plan for the April "Diary" were completed.

11. This is the title of an article mentioned a few entries later. Turgenev wrote a story called, "Hamlet of the Shchigrovsky District" (1849).

12. The paper reported that an eight-volume Chinese history of the Franco-German war had been given to the British Museum as a gift.

13. In the previous entry the lead article says a real improvement in the condition of the Turkish Christians is necessary, asserting that while Russia is only morally interested in this, Austria would oppose any independent Slavic state in the Balkans, even at the risk of war with Russia. Dostoevsky did not finish, or publish, the article.

14. An English religion propagandist, who preached that the sins of man are forgiven for anyone who truly believes. He visited Russia in 1874. Dostoevsky discusses him, very skeptically, in the March issue of his "Diary" (Brasol, pp. 267-8).

15. Yakovlev is the main character in A. F. Pisemsky's play *A Bitter Fate* (1858)—an honorable peasant type who ends tragically.

16. Pestel was one of the main leaders of the 1825 Decembrist Revolt. Soviet commentators regard this assertion about him as a lie.

17. The division of people into "humble" and "predatory" was taken over by Dostoevsky from his friend, the critic Apollon Grigoriev.

18. Paraphrase of a comment by Bismarck: "The great questions of the time are decided not by speeches and decrees, but by iron and blood."

19. Again, see the April *Diary of a Writer*, Brasol, pp. 273 ff.

20. This is developed in the April issue, Brasol, p. 285.

21. The hero of Turgenev's novel *Smoke* (see Volume II, pp. 69 ff., and notes).

22. O. A. Petrov was a famous singer, much written about in April 1876.

23. Vsevolod Krestovsky, a minor writer, considered his honor affronted by comments of a lawyer named Sokolovsky at Krestovsky's divorce trial.

24. The fourth and fifth items here were not finished.

25. This is the name of a character, a "paradoxalist" who appears in the *Diary of a Writer* in April 1876 and again in July-August 1876.

26. Tindal (1820-93) was an English physicist, whose book was translated into Russian; Dostoevsky singles out a section discussing charlatanism in the world of spiritism.

27. An eighth century monk and preacher.

28. See the section entitled "Unquestionable Democracy. Women." in the May issue of the *Diary of a Writer* Brasol, pp. 339-41.

29. "beauty of the gods...byliny" — This refers to Potugin's speeches in Chapter XV of *Smoke—byliny* are the Russian national folk epics. Ilya Muromets and Svyatogor are heroes in these epics.

30. Avseenko had said: "And suddenly they tell us that we have to follow this wanderer who hasn't chosen a road yet himself, that we should expect an idea and a model from this riddle, from this Sphinx who hasn't yet found either any idea or any model himself! Is this not irony?"

31. Notes for an unfinished, and in fact largely unwritten, novel.

32. This is material for the April issue. In it Dostoevsky mentions an unnamed friend (in fact Pobedonostsev) who advised him not to write about spiritism. The "springs" at Maikov's were poorly hidden springs used to move objects at one seance.

33. Nikolai Wagner (1829-1907) was a zoology professor who believed in spiritism.

34. Dostoevsky, along with fellow writers Leskov and Boborykin, attended a seance at A. N. Aksakov's on February 14, 1876.

35. Shchapov was once a colleague of Dostoevsky. Shchapov's wife Olga, according to memoirs, was a rare example of womanly self-sacrifice and staunch love in the face of all kinds of hardships. She died in 1874. Pisareva was a mid-wife who committed suicide. See Brasol, p. 341.

36. See Brasol, pp. 308ff.

37. Dostoevsky mistakenly thought Blagosvetlov was the author of a necrology of Shchapov.

38. Shchapov is defended in the April issue, "On Behalf of a Deceased Person", Brasol, pp. 308 ff.

39. A revised version of this is in the June issue, Brasol, pp. 350 ff.

40. Ivan Gagarin (1814-82), a Russian diplomat, later a Jesuit, who advocated submission of the Orthodox Church to the Vatican.

41. Orest Miller, in an article on Samarin, reprinted in the book *Slavdom and Europe* (1877).

42. A fairly detailed report, in his necrology, was given about Shchapov's alcoholism.

43. Refers to a statue of Peter the Great by M. M. Antokolsky (1872).

44. Foma Danilov was captured during military actions in Central Asia in 1875, and

executed after refusing to renounce Christianity and accept Mohammedanism. The incident was later made famous by Dostoevsky in *The Brothers Karamazov.*

45. Kairova had seriously wounded her lover's wife.

46. In the May issue of the "Diary" Dostoevsky writes about the Kairova case. It is fairly clear that Dostoevsky would not much approve of modern jurisprudence with its various psychological excuses, especially those which deprive one of responsibility for guilt, or good.

47. Ieroglifov was an editor, who made a scandal at the store of a bookseller (Bazunov) with whom he did business.

48. D. V. Grigorovich, once Dostoevsky's close friend, had ceased his active literary career much earlier, but until Chekhov's time remained a respected sponsor of the arts.

49. The article is sympathetic to special education for women.

50. The paper reported on the history of Stundism in the Ukraine. The Khlysts were flagellants.

51. Evgeny Utin was Kairova's attorney; Vladimir Sluchevsky was the prosecutor.

52. Velikanova was the wife whom Kairova attacked with a razor. Kairova was eventually released, though not really acquitted. Dostoevsky said in the May issue he was glad she was released, but he had considerable disagreement with the reasoning of the various parties.

53. The papers reported that Ekaterina Kornilova threw her step-daughter, a six-year-old girl, from a fourth-storey window. See the October and December issues of the "Diary." Dostoevsky took a particularly active role in this case.

54. Wilhelm Kaulbach (1805-74), German artist.

55. The suicide of Pisareva. See Note 35 above.

56. Notes connected with a visit which Dostoevsky made to an orphans' home in May 1876.

57. See Brasol, pp. 326 ff.

58. The girls, aged 10 and 11, were found murdered, one of them raped.

59. See Brasol, pp. 330 ff.

60. P. D. Boborykin (1836-1921), a prolific and popular novelist of the day.

61. See "The Utopian Conception of History," Brasol, pp. 360 ff.

62. *The Voice* said the April *Diary of a Writer* with its notes of a "paradoxalist" bore close resemblance to the ideas of Prince Myshkin on capital punishment.

63. Kh. D. Alchevskaya says in her diary that she told him the story of K's crime.

64. Hauser was an abandoned child found in Nuremburg in 1828 who could barely speak, and who seemed to defy efforts to educate him. He was murdered in 1833 by an unknown person.

65. The following did not appear in the May issue: "Environment," "Alchevskaya's story," "Turkey."

66. This was a favorable presentation of Redstock, defending him from attacks by Prince Meshchersky, who had accused him of ties with communists and Stundists. Favorable quotes about the Stundists and their sincerity are cited.

67. Dmitri Kartashov wrote Dostoevsky a letter of support; it is discussed in the May 1876 issue.

68. The June 1876 issue has two sections on George Sand.

69. Dostoevsky didn't carry out his intention to write about his early literary tastes; but Karamzin was one of his parents' favorite writers, and Ivan Shidlovsky, a romantic poet, and character, was one of Dostoevsky's early heroes and friends.

70. E. Guber was the translator of the first Russian version of the first part of *Faust* (1838).

71. A "Venetian" novel by George Sand. See Brasol, p. 348.

72. According to Dostoevsky, the popular Russian writer of the 1830s, O. Senkovsky, referred to Sand as "Egor Sand."

73. The line is a quote from "Dream", a poem by A. S. Khomyakov.

74. A novel by George Sand. See Brasol, p. 348.

75. The idea is discussed in the June issue of the "Diary," Brasol, pp. 344-50. The first section on Sand is entitled "The Death of George Sand," the second "A Few Words about George Sand."

76. Joseph Gibert was archbishop of Paris from 1871, later a cardinal.

77. The reference is inaccurate, but the "heretical article" mentioned in the next entry argued that forbidding remarriage to widowed Orthodox priests was an outmoded rule.

78. In the May "Diary," the section entitled "Unquestionable Democracy. Women," Brasol, pp. 339-41.

79. Bethel Strousberg (1823-84) was an important railroad builder in Russia, but in 1875 he went bankrupt and was deported. He is mentioned in the October "Diary," in the sections entitled "Best Men" and "About the Same," Brasol, pp. 480 ff.

80. A. N. Rober was a teacher in a Tver woman's school. His speech, published in No. 103, was about the difficulties facing women graduates and how they could overcome them.

81. The tarantula was in Florence seven years before this was written. Dostoevsky had to spend the night in the room with it because, after seeing it run in, no one could find it. *Piccola Bestia* is the title of the first section of the September "Diary," Brasol, pp. 427 ff., which deals with the Eastern question again.

82. In the June issue of *Diary of a Writer* Dostoevsky says the following: "Not in vain did Apollon Grigoriev, who also sometimes said rather sensitive things, say that 'were Belinsky to have lived longer, he would no doubt have joined the Slavophiles'. In this phrase there is thought."

In Grigoriev's "The Development of the Idea of Nationalism in Our Literature since the Death of Pushkin," published in Dostoevsky's magazine *Time* (No. 3, 1861), Grigoriev actually wrote: "Frequently the opponents failed to understand each other, especially the Westernizers the Slavophiles, which is the only way one can explain Belinsky's extremely harsh enmity to Slavophilism, enmity which, however, in the last period of his life, as some of his letters bear witness, began to shift to a completely opposite feeling."

83. In the October 1876 *Diary of a Writer* Dostoevsky wrote about Liza Herzen, who committed suicide after leaving a somewhat comical, but also angry, letter; a Petersburg seamstress jumped out of a window holding an ikon in her hands. See Brasol, pp. 468-70.

84. These topics are covered in the June issue again.

85. Senkovsky and Bulgarin were influential writers and editors of Pushkin's day, but also connected with the Tsar's secret police.

86. Dostoevsky received a letter from a man named Ragozin in which the phrase "to pierce the heart" is used.

87. Constantinople and the Eastern question are discussed in the June issue of the "Diary."

88. Mikhailovsky (1842-1904) was the most influential critic of his day, a Populist leader.

89. See Note 35 above and the May 1876 issue of the "Diary."

90. Dostoevsky, like many before and after him, believed Gogol's knowledge of the commonfolk, the Russian (as opposed to Ukrainian) commonfolk, was very poor. Gogol's early stories deal with "Little Russia," and critics such as Vengerov argued he transported Ukrainian folk into Russian works such as *Dead Souls,* or that he simply invented. In Gogol's *Selected Passages from a Correspondence with Friends* he discusses a number of problems which Dostoevsky is concerned with in the *Diary of a Writer.*

91. See Note 86 above.

92. Alexander Selin (1816-77), University of Kiev Professor of Literature, wrote Dostoevsky a letter containing ideas of the Russian common people and Russian history which Dostoevsky intended to refute later.

93. This and the following topics come up in the July-August issues of the "Diary."

94. Dostoevsky saw his first live orangoutang in the Berlin "Aquarium."

95. The sections on Zola and spiritism did not go into the July-August issue.

96. A local court had sentenced Dostoevsky to 48 hours in jail for publishing in *The Citizen* an article not passed by the censors, "The Kirgiz Deputies." According to Dostoevsky's wife he had a pleasant time in jail, rereading Hugo's *Les miserables* while his cellmate slept. His description of the event did not appear in the "Diary."

97. Strakhov published Grigoriev's works in 1876. In the Preface Strakhov does not mention circumstances which may have hastened Grigoriev's death—alcoholism and debtor's jail.

98. Strakhov wrote an essay called "The Woman Question" which was a critique of John Stuart Mill's "On the Subjugation of Women." Dostoevsky didn't agree with Strakhov's often optimistic analysis, and in the July-August "Diary" he quotes Strakhov praising English women, and proceeds to demonstrate the superiority of Russian women ("Briefly, I shall not defend the rights of the Russian woman to a high place among the women of all Europe, but I shall merely say this . . ."). See Brasol, pp. 408 ff. for the rest of this "briefly."

99. Smerdyakov's mother in *The Brothers Karamazov*.

100. In the final paragraph of Chapter XXV of *My Past and Thoughts* Herzen expresses his faith in the youth of Russia, who will make a great future for Russia possible.

101. The "Best People" is a section in the October "Diary."

102. The note is for the July-August issue, Brasol, pp. 369 ff.

103. See Chapter 3 of the July-August issue, Brasol, pp. 396 ff.

104. In his memoirs the Decembrist I. D. Yakushkin told how he gathered his peasants and offered to free them without land—but they said they would prefer things to remain the way they always had, "We're yours, but the land's ours."

105. The remarks were planned for the July issue, but did not appear. Dostoevsky had written his wife about admiring the children in Ems.

106. The girls who pass out the water from the springs in Ems. See Brasol, p. 391.

107. See "The Land and the Children" in the July-August "Diary," Brasol, pp. 416 ff.

108. In the July-August issue Dostoevsky says he went to Ems for reasons of health, not rest, and he quotes from K. Ryleev's poem "Voinarovsky."

109. *The Stock-exchange News* (July 4, 1876) reacted to Dostoevsky's June issue of the "Diary" and his thinking on the Eastern question, including the need to make Constantinpole part of Russia, as follows: "Mr. Dostoevsky is an abstract dreamer . . . but an extremely bad politician, and a naive one, whose words, the more he attempts to approve and console, sound all the more like malicious irony when applied to real facts."

110. A brochure published abroad, entitled "The Eastern Question from the Russian Point of View 1855," was attributed to Granovsky. Chapter II of the July-August "Diary deals with these matters (Brasol, pp. 379 ff.).

111. Nikolai Kireev (1841-76) was a retired officer, an extremely zealous Slavophile who organized volunteer troops for Serbia. He went himself, and was killed by the Turks.

112. Avseenko wrote a nasty review of Dostoevsky's novel, saying it was full of dirt and disgusting descriptions, "all the filth that is piled up in the underground." His criticism was of the first five chapters of Part I (which had appeared in a periodical), which do not contain the "mother's story."

113. The first issue of the journal for 1876 is meant.

114. See Note 98 above.

115. Reference to a brochure by A. Girshtorn, "Ems and Its Healing Springs" (St. P. 1874), found in Dostoevsky's library. It is mentioned in the July-August "Diary."

116. In Chapter II of the July-August issue, Dostoevsky praises the Germans in the section "The Germans and Work."

117. See the July-August issue, the section called "One of Those Benefited by Modern Woman," Brasol, pp. 408 ff.

118. "My Paradox" is the first section in Chapter II of the June 1876 issue of the "Diary," see Brasol, pp. 350 ff.

119. In her memoirs Catherine II tells a story about Peter III refusing to go to a bath-house, because he hated all native Russian customs and institutions.

120. Fyodor Stellovsky (died 1875) was a particularly nefarious publisher, who once signed an agreement with Dostoevsky under which Dostoevsky, if he failed to produce a novel by a certain date, would lose book publication rights to all his future works.

121. Dostoevsky did not follow this plan for the July-August issue.

122. In "Children's Secrets" (July-August "Diary") Dostoevsky discusses children, zero-population growth among the French bourgeoisie (according to Alexander Dumas), and, very briefly, Malthus. See Brasol, pp. 414-15.

123. "Dressing Gowns and Soap" is in Chapter I of the September issue of the "Diary." It is a discussion of the Eastern question, Kazan, the Turks, etc.

124. Dostoevsky discusses donations to the families of volunteers for the Serbian campaign in the September issue of the "Diary."

125. In Chapter II of the September issue of the "Diary" Dostoevsky engages in a polemic with the September issue of *The Messenger of Europe.*

126. Relates to "Combinations and Combinations" and "Dressing Gowns and Soap" in the September issue.

127. The paper had made fun of some of Nemirovich-Danchenko's boastful remarks (about speaking for all of the East of European Russia) in some sketches he had published.

128. See "Fears and Apprehensions" in Chapter II of the September "Diary" for expansion of these themes.

129. Dostoevsky cites Saltykov-Shchedrin (whom he had met in September or October 1876) in the December issue of the "Diary," without naming him. Brasol, p. 543.

130. Milan IV Obrenovich (1854-1901), the Serbian Prince, at first directed his troops in the Turko-Serbian war, then passed command to General Cherniaev, who in turn proclaimed Milan IV "King" of Serbia.

131. "Max" (pseudonym of B. M. Markevich) quoted Marlinsky in the attack on Nemiro-vich-Danchenko (see Note 127 above): "In order to judge any event correctly it is necessary for it to be separated from us by a historical shot."

132. An article by Evgeny Markov ("Ideas and Figures") argues that the Russian common people are ready to go to war to defend their fellow Slavs in the Balkans; he points out supposedly purely Russian virtues which Dostoevsky would approve of.

133. *The New Time* (Sept. 13, 1876) published a denial of Kraevsky's "International Telegraph Agency's" assertion about protests about Milan being proclaimed King of Serbia.

134. Fyodor Baymakov, a minor financier, leaseholder of *The St. Petersburg News.*

135. See Chapter I of the September "Diary" for development of the notes which follow here. Brasol, pp. 427 ff.

136. A summary of a *Times* story that the Russian volunteers for Serbia were political

extremists whom the Russian government were happy to see out of the country and in danger of being killed.

137. Lord Beaconsfield had said that the Russian volunteers were "socialists, communists and communards," whom the Russian government had purposely dumped out of Russia. In the September "Diary" (Brasol, p. 430 etc.) Dostoevsky denies this vehemently—first pointing out in his quaint and antisemitic way that Beaconsfield was "born a Jew" (which for Dostoevsky and many of his Russian readers decided the matter without further argument), and going on to deny the presence of socialists. This crazy area of discussion and prejudice is continued by the Soviet commentators to Dostoevsky's Notebooks, who insist of course that there were too socialists there—presumably fighting for their brothers in the Eastern Block.

138. Mikhail Stasyulevich (1826-1911), publicist, historian, publisher of *The Messenger of Europe.*

139. Around 1876 England became de facto owner of the Suez Canal. There was an English squadron stationed in the Gulf of Bezik near Turkey.

140. These four entries are in the September issue of the "Diary."

141. Kifa Mokievich and Moky Kifovich are two peripheral characters in Gogol's novel *Dead Souls,* symbols of useless cogitation on the one hand and destructiveness on the other.

142. K. I. Maslennikov, a justice official, was one of those who urged Dostoevsky to help Kornilova—who was sentenced to over two years in prison for throwing her step-daughter out a window. Dostoevsky argued she was not responsible, and he played a major role in helping her win an appeal, and be freed. See the October 1876 "Diary."

143. Of the items here Dostoevsky did not complete the one on Selin, or the one on Pechorin and the duel. Herzen's daughter's suicide is discussed in the October issue.

144. The retelling of this article emphasized the liberal English plan to use an independent Slavdom as a tool against the Russians.

145. This is one of the questions pondered by Kifa Mokievich (see Note 141 above).

146. Only the final item in this early plan for the October issue was actually used.

147. The deletion before "merchants" here (and in subsequent entries) is almost certainly Soviet censorship of Dostoevsky's abuse of Jews as "Kikes."

148. See Note 83 above. The girl was also the model for the heroine of Dostoevsky's story "A Gentle Spirit," first published in the November 1876 issue of the "Diary."

149. A "Popovka" was a special kind of warship designed by A. A. Popov, a round ship which was not judged very successful.

150. The Russian paper had a story translated from a German paper about a kind of sermon in which the Turks called for the destruction of the Christians.

151. Larosh went along with the point of view that Russia's many internal problems, including poor schools, deserved primary attention—and not just a foreign war.

152. Apparently this refers to a letter in which the efforts of simple peasants to make a collection for the Slavs are described—they decided to take up the collection after being told of brutalities against the Christians by the Turks.

153. The article discussed the possibility of making Constantinople a neutral city, but giving Russia access to the Dardanelles.

154. Pozzo di Borgo (1764-1842) was a Russian diplomat. The article Dostoevsky refers to presents a conversation between di Borgo and Tsar Nicholas I about the fate of Constantinople if the power of the Sultan were to collapse. The general idea was that Russia could never totally give up Constantinople, and even if it became a neutral city there would have to be a Russian garrison there.

155. The item reads: "Is not the proposal that the English ambassador at court go to Livadiya [a Black Sea resort] a sign of the total helplessness of England on the European

continent, helplessness all the more perceptible since even Bismarck himself has an ironic attitude towards England's continental might, having observed, according to the "Daily News,"
that England is not taken into consideration by European politicians."

156. A congress of workers took place in Paris in October, the first after the fall of the
Paris Commune. The Moscow newspaper drew a parallel between the "rebirth of socialism" and
the activities of the bashi-bouzooks going wild in the Christian parts of Turkey.

157. A discussion of how best to have good medical care in areas of military hostilities.

158. The Moscow paper asserted that the English were assisting the Turks in continuing
their vile practice of selling Christian women and children.

159. The English ambassador Loftus was going to talk with the Tsar in Livadiya, to present English conditions which were not negotiable.

160. The report said the police in Pest had to forbid a student demonstration in favor of
Turkey.

161. Here Dostoevsky uses a peculiar verb—"stushevat'sia"—which he explains in the November issue of the "Diary," see Brasol, pp. 882 ff.

162. The "triangular wound" and the "sword" and "dragonfly" are paraphrases from
Pushkin's one-act tragedy "The Stone Guest" (the words of Don Juan).

163. This is a discussion of Pushkin's "The Stone Guest."

164. On "artlessness" or "simplicity" see the October "Diary," Brasol, pp. 469 ff.

165. The article argues that the patriotic feelings inspired by the affairs in the Balkans
are temporary, and that basically social consciousness is lower than it was in Russia during the
1860s.

166. During the decisive battle of the Serbian-Turkish war the Serbian artillery refused
to submit to the commands of General Chernyaev. This was naturally commented on widely in
the Russian and world press, particularly the English, who apparently exaggerated the importance and seriousness of the event. Poletika was a writer who said that Chernyaev had inspired
various sketches in which the Serbian soldiers are presented as cowards.

167. There was a false report in the papers that Chernyaev had challenged the Serbian
War Minister to a duel.

168. The Serbian War Minister.

169. Here and in the immediately following entries there are several omissions which are
probably examples of Soviet censorship—probably slurs on the Jews or other nationalities.

170. Garibaldi and Cavour played important roles in the developing unification of Italy.

171. Gambetta was Minister of Internal Affairs in the "people's" government formed after
the overthrow of Napoleon III; he escaped the German encirclement by flying out in a balloon
to organize resistance against the Germans. Dostoevsky also considers him brilliant for supporting
his former enemy Thiers against the monarchist majority in 1871-73.

172. See the "New Phase of the Eastern Question" in the October "Diary."

173. An international conference to discuss the Balkan situation; it was proposed by
Alexander II, held in Constantinople in December.

174. See "Two Suicides" in the October "Diary."

175. In March 1878 Dostoevsky wrote a letter saying he had the idea for a novel entitled
Children; apparently, judging by this entry, he had the idea several months earlier.

176. On October 29, 1876 Tsar Alexander II made a speech in the Kremlin stating Russia's firm intention to go to war. It is mentioned in the February 1877 issue of the "Diary."

177. The author proposed giving Constantinople to Bulgaria, because the question of
water rights was not really very important to Europe anyway. The March 1877 issue of the
"Diary" has more on the Eastern question.

178. Dostoevsky uses a Russian proverb which has roughly the same idea as "Don't put off until tomorrow..."; translated roughly it comes out: "Catch Peter at dawn; if you give him the day to think, he'll begin to stink." Apropos of the Eastern question and another of his slurs on the Jews, Dostoevsky uses the proverb in the December "Diary," Brasol, p. 558.

179. Photius (Pyotr Spassky, 1792-1838) was a priest skilled in asceticism and court intrigues—a favorite of reactionaries.

180. Plans for an unwritten novel called *The Dreamer.*

181. "The Pugachevtsy" (Pugachevians) was a novel by E. A. Salias.

182. I. N. Skobelev commanded the punishment of rebels in the military colonies in 1831. Nabokov—presumably General Ivan Nabokov (1787-1852), brother of Vladimir Nabokov's great grandfather, commander of the Peter-Paul Fortress when Dostoevsky was arrested and held their in 1849.

183. Letters by V. P. Meshchersky, printed under the title " 'The Truth' about Serbia."

184. Nikolai Semenov was a high government official, but also a specialist in botany.

185. This strange psychology and logic still has some applicability today.

186. Proudhon wrote a treatise entitled "War and Peace" (1861). It ends with the statement that "mankind does not want war any more."

187. A Colonel MacIver authored a brochure devoted to Gladstone, in which among other things he says that the mere presence of Chernyaev inspires great respect (MacIver was a volunteer in the Serbian army himself), and otherwise praising him in ways with which Dostoevsky would agree.

188. These notes are for the future story "A Gentle Spirit" ("Diary," November).

189. This refers to a published comment on the use of French for business correspondence in Russian ministries under Alexander I.

190. The Moscow paper reported that English missionaries were going around to the Bulgarians blaming all their troubles on their belonging to Orthodoxy, not Protestantism.

191. An article advocating privateering if the English did not agree to the principle of inviolability of property during wartime. The guild duties referred to were supplementary ones set for the duration of the war.

192. The report argued there was a difference between simple cruising and privateering.

193. Dostoevsky has in mind the refusal of Germany and other countries to participate in the Paris World Exhibition of 1878.

194. A report on thieves among the upper classes—mentioning among others the sons of two generals who had been arrested.

195. This entry is a polemic with an article by L. Polonsky, who argued that a free federation of Balkan states had to be established, European Turkey liquidated, and the sea rights controlled not by Russia, but by "our friends."

196. The cited article says Russia's main concern in the Balkans is a moral one, that material considerations are secondary.

197. M. A. Yurkevich wrote Dostoevsky in late 1876 telling him about the suicide of a 12-year-old student. See the January 1877 issue of the "Diary," Brasol, pp. 590-91.

198. "A fantastic story" does not appear as part of the title of the final version.

199. The ad for this book read as follows: "A book on the use by Jews of Christian blood for religious purposes. Its author has been vouchsafed the most elevated gratitude of His Majesty the Crown Prince, for giving him the book. It contains 150 facts about the torture and murder of Christian babies, it describes this vile rite and its purpose."

200. Robert Salisbury (1830-1903), Disraeli's minister for Indian affairs, was the English representative at the December 1876 conference in Constantinople. The Russians saw his trip to various countries first as an attempt to build anti-Russian policy.

201. A speech by Gladstone suggested Christians in Turkey would prefer English to Rusian aid.

202. Journalist Dmitri Girs reported Russian soldiers departing from Serbia were required to surrender their Serbian uniforms.

203. Baimakov's company's bankruptcy ruined 3,000 small investors; he blamed the government for not helping him.

204. Nikolai Demert (d. 1876) was one of Dostoevsky's liberal adversaries in *Notes of the Fatherland.* Pomyalovsky was a well-known liberal prose writer, Kurochkin a radical poet. All had drinking problems.

205. Lermontov wrote a verse narrative called, "The Song of the Merchant Kalashnikov," set in Ivan the Terrible's reign. Kalashnikov is executed for justifiable homicide. Belinsky was indignant at Ivan's sentence, Dostoevsky was not.

206. V.P. Burenin wrote a feuilleton about a forgery case in which N.N. Panteleev was involved. Panteleev left 900,000 rubles to pay off obligations of his former serfs.

207. Chernyshevsky's novel *What is to be Done* was translated into French and reviewed negatively.

208. This ellipsis has the smell of censors' ink. Dostoevsky's remarks on Communism here were probably too strong for print in the USSR.

209. An article by P. Sokolovsky argued that a government plan to switch to personal land ownership from ownership by the peasant commune (*mir*) was very dangerous. Farm land was traditionally owned and shared by communities of peasants together.

210. Again, this may be a censored passage.

211. Boborykin gave a lecture saying Griboedov's satire in *Woe from Wit* was more universal and less dated than Gogol's in *The Inspector General.*

212. *The Voice* would shortly publish a very favorable review of Dostoevsky's story, "A Gentle Spirit."

213. V. Burenin published a review of a variety of works by "national" or "people's" writers, including Fyodor Reshetnikov (1841-71).

214. The Constantinople Conference begun Dec. 11, 1876 at the initiative of England found a peaceful solution to the current Balkan problems. But Western troops were stationed in Turkey as observers to see that Christian rights were upheld.

215. Dostoevsky did not finish a long section on satire he planned for the "Diary." As suggested on the next page (115), Dostoevsky believed Gogol's satirical town in *The Inspector General* was a microcosm of all Russia. —Cuvier (1769-1832) reconstructed whole animals from a few bones.

216. Words of Chatsky in *Woe from Wit.*

217. Words of Chatsky in *Woe from Wit.*

218. Aleko was the hero of Pushkin's *The Gypsies.* He murdered his beloved, showing he didn't truly believe in freedom.

219. In a letter, Pushkin had said Chatsky was wrong to waste his wit on ignoramuses.

220. Another quote from Chatsky.

221. Famous words of Chatsky at the end of the play.

222. Dostoevsky is referring to Saltykov-Shchedrin.

223. Dostoevsky completed only points 1 and 5 for the "Dairy."

224. A revolutionary demonstration by the new Land and Freedom group in St. Petersburg. Plekhanov was one of the organizers.

225. See the December "Diary."

226. Alexander Ostrovsky (1823-86), the prolific dramatist.

227. See the December "Diary," Brasol, 542-45, "A Few Words on Youth."

228. A (Buda)Pest newspaper article led right-wingers to see the December 6 demonstration as inspired by foreign agitators.

229. See the December "Diary." Brasol, 553 ff.

230. *Dead Souls* was published in 1842 to very mixed reviews.

231. Alexander Bestuzhev-Marlinsky was extremely popular for his society tales and romantic adventure stories about the Caucasus. Pushkin's "A Queen of Spades" (1834) came after Marlinsky was a hit.

232. The knightly hero of ancient Russian epic songs.

233. See Note 206 above.

234. See "Arbitrary Assertions" in the December 1876 "Diary."

235. Saltykov-Shchedrin.

236. See "Russian Satire" in the January 1877 "Diary." Brasol, 582 ff.

237. See the last section of the December "Diary." Brasol, 557 ff.

238. Boborykin (December 1876) said England had many good characters for historical drama.

239. See the last section of the December "Diary." Brasol, 557 ff.

240. Dostoevsky didn't finish the items on the commune, the soldier and Martha, idealists and realists, or Litke. Or respond to the review of "A Gentle Spirit."

241. The character in *The Devils.*

242. Stasov defended Repin's views on European artists.

243. The apples and realism refer to Chernyshevsky. See Notes 2 and 63 to Notebook I and Note 32 to Notebook IV.

244. In the journal publication of the novel, on page 92, Turgenev says: "He was very intimate with the Petersburg revolutionists, and was to a certain extent in sympathy with them, since he was himself one of the people; but he realised the instinctive aloofness from the movement of the people, without whom 'you can do nothing,' and who need a long preparation, and that not in the manner nor by the means of these men. And so he stood aside, not in a hypocritical or shifty way, but like a man of sense who doesn't care to ruin himself or others for nothing."

245. See Brasol, pp. 567-79.

246. See Brasol, pp. 569 ff.

247. Here and below Dostoevsky is talking about Zola and characters in the work named.

248. A play (1838) by Nestor Kukolnik.

249. Strakhov held two important official posts related to books simultaneously. Dostoevsky and he had been friends and collaborators in the past, but this entry shows Dostoevsky's change. Some years after Dostoevsky's death, Strakhov offered biographical details about Dostoevsky's moral character and sexuality which greatly offended Dostoevsky's widow.

250. Mikhail Speransky's projects for Russia (during the reign of Alexander I) included a two-house parliament based on the English model.

251. See Chapter 2 of the May-June "Diary," Brasol, pp. 710 ff.

252. Areopagus—the governing "Council" in Ancient Greece.

253. Here and in subsequent entries the Soviet editors have apparently censored out symptoms related to sex or bowels.

254. See Note 151 above.

191

255. A reference to the poet and editor Nekrasov. *The Contemporary* had a division called "Science and Art," 1847-58.

256. G.E. Blagosvetlov, editor 1860-66, of the radical journal *The Russian Word.*

257. Pushkin's first popular narrative poem was *Prisoner of the Caucasus* (1822).

258. Dostoevsky took up Zola in Ems in July 1876, telling his wife he had been neglecting European literature. "...And imagine, I could scarcely read it, such filth. And they shout about Zola as a celebrity, the luminary of realism."

259. Hermann is the mad hero of Pushkin's story "The Queen of Spades" (1834), a model for Raskolnikov.

260. Dostoevsky's first publication was a loose translation of Balzac's *Eugénie Grandet.*

261. A very popular French writer (1832-?).

262. In the original, Dostoevsky's poem here is in rhymed trochaic tetrameter.

NOTEBOOK XI

1. Nikolai Leskov wrote many works about Orthodox characters, notably his novel *Cathedral Folk* (1872).

2. Vasily Vereshchagin (1842-1904), one of the "Peredvizhniki" ("Wanderers"), a well-known school of artists.

3. Comments critical of various positions of Dostoevsky's "Pushkin Speech" (June 8, 1880) came from Saltykov-Shchedrin, Gleb Uspensky and Nikolai Mikhailovsky, all in *Notes of the Fatherland.*

4. Saltykov-Shchedrin.

5. In Russian, "vsechelovek."

6. *The Country* was a liberal newspaper. Like *The Messenger of Europe* it printed very critical remarks on the "Pushkin Speech."

7. There was a controversy over high prices and low supply of these products—which were supposed to be so plentiful they could be exported.

8. There were articles on high fees being collected by the heads of the *mir*, or communes, and the money was often misused.

9. Two pieces in October issues of *The New Time* were favorable to "unification" of Poland and Russia.

10. Saltykov-Shchedrin's satirical sketches *Abroad* had begun to appear, including one where he presents a self-satisfied German policeman.

11. The title is a part of Herzen's *My Past and Thoughts.* Saltykov had once been lightly punished by "exile," which Dostoevsky finds insignificant.

12. The Baron invited Russia to join Austria and Germany against France.

13. Molchanov, *The New Time* Paris reporter, was too favorable to Gambetta for Dostoevsky. Felix Piat was editor of *La Commune*, whose calls for revolution were quite open.

14. Kvyatkovsky and Presnyakov, members of The People's Will, were executed (November 4, 1880) for murder. Their co-defendants got life imprisonment.

15. Goldenberg was a terrorist murderer who committed suicide during the trial (Note 14 above), after testifying to the growing popularity of the idea of assassinating the Tsar. Loris-Melikov was a relatively liberal Minister under Alexander at this time.

16. This note was published not long after Dostoevsky's death, and Saltykov-Shchedrin said the policeman he feared when writing was the one who lived inside of every Russian.

17. It was announced that a new political newspaper called *Order* would be put out under the editorship of *The Messenger of Europe.*

18. D. I. Mendeleev had been refused election to the Academy of Sciences—according to the article because of the nationalism of its German professors.

19. I. F. Gorbunov's stories about the commonfolk were often read at Suvorin's evenings.

20. The paper reported that during a performance of the play *Garibaldi* socialists did bad things from the upper balcony onto the main floor.

21. Konstantin Kavelin published an "Open Letter to F. M. Dostoevsky" in No. 11 (1880) of *The Messenger of Europe.* Dostoevsky answers him in these entries. Among other things Kavelin wrote: "Renunciation of the world, humiliation of the flesh, spiritual contemplation as the highest good and perfection have long seemed to the East the only escape from the miseries and misfortunes of earthly life."

22. Kavelin wrote: "Perhaps you find another person's answer mistaken, you say he's calling good bad and vice versa, but in his conscience, in his feelings he is a moral person."

23. Liberty-loving hero of Adam Mickiewicz's long poem *Konrad Wallenrod.*

24. Pope Pius IX agreed to various reforms after the revolutions of 1848.

25. Beketov was Rector of St. Petersburg University. He objected to a letter published in *The New Time,* signed only "A Student." Beketov called the letter slanderous, suggested the editors wrote it, and threatened to go to the Ministry of the Interior over it.

26. A soldier turned robber in *Dead Souls.*

27. Dostoevsky planned a satire on a liberal minister whose "program" or "plan" of reforms in Russia works only to the advantage of bourgeois Europe. It was a satire on Loris-Melikov, who had an unannounced "program" when he became Minister under Alexander. Both liberals and conservatives hoped he would help their cause.

28. Professor Gradovsky had written a piece (1879) saying the idea of Orthodoxy was vague until Khomyakov explicated it, but that even Khomyakov—poet and theologian—left them only an "ideal."

29. The Tver *zemstvo* speech supported Loris-Melikov warmly. The Kolyavich article was on Russo-Polish relations *(The New Time).*

30. Ivan Krylov's fable (1825) has a pig destroying the roots of the oak which feeds him acorns.

31. K. S. Veselovsky was singled out as one who had been in the Academy for 27 years, and written one mediocre book on the Russian climate.

32. *The New Time* made the suggestion of reducing military expenditures to cover the budget deficit. Dostoevsky reacted like Solzhenitsyn in the United States or Spain.

33. A quote from Krylov's fable "The Quartet."

34. See "The Chatter-Mill and Chatterboxes" in the January, 1881 "Diary."

35. "Radical medicine..."—a quote from Repetilov in *Woe from Wit.*

36. A Swedish scholar and explorer who came to Russia to arrange a Siberian island expedition.

37. In *Woe from Wit* Repetilov says this of a vaudeville instead of a Jesuit.

38. Ermak was Russia's Columbus of Siberia.

39. Ivan Goncharov wrote a famous article on *Woe from Wit,* called "A Million Torments."

40. Here Dostoevsky combines lines from two poems by Pushkin.

INDEX
(Bracketed numbers refer to Footnote pages)

Aesop: II: 142, 155
Akhsharumov, P.N. I: 47, 99 [137, 138, 143]
Aksakov, A.N. II: [193] III: 22, 157 [182]
Aksakov, K. II: 119, 131, 132
Aksakov, Sergei: I: 99 II: 81, 141 [195]
  A Family Chronicle: II: 167
Alarmclock (Teapot) I: 109, 115 [144]
Albertini: I: 14
Alchevskaya, Kh. D. II: [195] III: 39, 40, 41 [183]
Alcibiades: II: 82
Alexander I: II: 29, 31, 36, 65, 82, 86, 171 [189]
Alexander II: I: [137] II: 77, [188, 192, 193]
Alfonso, King: II: 159
Altay: II: 6
Andrew of Crete: III: 18
Anna, Tsarina: I: [136]
Antolsky, M.M. III: 28 [182]
Antonovich, M.A. (Mr. Outside Satirist) I: 31, 101-104, 129 [136, 140, 143, 144]
  "An Asmodeus of Our Time": I: [143, 146]
  "The Thrushes" I: 100-105 [140, 143, 144]
Aristotle: II: 30, 79 [188]
Artemievna: III: 125
Askochensky, V.I. I: 17 [134]
Atkinson, J. Beavington: II: 55, [183]
Auerbach: I: 62
Augustenberg, Prince: I: 70, 71
Augustine, St. II: 171 [196]
Avdeev, Mikhail V. II: 120 [191]
  The Underwater Rock: I: 98 [143]
Averkiev, D. I: 48, 49, 59, 60, 90 [139] II: [190]
Avseenko, V. G. II: 64, 97, 120, 165-171 [179, 184, 195] III: 11, 12, 13, 14, 15, 16, 17, 18, 19, 21, 26, 56, 57, 130, 137 [181, 182, 185]
Avvakum, Archpriest: II: 6 [178]

Bacon, Francis: I: 42
Baimakov: III: 109, 139 [186, 190]
Bakanin: I: 8, 32
Balakirev, I.A. I: 29 [136]
Babikov: I: 60, 61
Balzac, Honoré
  Eugénie Grandet: III: 139 [192]
  Goriot: III: 42
Baymakov, Fyodor: III: 63 [186]
Bazarov: I: 32
Bazunov, Alexander F. I: 48 II: 119, 122, 132 [191] III: 30 [183]
Bebel: II: [184]
Beketov: I: 14 [134] III: 155 [193]
Belinsky, Vissarion: II: 3, 28, 29, 69, 77, 100, 123, 130, 144, 163, 170, 171 [190, 195] III: 12, 13, 22, 27, 36, 43, 58, 64, 74, 110, 112, 131, 139, 148 [184, 190]
  Selected Philosophical Works: [195]
Belkin, Ivan—see Pushkin, Alexander
The Bell: I: [135]
Belot: II: 58
Belov: II: 16, 18, 20
Belyaev: I: 48 II: 63 [184]
Berezin, I.N. II: 97, 107, 110, 111,
  Russian Encyclopedic Dictionary: II: [189]
Bergman, Avgust Alexandrovich: I: 48 [138]
Bismarck: I: [142] II: 82, 97, 147, 149, 151, 157, 158, 159 [179] III: 35, 39, 45, 69, 74, 166, 170 [182, 188]
Blagosvetlov, G. I: 59, 129 III: 24, 137, 138 [182, 192]
Blanc, Louis: II: 156, 157
Boborykin, P. I: 71 [141] II: 159 [192, 193, 194] III: 36, 40, 112, 122 [182, 183, 190, 191]
Bobrovsky: II: 20 [181]
Bogdanov, I. II: 16, 17, 18 [179, 180]
Bogdanovich, M.I. II: 36, 171, 172 [195]
Boreisha, Anna Petrovna: III: 113
Borgo, Pozzo di: III: [187]
Borodkin: I: 13
Boswell: II: [192]
Bov—see Dobrolyubov
Božić: III: 105
The Brand—see *The Spark*
Brasol, Boris: II: [178, 179, 189, 191, 192, 193, 194, 195] III: [181, 182, 183, 184, 185, 186, 187, 189, 191]
Bryullov, K.P. II: 121, 140 [192]
Buckle: I: 32, 106 [144]
Budaevsky: I: 60
Bulgakov: II: 17
Bulgarin: II: 79 III: 46 [184]
Bulkin: I: 62
Bunakov: I: 61, 62
Burdin, F. A. I: 62 [139]
Burenin, V.P. II: 6 [179] III:110, 112, 113, 121 [190]
Buslaev, F.I. I: 18 [134]
Butagov: II: 17
Byron, George: II: 70, 71, 77, 94, 120
  Don Juan: II: 73 [187]

Carlos, Don: II: 140-141, 146, 153, 155, 158, 159, 160 [192]
Carlyle, Thomas: II: 171 [196]
Casanova: II: 69

Catherine, Tsarina: II: 77, 166
Catherine II: III: 125 [186]
Cavour, Camillo: I: 5, 19, 27, 28, 31 [133]
 III: 69, 90,[188]
Chaev, N.A. I: [140]
Chambord: II: 160
Chekhov, Anton: III: [183]
Chernyaev, Mikhail G. II: 63, 65 [184] III:
 72, 73, 87, 88, 89, 90, 91, 92, 93, 94, 99,
 105 [186, 188, 189]
Chernyshev: II: 162
Chernyshevsky, N.G. I: 3, 4, 14, 18, 27-30, 31,
 100 [133, 134, 136, 138, 140, 143, 145, 146]
 II: 29, 172 [179, 196] III: [191]
 "On the Esthetic Relation of Art to Reality"
 I: [133, 135]
 "Polemical Beauties": I: [134, 135, 136]
 What is to be Done? I: [133, 144, 145]
 III: 111, [190]
Chikhachev: II: 147 [193]
Church and Society Bulletin: III: 13, 41, 43,
 46, 54
Churilo: II: 161 III: 21
Citizen, The: II: 3, 6, 10-19, 20, 21, 66, 67, 69,
 96, 97, 98, 103, 142 [178, 179, 180, 181,
 183, 190] III: 63 [185]
Cohen, Joseph: I: 95 [142]
Commune, La: III: [192]
Condiore: III: 65
Contemporary, The (Timely): I: 3,4, 21, 30, 31,
 38, 43, 60, 61, 69, 99, 101, 102, 105-6, 107,
 109, 110, 115, 123, 127 [133, 134, 136, 137,
 140, 142, 143, 144, 145] III: [192]
Contemporary Annals: I: 27
Contemporary Chronicles: I: 27
Contemporary News: II: 96 III: 74
Contemporary Review: I: 68
Country, The: III: 146 [192]
Cuvier: III: 114, 115
Daily News: III: 75 [188]
Danchenko: II: 17
Danilevsky, Grigory: II: 102, 103 [190, 196]
 III: 81
Danilevsky, N. II: 172
Danilov, Foma: III: 29, 35, 124, 125 [182]
Darwin, Charles: II: [181]
 Origin of the Speicies: II: [181]
Davidov, Dennis: I: 81 II: [184]
Day, The: I: 60, 106 [139, 144]
Delvig, Baron: II: 118
Demert, Nikolai: III: 109 [190]
DeRobert: III: 159
Descartes, Rene: I: 42
Dickens, Charles: II: 143, 153 III: 125
 The Pickwick Papers: II: 120
Diderot: II: 64
Diogenes: I: 21

Dionysius: III: 132
Disraeli (Beaconsfield): II: [184, 190] III:
 70-71, 93, 109 [187, 189]
Dobell, Sydney: II: 159-160
Dobrolyubov, N.A. (Bov): I: 17-18, 20-26, 29,
 30, 32, 104 [133, 134, 135, 136] II: 140
 [192]
 "Jumping into the Water to Get Out of the
 Rain": I: [134, 136]
 "Pan-Russian Illusions Destroyed by Birching":
 I: [134, 135]
 "The Sad Thoughts of a Student of the Lu-
 theran Faith but not of the Kiev School
 District": I: [135]
Dolgomostiev, I. G. (Igdev): I: 49, 90, 115 [145]
Donskoy, Dmitri: I: [137]
Dostoevsky, Fyodor: I: 102 II: 65, 97, 98, 117
 III: 67, 113, 140 [Footnotes passim]
 "Again the Young Pen": I: [140]
 "Books and Literacy": I: [136]
 The Brothers Karamazov: I: [139] II: 143
 (Smerdiashchaya), 175 (Grand Inquisitor),
 [179, 180, 183, 191, 192, 193, 194, 196]
 III: 51 (Smerdiashchaya), 153 [183, 185]
 Children: III: 94 [188]
 Complete Collected Works of Fyodor Mikhai-
 lovich Dostoevsky. 1865-1870: I: [138]
 Complete Collected Works of Fyodor Mikhai-
 lovich Dostoevsky [in progress]: I: [141]
 Crime and Punishment: I: [138, 139, 141]
 II: 108, 149, 166 [189 (Raskolnikov)
 190] III: 38 (Raskolnikov) [192 (Ras-
 kolnikov)·]
 The Crocodile: 95 (Zakhozhev) [133, 137,
 140, 141, 142, 144, 145]
 "Dead Powers and Future Powers": II: [192]
 The Devils: II: 3 (Kirillov), 9 (Kirillov), 135,
 144, 147 (Kirillov), 149 [178, 179, 182,
 183, 185, 186, 192 (Shatov), 193, 194]
 III: 125 (Kirillov), 150 [191]
 Diary of a Writer (Notebook): I: 70 [141]
 II: 15, 16, 18, 19, 63, 67, 79, 90, 99, 117,
 120, 158 [178, 179, 180, 183, 184, 185,
 187, 188, 189, 191, 192, 193, 194, 195,
 196] III: 23, 146 [181, 182, 183, 184,
 185, 186, 187, 188, 189, 190, 191]
 The Double: I: 14-17, 45-46 [134] II: 28,
 64-65 [181]
 The Dreamer: III: [189]
 "Dreams about Europe": II: [192]
 The Drunkards—see Crime and Punishment
 Fathers and Children: II: 149-150
 "A Fix in the Village Izmailov": II: [181]
 "From the Editor": I: [138]
 The Gambler: II: [194]
 "A Gentle Spirit": III: 100, 108, 124 [187,
 189, 190, 191]

196

Dostoevsky, Fyodor (cont.)
    House of the Dead—see Notes from the
        House of the Dead
    The Idiot: I: [137] II: [179, 183, 192,
        193] III: 38, 112 [183 (Myshkin)]
    The Insulted and Injured: I: 56
    "A Little Boy at Christ's Christmas Tree":
        II: [189]
    "Making an End to It": I: [140]
    Marriage: I: 123-125
    "Mr. -bov and the Problem of Art": I: [136]
    A Nasty Anecdote: I: 56 [134]
    "A Necessary Declaration": I: [138, 139,
        143, 145]
    A Nest of Gentlefolk: I: 56 III: 117
    Notebook—see Diary of a Writer
    Notes from the House of the Dead: I: 16,
        56 [133, 136] II: [182, 188] III: 100,
        113, 135
    Notes from the Underground: I: 56 [133,
        139, 140, 144, 145] II: [187]
    "Notes of Semyon Zakhozhev": I: 95. See
        also The Crocodile.
    "The Peasant Marey": II: 98, 110, 111, 112,
        115, 116, 122, 133 [190]
    "Poor Folk": II: 106-107
    The Possessed—see The Devils
    "Puns in Life and Literature": I: [140]
    A Raw Youth: II: 66, 83, 146, 156, 158,
        159 (Versilov), 167 [178, 180, 183, 184,
        187, 188, 190, 194, 195] III: 57
    "Shchedrodarov": I: [143]
    "The Story of Father Nil": II: [181]
    The Unpublished Dostoevsky: I: [141]
        II: [178]
    "Wall to Wall": II: [181]
    "A Weak Heart": II: 107, 108
    "A Whistle": I: [133]
Dostoevsky, Maria Dmitrievna: I: 39, [137]
Dostoevsky, Mikhail: I: 56 [134, 136, 138]
    III: 24
Dostoevsky, Nikolai: I: [134]
Dragomanov, M.P. I: 20, 23 [135]
Droz, Gustave: III: 139
Druzhinin, Alexander: II: 154 [194] III: [137]
Dudyshkin: I: 14, 54 [136]
Dukhinsky: I: 95, 107
Dumas, Alexandre: II; 58 [186]
Dumas-fils, Alexandre: III: 60
Dziennik Warszawski: I: 142]

Ecclesiastical and Civic Herald: II; 152
Élie de Beaumont, Jean Baptist: I: 15, 16 [134]
Eliseev: II: 76, 100 [187]
The Epoch: I: [136, 137, 138, 139, 140, 141,
    143, 144, 145, 146] II: [179]
Erckmann-Chatrian: II: 58

Ermck: III: 170 [193]
Ermolov: II: 132
Excerpts—see Notes of the Fatherland
Fadeev, Rostislav: II: 16, 28, 29, 33, 34, 36,
    64, 154, 161 [179, 182, 184] III: 13
Fateev: I: 48
Fermor: I: 32
Fet, A.A. II: 141 [193]
Feuerbach: I: [137]
Feuillet, Octave: II: 58
Filippov, O. A. I: 43, 44, 48, 59, 60, 61, 62
    [137, 139, 140] II: 16, 18, 19, 120 [179,
    180]
Filonov, Andrei G. II: 64, 75, 99 [184]
The First Step: II: [195]
Flaubert, Gustave: II: 58
Fourier: II: 29
Fraternal Aid: II: 131
Friedrich, Prince: I: [141]

Gagarin, Ivan: III: 27, 31 [182]
Gagarintsev: III: 55
Gaius Gracchus: II: 91, 94 [188]
Gamaliel: I: 38
Gambetta: III: 90, 148, 156, 157, 166, 170,
    173 [188, 192]
Gamma—see Granovsky, G. K.
Gandaev: I: 94
Garibaldi: I: 27, 45, 46, 93 [141] III: 65, 67,
    69, 90, 91 [188]
Garland: III: 147
Gavrilov: I: 13
Gaydeburov: III: 78
The Gazette: II: [191]
Geilovich: I: 32
Genike: II: 17
Gensler, I. S. II: 17 [180]
Ghengis Khan: I: [137]
Gibert, Joseph: III: 43 [184]
Girardin, Emile: I: 47, 93 [141]
Girs, Dmitri: III: 109 [190]
Girshtorn, A. III: [186]
Gladstone: III: 109 [189, 190]
Glebov: III: 146
Goethe: I: 31 [136] II: 87, 145 III: 129
    Faust: II: 86 III: 41, 99, 103, 129, 145
        [183]
Gogol, Nikolai: I: 4, 13, 30 [134, 145] II: 32,
    65, 75, 89 [182, 183, 185, 190, 195] III:
    49, 115-118 [184]
    Dead Souls: I: 14, 15 [134] II: 106 (Chi-
        chikov) [185, 190 (Chichikov)] III: 72
        (Mokievich, Kifovich) 77 (Mokievich, Ki-
        fovich), 118, 155-156 (Kopeikin) [184,
        187, 191, 193]
    "Departure from the Theatre": II: [188]
    Inspector-General: I: 31, 38 (Derzhimorda),

Inspector-General (Cont.)
    [137] II: 63 (Khlestakov), [184 (Khlestakov), 190 (Skvoznik-Dmukhanovsky)]
    III: 112, 114, 115, 118 [190]
Mirgorod: II: [186]
"Nevsky Prospekt": II: 74 (Pirogov), 94
    (Pirogov) [187]
"The Nose": I: 118 [145]
"Notes of a Madman": I: 14 (Poprishkin)
    [134]
*Selected Passages from a Correspondence
    with Friends:* II: [182] III: [184]
"Tale of Terror": II: [186]
"Testament": II: [183]
"Viy": II: [186]
Goldenberg: III: 149 [192]
Golovachev, Alexei Andreyanovich: I: 37, 60,
    61, 62
Golts-Miller, Ivan (G.M.) I: 129 [137, 143, 145,
    146]
Golubev, Victor F. II: 99, 112-113, 114 [189]
Goncharov, Ivan: I: 31 [136, 146] II: 149
    [194] III: 11, 44, 150, 179 [193]
Oblomov: I: 127, 146
Gorbunov, Ivan Fedorovich: II: 16, 86, 118
    [180] III: 150 [193]
Gorchakov: III: 95
Gorsky, P. N. I: 59 [139]
Government Messenger, The: II: [191]
Gradovsky, A. D. III: 154, 155, 158, 177-78
    [193]
Granovsky, G.K. (Gamma): II: 108, 120, 153,
    155 [190, 191, 194] III: 57, 68, 74, 127,
    [185]
Grekov: II: 4
Griboedov, Alexander: I: [137] III: 114, 118
Woe From Wit: I: 37, 115 (Chatsky) III:
    114-118 (Chatsky), 136 (Chatsky), 179
    [190, 193 (Repetilov)]
Grigoriev, Apollon: I: 31, 48, 49, 59, 61 [136,
    137, 138, 139] II: 74, 114 III: 45, 47, 51,
    54, 57, 82, 84 [182, 183]
"Art and Truth. Elegy-Ode-Satire": II: [189]
Grigoriev, I. I: [137]
Grigoriev, Peter: II: 105 [190]
Grigoriev, Vasily V. II: 113, 119, 164 [191]
Grigorievich, Mikhail: III: 70
Grigorievich, O. V. II: [189] III: 30, 113,
    168 [183]
Gromeko, S. S. I: 27 [135]
Grunilyon, Mrs. II: 17
Guber, E. III: 41, 103 [183]
Gusev, A. F. II: 97 [189]

Hair, The: I: 107, 109, 110, 112, 123 [144]
Hegel: I: 14 [134] II: 102
Heidelberg, Countess: II: 7

Heine, Heinrich: II: 120
Herzen, Alexander: I: 99 [135, 136] II: 29,
    [189] III: 42, 48, 51, 52, 54, 58, 60, 61,
    64, 89, 112, 121
"Appel a la pudeur": I: [135]
My Past and Thoughts: III: [185, 192]
"Prison and Exile": III: 147
Herzen, Liza: III: 45-46, 47, 58, 73, 78, 84
    [184, 187]
Holbein: II: [193]
Holbein the Younger: II: [182]
Holstein: I: 127. See also Schleswig-Holstein.
Homer: II: 119
Hübner, Baron: III: 148
Hugo, Victor: II: 93, 108, 115, 168 [190]
    III: 14, 37, 43, 126, 138
Les Miserables: II: 120, 143, 153 [190]
    III: [185]
Notre Dame: II: 120
Humboldt: III: 99

Ieroglifov: III: 30 [183]
Igdev—see Dolgomostiev, I. G.
Ignatiev: III: 81
Iliad, The: II: [189]
Illustrated Gazette, The: II: 117, 118, 121, 164
Independance Belge: II: 68
Isabella, Queen: II: 9 [181]
Isaev, Pavel (Pasha): I: [133]
Isaeva, Maria Dmitrievna: I: 39, 41, 56 [133]
Ishchenko, Mlle. II: 29
Ivan, Tsar (The Terrible): III: 61, 110, 134,
    [190]
Ivanova, Sonia A. I: [137]
Izvoinikov: I: 118

Journal des Débats: I: 93 [142] III: 75, 115,
    116, 119, 121, 133
Journal de St. Pétersbourg: I: 94 III: 83, 88
Jungdorf: II: 4

Kaidonov, I. K. II: 146, 155 [193]
Kairova: III: 29-30, 31-32, 34, 35, 36, 38, 40,
    45 [183]
Kalatuzov: I: 61
Kambeck, Lev L. I: 118 [145]
Kant, Immanuel: I: 14 [134]
Karamzin, N. I: 39, 113, 115, 121 [145] II:
    65, 70, 82, 86, 140 III: 41 [183]
History of the Russian State: II: [192]
Karlov: III: 52, 117
Kartoshov, Dmitri: III: [183]
Kartsov: III: 88
Kashin: I: 32
Kasparovich, E.L. II: [190]
Katkov, Mikhail: I: 4, 38, 54, 99, 105, 106,
    115 [133, 136, 138] II: 20, 70, 103, 140 [181,

Katkov (cont.)
 184] III: 13, 145
Kaulbach, Wilhelm: III: 33 [183]
Kavelin, Konstantin: III: 151, 154, 155-157,
 174-176 [193]
Kazantsev: II: 18
Kelsiev, Vasily Ivanovich: II: 16, 18, 19 [179, 180]
 180]
Kempis, Thomas à: II: 171
Keronsky: III: 23
Khomyakov, A. S. I: 94 [142] II: 171 [196]
 III: 31, 158 [184, 193]
Kiev Telegraph, The: II: 67, 85
Kievan, The: II: [183]
Kireev, Nikolai: III: 57 [185]
Kishensky, D. O. II: [179, 180, 181]
Kokhanovskaya, Nadezhda Stepanovna: I: 31,
 37, 38 *(Roi)* [136, 137] II: [179]
Kokhovsky: II: 17
Kolontarov, Sergei Nikitich: III: 72
Koloshin: I: 48, 59, 60, 61
Komarov, Matvey: III: 181
Koni, A. F. II: 90, 94, 95, 126, 130 [183, 188]
Konrady: III: 122
Konstant, Varvara Dmitrievna: I: 37 [137]
Konstantinov, N. II: [180]
Korablev: III: 108
Kornilov, Stepan Kornilovich: III: 95
Kornilova, Ekaterina: III: 94, 98, 115, 116
 [183, 187]
Koshkarev: I: 62
Kositsa—see Strakhov, N.
Kostomarov, N.I. I: 38 [137] II: 11, [179]
Kotlubai, Eduard: II: 91 [188]
Kotzebue, August von: II: 76 [187]
Kovalevsky, M.E. II: 90
Koyalovich: I: 59, 61 III: 159 [193]
Kozhanchikov, G. F. II: [182]
Kozlov: II: 35
Kraevsky, Andrei Alexandrovich: I: 71, 72-73,
 95, 115, 118, 130 [140, 141, 142, 144, 145]
 III: 62, 63, 88, 105, 112
Krestovsky, Vsevolod V. I: 31, 121 [139, 145]
 II: 32, 64, 170 [184, 195] III: 13, 18 [182]
Kritsky, Andrey: II: 170
Kroneberg: II: 170, III: 122-131, 136-138, 150,
 [191, 192]
Kryatkovsky: III: 148 [192]
Krylov, Ivan: III: 162, 174 [193]
 "The Pig under the Oak Tree": III: 160,
 162
 "The Quartet": III: 165 (Yakova)
Kryukovskaya, Olga: I: 62, [139]
Kukolnik, Nestor: III: 129 [191]
Kupernik: II: 143, 152, 153, 154, 155, 163
 [193]
Kurochkin, Nikolai: I: 31 III: 110 [190]

Kusheleva, Countess: III: 57
Kutorgi: II: 79
Kvashin-Samarin: I: 118

Labor-Rest: II: 17
Lacenaire, Pierre Francis: I: 59 [139]
Lacordaire, Jean Baptiste: I: 93 [142]
Lamartine: II: 65, 126 [185]
Lamennais, Felicité Robert de: I: 93 [142]
Lamp, The: 4, [133]
LaRoche, G. R. II: 68 [186] III: 80, 83, 84,
 137 [187]
Lasalle, Ferdinand: II: 171 [184, 196] III: 157
Laube: I: 118
Lavrov, Pyotr Lavrych: I: 32 [136]
 Philosophical Dictionary: I: [136]
Lebedev: III: 52
Ledru-Rollin, Alexandre Auguste: I: 121 [145]
 II: 55 III: 46
Lemoin, Jean: II: 66 [185]
Leontiev, K. N. II: 103 [184, 190] III: 145
Lermontov, Mikhail: II: 30, 71, 77, 94, 96, 118,
 120 [182, 189] III: 58, 110
 A Hero of our Time: II: 91 [185, 188]
 III: 73 (Pechorin), 78 (Pechorin), [187
 (Pechorin)]
 "Masquerade": II: 30 [182]
 "Princess Mary"—see *A Hero of our Time*
 "The Song of Merchant Kalashnikov": III:
 [190]
Leskov, Nikolai: I: [141, 143, 144] II: 60
 [193] III: 146 [182, 192]
 Cathedral Folk: III: [192]
Lewes, George Henry: II: 171 [195]
Liberté: III: 119
Library for Reading (The Reading Room): I:
 109, 110 [141, 144]
Liebknecht: II: [184]
Lisovsky, N. I: [138]
Litke: III: 126
Loboda, S. M. II: [179]
Loftus: III: 83, 84, 106 [188]
Loris-Melikov: III: 148-149, 159, [192-193]
Louis XVI: I: 15
Louis XVII: II: 124 [192] III: 14
Lugagnan: I: 59
MacIver, Colonel: III: 99, 105 [189]
MacMahon, Edme Patrice Maurice de: II: 90,
 105, 118, 121, 156 [188]
Maikov: III: 22, 23, 130, [182]
Makary: II: 36
Maksimov: II: [180]
Malkov: II: 149
Malthus: I: [138] II: 84 III: 60 [186]
 "An Essay on the Principle of Population":
 I: [138]
Marbr: I: 12

Markevich, B. M. III: [186]
Markov, Evgeny: II: 34, 91, 158 [182, 194] III: 60, 61, 62 [186]
Marlinsky, Alexander: III: 62, 119 [186, 191]
Martin, Henri: II: 172
Marx, Karl: II: [184]
Maslennikov, K.I. III: 72 [187]
Matthew the Apostle: I: [137]
Maximov: III: 127
Maximovich: III: 45
Maykov: II: 32
Mendeleev, D. I. II: 78, 143 [187] III: 99, 150 [193]
Menshikov, A.S. II: 74, [187]
Meshchersky, V.P.: II: 16, 17, 18, 19, 21 [179, 181] III: 13, 98, 107, 109, 129 [183, 189]
Messenger of Europe: II: 87 [178] III: 60, 61, 62, 63, 64, 65, 73, 74, 75, 79, 83, 134, 146-147, 150, 152, 174 [186, 192, 193]
Michelet: I: 95 [142]
Mickiewicz, Adam: I: [141]
"Konrad Wallenrod": III: 152 [193]
Mikhailovsky, Nikolai K. II: 4-5, 6, 8, 10, 27, 75, 76, 85, 118, 143, 156 [178, 187, 193] III: 48, 146 [184, 192]
Mill, John Stuart:
"On the Subjugation of Women": III; [185]
Miller, Orest: III: 28, 33, 126, 138 [182]
Milon, Prince: III: 88
Milyukov, Alexander P. I: 4, 43, 48, 116 [133, 145]
Minaev, D.D. I: 31 [137] II: [191]
Mitrofaniya, Mother Superior: III: 29
Minutes: III: 155
Molchalin: III: 82, 83
Molchanov: III: 148, 157 [192]
Moleschott, Jacob: I: 32 [145]
Moleyer, Richard: III: 103
Molière: III: 116
Moller: I: 7, 8
Moltke: III: 126
Mombelli, Nikolai: II: 164 [195]
Mordvinov, Nikolai S. II: 29 [181]
Morning Post: I: 93 [142]
Moscow News: I: 93, 94 [142] II: 9, 18, 20, 34, 36, 53, 63, 66, 67, 68, 78, 85, 95, 100, 103, 108, 109, 117, 118, 121, 140, 141, 142, 143, 146, 152, 156, 157, 158, [185] III: 11, 12, 35, 44, 50, 51, 54, 58, 63, 66, 68, 70, 72, 79, 81, 83, 86, 91, 105, 108, 109, 111, 113, 115, 116, 117, 119, 122, 125, 174
Münchausen: I: 4
Murat: III: 39
Murillo: I: 113
Muromets, Ilya: I: 93 [142] II: 157, [189, 194] III: 21, 79, 120 [182]
Musset, Alfred: II: 58

Nabokov, Ivan, General: III: 98 [189]
Nabokov, Vladimir Vladimirovich: III: [189]
Nadein: II: 133 [192, 196]
Napoleon I: I: 93 [137, 142] II: 31, 72, 90 III: 50, 63, 65, 67, 69, 121, 173
Napoleon III: I: [142] II: 35, 99, 152 III: 69, [188]
Nazimov, N. A. II: 114
Nechaev, S.G. II: 3, 4, 11, [178]
Nekrasov, I.Y. II: [181, 184] III: 79, 128, 133
Nekrasov, Nikolai: I: 99 [134] II: 64, 75, 85, 100 [179, 184, 189] III: [192]
"Bashfulness": I: [134]
Nemirovich-Danchenko: II: [180, 181] III: 62 [186]
Nesterov: II: 120
Neuletika, Poletika: III: 87, 88
New Time: II: 71, 98, 140, 141, 142, 143, 152, 158, 163, 171 [193, 194] III: 13, 21, 26, 28, 29, 30, 34, 35, 41, 43, 45, 48, 52, 63, 66, 70, 74, 75, 76, 77, 80, 81, 82, 83, 84, 85, 86, 87, 88, 89, 92, 95, 96, 98, 105, 106, 107, 108, 109, 112, 113, 118, 122, 124, 125, 147, 148, 149, 150, 151, 155, 157, 159, 161, 173, 174 [186, 192, 193]
News, The—see *St. Petersburg News*
Nezlobin, A. II: [186]
Nicholas I: II: 77, 121 [187, 192] III: [187]
Nicholaevna, Anna: III: 161
Nikolić, Minister: III: 89
Nikolsky, Priest Ioann: II: 17
Noise, The: I: 73
Nordenskjöld: III: 167
Noreyk: III: 84
Notes of the Fatherland (Excerpts): I: 20, 26, 27, 71, 72, 95, 110 [133, 135, 136, 140, 141, 142, 143, 144] II: 30, 76, 91, 96, 98, 118 [178, 179, 184, 186, 187, 188, 189, 190, 193] III: 54, 146, 147 [190]
Novorossisk Telegraph: III: 174
Novoselov: III: 88, 92

Obolensky, D. A. II: 133 [192]
Obrenovich, Milan IV: III: 62 [186]
Odoevsky, Vladimir: II: 171 [195] III: 14, 76
Ofrosimov: III: 12 [181]
Opinion National: I: 70
Order: 149 [193]
Orsini: III: 67, 69
Ostrovsky, A. N. I: 13, 61, 71 [139] III: 75, 97, 141 [189, 192] III: 115-117, 122, 168, [191]
Otto, Alexander: II: [195]

200

Our Time: I: [134]
Outside Satirist—see Antonovich, M. A.

Palaetsky: III: 65
Palkin: II: 14
Palmerston: I: 93 [141-142]
Panteleev, N. N. I: 59 III: 110, 112, 117, 121 [190]
Papkova, L. II: 9 [180]
Parfeny, Hermit: III: 151
Pavlov, N. F. I: 14, 29 [134, 136]
Pechatkin, V.P. II: [182]
Penkovich, Churila: II: 82
Pericles: I: 15
Persigny, Jean: I: 70 [141]
Persini: I: 95
Pertsov: II: 17
Pestel: II: 77 III: 14 [181]
Pestrina: I: 3
Peter I (The Great): I: 54 [138] II: 6, 7, 29, 30, 31, 32, 36, 60-61, 79, 83, 103, 134, 142, 144, 166, 168, 169, 171, [178, 182] III: 16, 26, 28, 31, 37, 58, 60, 73, 96, 97, 111, 137, 148, 156, 157, 162, 172, [182, 189]
Peter III: I: 59 [186]
Petersburg Gazette: II: 118, 120 [191]
Petersburg Leaflet: I: 110, 112 II: 17
Petersburg News—see *St. Petersburg News*
Peterson, Nikolai: II: 157 [194]
Petrov, O. A. III: 18, 35 [182]
Petrov, Peter: II: 55, 120
Photius: III: 96 [189]
Piat, Fèlix: III: 148, 149, 151 [192]
Pilate, Pontius: I: 129
Pirogov, N.I. I: 4, 5, 17,26, 28, 30 [133, 134, 135]
Pisarev, Dmitri: I: 28, 99 [136, 138, 143, 144, 145] II: 70, 83, 153 III: 23
    "Nineteenth-Century Scholasticism": I: [135]
Pisemsky, A. F. I: 127 [145] II: 165 [179, 195] III: 168
    A Bitter Fate: III: [181]
Pius IX, Pope: III: 153 [193]
Plekhanov: III: [190]
Pobedonostsev, K. P. II: 117, 119, 141, 142, [178, 180, 182, 191, 196] III: 22, 51, [182]
Pogodin, M. P. I: 54 [137, 138] II: 16, 71, 78 [179, 182, 186, 188]
Poletika: III: 105 [188]
Polevoi, A. II: 16, 171 [180]
Polevoi, P. N. II: 92
    History of Russian Literature: II: [189]
Polonsky, Lev: III: 106, 107 [189]
Polonsky, Ya. P. I: [138] II: 87, [188] III: 106
    "Discord": I: 48

Polyakov: I: 12
Polyana, Yasnaya: II: 29
Polyansky: III: 78, 85
Pomyalovsky: III: 109-110 [190]
Popov, A. A. III: [187]
Popov, Nil: II: 36 [182]
Popov, R. II: [180]
Poretsky, A.U. I: 49, 59, 60, 61 [138] II: 18, 67 [185]
Postel, Karl—see Postl, Karl
Postl, Karl: I: [137]
Potekhin: III: 113
Potulov: III: 50
Prachkov: III: 60
Presnyakov: III: 148 [192]
Prescott, William H. II: 172 [196]
Prezhevsky: II: 17
Pribytkova, Varvara: II: 145 [178, 179, 193]
Proudhon: I: 21, 32, 53, 54 [137] II; 58, 90 III: 99 [189]
Prutkov, Kuzma: I: 16, 31, 123 [134, 145-146] II: 145 [193]
Pseldonimov: I: 16
Pugachev: III: 96, 98
Pushkin, Alexander Sergeevich: I: 31, 38, 39 (Belkin) [136, 137, 140] II: 32, 35 (Belkin), 75, 77, 91, 95, 108, 118, 120, 155, 170, [182, 187, 190, 191, 195] III: 42 (Belkin), 85, 114, 129, 150 [184, 193]
    "The Bridegroom": III: 130
    "The Captain's Daughter": II: 32
    Eugene Onegin: II: 170 (Tatyana), 171 (Tatyana) III: 133 (Tatyana)
    "The Fountain of Bakhchisarai": I: 100
    "Geneology of My Hero": II: [188]
    "The Gypsies": III: 114-118, [190]
    History of Peter the Great: II: 182
    "The Poet": II: [192]
    "A Poor Knight": II: [193]
    Prisoner of the Caucasus: III: 138 [192]
    The Queen of Spades: III: 119, 139 (Hermann) [191, 192]
    "The Shot": II: 91 (Silvio) [188]
    "The Stationmaster": II: [182]
    "The Stone Guest": III: [188]
Putsykovich: III: 16, 18, 19 [180]
Pypin, Alexander: I: 68, 99, 129 [137, 143] II: 5, 9, 171, 172 [178, 195]

Quixote, Don: II: 85, 102, 120, 145, 146, 153, 159

Raevsky: III: 66
Ramel-Plan, K. II: 171
Raphael: I: 110 [144] II: 94
Raspail, Francois Vincent: II: 151, 156 [194]
Ratkov-Rozhnov: III: 35

Ratynsky: III: 100
Raumer, K., von: II: [196]
Reading Room, The—see *Library for Reading*
Redstock, Lord: II: 161-162 III: 13, 25, 28,
    37, 41, 43, 54, 58, 127 [183]
Renan, Joseph Ernst: I: 96 [137, 138, 143]
    II: 27, 89
Repin: III: 125, 126 [191]
Reshetnikov, F. M. II: 64 [184, 190]
Revile, A. I: [138]
Revue des deux Mondes: III: 111
Rober, A. N. III: 45 [184]
Rodić, Baron: III: 11, [181]
Rogov: II: 17
Rosen: II: 153
Rostovstsev: II: 120 III: 98
Rousseau, J-J. I: 47, 93, 94 [144] II: 64, 170
    III: 51
Rückert, Richard: II: 95 [189]
Rurik: II: 78
Rus: III: 156, 157, 163
Rusakov: I: 13
Russia: III: 147
Russian Antiquity: III: 98
Russian Archive, The: III: 105
Russian Herald: II: 141
Russian Invalid, The: I: 115
Russian Literature Triquarterly: II: [194, 195]
Russian Messenger, The: I: 4, 5, 14, 26, 34
    [133, 138, 144] II: 55, 64, 71, 75, 79, 100-
    101, 165, 166, 167, 170 [180, 184, 186, 187,
    188, 193, 195] III: 16, 57
Russian News, The: II: 20 [184]
Russian Past: II: [182]
Russian Talk: 31 [135]
Russian Word, The: I: 107, 118 [136, 145, 146]
    III: [192]
Russian World: II: 64, 65, 66, 67, 85, 95, 96,
    97, 103, 117, 121, 157, 158, 163 [184, 191]
    III: 13, 77, 82, 87, 90, 91, 105, 108, 125
Ryleev, K. I: 39 III: 56 [185]
Ryumin: III: 12

Saburov, A. A. II: 94 [187]
Sade, Marquis de: I: 95 III: 152
Sadovaya: III; 108
Saint-Beuve, Charles: II; 172 [196]
St. Petersburg Gazette: I: 70
*St. Petersburg News (The News) (The Petersburg
    News):* I: 73, 107, 118, 122 [141, 144]
    II: 20, 46, 55, 103, 140, 152 [180, 183]
    III: 85, 89, 90, 91, 109, 110, 161 [186]
Salias, Evgeny: II: 17 [180] III: [189]
Salias de Turnemir, E.V. I: [140] II: 64 [184]
    See also Tur, Evgenia.
Salisbury, Robert, Marquis: III: 108 [189]
Saltýkov-Shchedrin, M. E. I: 53, 69, 99, 101,

Saltykov-Shchedrin (cont.)
    104, 105 [137, 138, 140, 143, 144] II: 6,
    96 [186] III: 62, 84, 109, 115, 126, 140,
    146, 147, 149, [186, 190, 191, 192]
    Abroad: III: [192]
    The Golovlyovs: I: [138]
    "The Impolite Koronat": II: [186]
    "Mrs. Muzovkina": I: 43, 102, 104
    Provincial Sketches: I: [137]
Samarin, Yury: II: 21, 36, 161, 163, 164 [195]
    III: 31, 33 [182]
Sand, George: II: 58, 100, 120, 153 [185]
    III: 41, 42, 43, 45, 46, 47, 129, 139 [183,
    184]
Saper: I; 31
Saturday Review, The: I: [141]
Savalev: III: 173
Savich: I: 59
Schiller, Gustave: II: 123 [192] III: 138, 139
Schleswig: I: 127 [141] See also Holstein.
Schlözer, August Ludwig von: II: 172 [196]
Schmidt, Julian: II: 172 [196]
Schmidt, K. A. II: [180]
Schnapps, Schlimmer: I; 70
Scott, Walter: II: 120
Sealsfield, Charles, pseud.—see Postl, Karl
Sebastiani, Comte Horace François: II: 149,
    155 [194]
Sechenov, I.M. I: 54 [138] II: 134, [192]
    III: 23
Selin, Alexander: III: 50, 52, 58, 60, 62, 73
    [185, 187]
Semenov, Nikolai: 98 [189]
Senkovsky, O. III: 46 [184]
Serov: I; 43, 59 [137]
Shakespeare, William: I: 3, 96 [133, 143]
    II: 94, 96, 108, 119, 145, 146, 153 [189]
    III: 42, 83, 104, 122
    Hamlet: II: 85, 153
Shalfeev: II; 17
Shalikova: II: [179]
Shchapov: III: 23, 24, 28
Shchedrin—see Saltykov-Shchedrin
Shcheglov, Dmitri M. I: 3 [133]
Shcherbinskaya, Olga: II: 94 [190]
Shchukin: I: 61
Sheller-Mikhailov: II: [188]
Shestakov: I: 37
Shidlovsky, Ivan: III: 41 [183]
Shore, The: III: 177
Shpilhagen: I: 48
Shtrandman: I: 32
Sidoratskaya: III: 148
Siecle: I: 70
Siedo-Ferrotti: I: 93 [141]
Sikevich: I: 62
Sineus: II: 78

Skabichevsky: II: [188, 192-193]
Skapidarova, Afimia: I: 70 [141]
Skariatin: I: 130 [146]
Skobelev, I.N. III: 98 [189]
Skobeltsyn: I; 3
Skyler: II: 157 [194]
Sluchevsky, Vladimir: II: 31 [183]
Smirnov: I: 32
Socrates: I: 113, 123
Sokolov: II: 16
Sokolovsky: I: 61 [138] III: [190]
Solon: II: 82
Soloviev, Nikolai Ivanovich: II: 16 [179]
Soloviev, S. M. II: 36, 171 [182, 196] III: 94
Soloviev, Vladimir: II: 171
Soloviev, Vsevolod: II: 16, 85, 164 [179, 182-183, 188, 195] III: 81
Solovyov, N. I: 95 [138, 143]
Solzhenitsyn, Alexander: III: [193]
Son, The—see *Son of the Fatherland, The*
Son of the Fatherland, The (The Son): I: 121, 127 [146]
Spark, The (The Brand): I: 115, 121 [137, 144, 145]
Spasovich, V.D. II: 119, 120, 122-132, 135, 136-140 [191, 192]
Speransky, Mikhail: II: 29 [182] III: 132 [191]
Spielhagen, F. I: [138]
Stanley, Henry? II: 16 [180]
Stasov: III: 125, 126 [191]
Stasyulevich, Mikhail: III: 71, 79, 134 [187]
Stechkina, L. II; 70, 79 [186]
Stellovsky, Fyodor: I: [138] III: 59, 84 [186]
Stepanov, N. A. I: 109, 120, 121 [144]
Stillman, Beatrice: II: [194]
Stock Exchange: II: 69
Stock Exchange News: II: 72, 78, 81, 87, 91, 117, 119, 132, 141, 152 III: 52, 54, 57, 84, 87, 88, 89, 90, 91, 92, 112, 123 [185]
Strakhov, Nikolai (Kositsa): I: 43, 48, 49, 60, 61, 104-105, 106, 115 [137, 138, 144, 145] II: 16, 18, 19, 20, 30, 35, 171 [178, 179, 181, 195] III: 51, 54, 59, 130, 139-140 [185, 191]
Strauss, David Friedrich: II: 88 [188]
Strekalov: I: 62
Strousberg, Bethel: III: 44, 78, 82, 83, 85, 89, 92, 93 [184]
Sudovshchinov, E. I: 20 [135]
Sukhovo-Kobylin, A. V. I: 102 (Krechinsky) [144]
Suslova, Apollinaria: I: [138] II: 129 [194]
Suslova, Nadezhda: II: 150, [194]
Suslova, Polina: II: [194]
Suvorin, A.S. II: 69, 76, 78, 81, 85, 87-88, 91, 117, 118, 140, 141 [179-180, 186, 187, 188,

Suvorin, A. S. (cont.)
189, 192, 193] III: 61, 62, 83, 150
Suvorov: I: 105 III: 88
Svetlozanov, Prince: II: 66
Svistunov, P.N. II: 114
Svyatogor: III: 21 [182]
Swedenborg: II: 90

Tacitus: II: 93, 94, 97, 171 [189] III: 55
Taine, Hippolyte: II: 172 [195, 196]
Talk: II: [179]
Tallyrand: I: [137]
Teapot, The—see *The Alarmclock*
Tebrikova, Marina: II: 75 [187]
Temps: III: 76
Terner: III: 29, 30, 31, 33, 36, 41
Thierry, Augustin: II: 172
Thiers: I: 70, 99 [143] III: 69, 90 [188]
Tiblin, Nikolai Zvovich: I: 3, 59
Time: I: [133, 134, 136, 138, 139, 146] III: 24, 25
Timely—see *The Contemporary*
Times, The: I: 70, 113 II: 9, 20, 95, 135, [181] III: 70 [186]
Timkovsky: I: 45
Tindale, John: III: 18 [182]
Tokarev: III: 83, 84, 88, 92
Tokhtamysh: I: 38 [137]
Tolstoi, Alexei: I: [134] II: 29, 64 [185, 194]
Tolstoi, Lev: I: 15 [145] II: 27, 30, 92, 98, 100-101, 141, 144, 149, 153, [181, 182, 189, 194] III: 44, 167, 178
    Adolescence: II: 153
    Anna Karenina: II: 120, 140, 171 [194] III: 14
    Childhood: II: 76-77
    "On Educating the Commonfolk": II: [189]
    War and Peace: II: 16, 120, 144 (Karataev), 168 (Bezukhov, Bolkonsky), [193 (Karataev), 195 (Bezukhov, Bolkonsky), III: 189
Torchinsky: I: 59
Trollope, Anthony: II: [188]
Truvor: II: 78
Tur, Evgenia (pseud.): I: 70, 112, 113 [140]
    See also Salias de Turnemir, E. V.
Turgenev, Ivan: I: 14, 99, 102, 129 [138, 139, 140, 141, 146] II: 64, 65, 69-70, 71, 72-73, 75, 81, 82, 85, 87, 92, 108, 120, 121, 131, 144, [185, 186, 188, 191, 195] III: 11, 47, 167, [191]
    "Bezhin Meadow": II: [179]
    "The Dog": II: 72, 74 [187]
    "Fathers and Sons": I: [136, 143]
    "Hamlet of the Shchigrovsky Region": III: 181
    Nest of Gentlefolk: II: 76-77, 153, 168 (Lav-

Nest of Gentlefolk (cont.)
retsky), [195]
"On the Eve": I: [144]
"Phantoms": I: [140]
Rudin: I: 48 (Volyntsev) [138]
Smoke: (Potugin) II: 69, 71-72, 73-74, 75,
77, 81, 82-83, 85, 86, 104, 109, 115, 118,
121, 131, 144, 149, 159, 167, [186, 187,
191, 192, 194 III: 11, 16, 21, 127 [182]
Sportsman's Sketches, A: I: 72 [141] II:
70, 85 [179]
"Vernal Waters": II: 118
Virgin Soil: III: 125, 126, 127
Turunov: I: 48
Tyutchev, F. I. II: 108 [190, 191]

Ungern-Sternberg: II: 35
Ushakov: I: 62
Uspensky, Gleb: III: [192]
Ustrialov: I: 90
Utin, Evgeny: III: 31-32, 34, 35, 38, 39, 40,
47 [183]
Utin, L. I: [138]

Valjean, Jean: II: 102, 125
Vasilchikov: II: 161
Vasiliev: III: 146
Velikhanov: I: 32 III: 38
Velikhanova: III: 31-32, 38, 39, 40 [183]
Velsky, Prince: I: 95 II: 153
Vengerov, S. A. II: [193, 195] III: [184]
Vereshchagin, Vasily: III: 146 [192]
Veselitsky-Bozhidarovich, G. S. II: 109
Veselovsky, K. S. III: 160 [193]
Viardot, Pauline: II: 69 [186]
Victoria, Queen: II: 155
Viskovakov: III: 61, 62
Villemain, Henri: II: 172, 196
Vladislavev, M. I: [138] II: [196]
Vlas: III: 125, 126
Voice, The: I: 47, 59, 70, 71, 72-73, 93, 94,
118, 130 [140, 141, 142, 144, 145] II: 7,
17, 20, 30, 34, 63, 64, 67, 68, 69, 72, 75, 78,
81, 84, 85, 90, 91, 92, 93, 94, 95, 100, 102,
105, 106, 109, 110, 113, 117, 118, 120, 122,
127, 131, 132, 137, 141, 142, 143, 152, 153,
158, 162 [180, 182, 184, 185, 189, 192]
III: 11, 12, 13, 14, 18, 29, 38, 61, 62, 66, 75,
79, 82, 83, 84, 86, 88, 93, 112, 123, 125, 134,
177 [181, 183, 190]
Volf: I: 120 II: 81 [187, 188, 190]
Voltaire: II: 64
Vorobiev: II: 111, 112-113, 114, 115
Voronezh Telegraph: II: [188]
Vovchok, Marko: I: 29 [136]
Vrangel: I; 62 [139, 141

Vtorov, Nikolai Petrovich: I; 48

Yakushkin, E. II: 171
Yakushkin, I. D. II: 32 III: 54, 57, 58 [185]
Yanyshev: III: 29, 30, 146
Yazykov: III: 127, 157
Yurev: III: 160
Yurkevich, M. A. III: 107
Yurkevich, Pamfil Danilovich: II: 16, 18 [179]
III: [189]

Zaguliaev, M. A. I: 70, 71, 118, [140, 141, 145]
Zaitsev, V. A. I: 99, 112, 122 [144, 145]
III: 63
Zasulich: III: 153
Zhemchuzhnikov, Alexei: II: 150 [194] III:
86, 89, 90, 92
Zhivio: II: 110
Zhukovsky: III: 138
Zimenko: I: 62
Zimmermann: III: 125
Zinoviev: II: 20
Zlatoust, Ioann: III: 25, 28
Zola, Emile: II: 58, 171 III: 50, 51, 54, 129,
139 [185, 191, 192]
Zotov, Vladimir Rafailovich: II: 95, 97, 100,
106-108, 117, 118, 121, 122, 131, 164 [192]
Zubov, Platon: III: 96, 98